~~SECRET~~

THE AIR FORCE IN SOUTHEAST ASIA

Tactics and Techniques

of

Close Air Support Operations

1961 - 1973

by

Lt. Col Ralph A. Rowley

OFFICE OF AIR FORCE HISTORY

February 1976

~~SECRET~~

FOREWORD

This historical study deals with U.S. Air Force close air support operations within the Republic of Vietnam, with the emphasis on tactics and techniques. The author, Lt. Col. Ralph Rowley, previously wrote two monographs dealing with the important role played by Forward Air Controllers (FAC's) in South Vietnam. In this study, he examines such operations from the viewpoint of the pilots and crews of the attack aircraft. These included T-28's, A-1E's, A-26's, A-7's, F-100's, B-26's and B-57's. The role of Air Force gunships--the AC-47, AC-119, and the AC-130--and the armed FAC also are discussed by the author. In addition, he describes the key role played by the Tactical Air Control System, which the Air Force established in Vietnam in the early 1960's. Colonel Rowley's monograph is the twentieth classified historical study on the war published by the Office of Air Force History since 1962.

STANLEY L. FALK
Chief Historian
Office of Air Force History

PREFACE

This study traces the chief developments in close air support tactics and techniques from 1961 to 1973. It dovetails with previous Office of Air Force History studies treating forward air control, gunship, and night operations.*

As depicted in Chapter I, the historical development of close air support shows a succession of peaks and valleys stretching back to World War I. The valley after the Korean War mirrored the U. S. strategy of massive nuclear deterrence. Specifically, the Strategic Air Command's expanding bomber force and a powerful intercontinental ballistic missile program were emphasized to deter a general war. In the past-Korean War period, the Tactical Air Command (TAC) concentrated its efforts on a modernization program, which included introduction of the F-100 and F-105 fighters and light bombers such as the B-57's. All tactical fighters and light bombers were equipped to carry TNT or atomic bombs and play a role in discouraging limited war or brushfire incidents.

Stepping up support of the South Vietnamese forces in 1961, the Air Force saw that the use of tactical nuclear weapons was impractical. The enemy was waging a low-key counterinsurgency conflict, striking swiftly and slipping away--preferring to move at night and hide by day. Lacking a tested tactical doctrine to deal with such warfare, the Air Force had to hammer out one in combat. Hence, the central theme of this study is how close air support tactics and techniques were forged by the men in the field. It tells how they

---

 * Maj Ralph A. Rowley, USAF FAC Operations in Southeast Asia, 1961-1965 (S), January 1972; Maj Victor B. Anthony, Tactics and Techniques of Night Operations, 1961-1970 (S), March 1973; Lt Col Jack S. Ballard, Development and Employment of Fixed-Wing Gunships, 1962-1971 (S), January 1974; Lt Col Ralph A. Rowley, FAC Operations, 1965-1970 (S), May 1975. These and the present study will eventually be combined in book form.

improvised, innovated, or simply made do until supplied with the necessary aircraft, munitions, detection devices, and other equipment for countering Communist aggression.

The early war years (1961-1964) laid the ground work for later close air support. A striking feature of the period was the extent that the Air Force relied upon aging aircraft and equipment to meet immediate needs. Initially, propeller-driven slow movers dominated the scene. Forward air controllers took to the air in the 0-1, while strike pilots flew the T-28, B-26, and later the A-1. C-47's and C-123's dispensed flares during night operations. Step by step new FAC fighter and flareship tactics were built. A revamped Tactical Air Control System was introduced into South Vietnam. More types of convention munitions became available, and in December 1964 the AC-47 gunship arrived to help cope with the upsurge of Communist attacks on hamlets and outposts. Most important, ground commanders began to believe in tactical air power.

The Gulf of Tonkin Crisis in August 1964 triggered a steady buildup of U.S. forces in Southeast Asia that did not tail off until the onset of Vietnamization in 1969. Jet aircraft (B-57's, F-4's, F-100's, and F-105's) flew close air support missions, cutting down response time. AC-130, AC-119G, and AC-119K gunships, fitted with the latest in detection and fire control systems, pummeled and at times decimated enemy units. High-flying B-52's dumped massive bombloads on Communists troops. The role of the FAC expanded as he moved from the 0-1 to the 0-2A and thence to the OV-10 aircraft. The starlight scope, infrared detectors, and side-looking airborne radar pinpointed the enemy at night and in bad weather. A highlight of these years was the perfecting of close air support and the full acceptance of tactical air power by ground commanders.

Vietnamization got under way in 1969, and was marked by a phased withdrawal of American forces and a corresponding increase in those of South Vietnam. All through the drawdown, the Air Force went on supplying air support. Tactical air power became a key element in the Allied incursions into Cambodia in 1970--it was crucial at the battle for Tchepone and the pullback of the ground troops to South Vietnam. Moreover, USAF strike aircraft, gunships, and B-52's helped break the enemy's 3-pronged offensive into the South during 1972--saving the day at Hue, Quang Tri City, Kontum City, and An Loc. With the signing of the cease-fire agreement in late January 1973, fighting in Vietnam was halted. Subsequently, except for airlift support in Cambodia, U. S. combat operations in Southeast Asia ended on 15 August 1973.

Although out of the war, the Air Force did not intend to let the sharp edge of tactical air power grow dull. In 1966 the Chief of Staff had given the green light to planning for a purely close air support aircraft. Hence in 1973 the Air Force selected the Fairchild A-10A, with final acceptance coming in 1975. It also set about tailoring the Tactical Air Control System to the evolving demands of modern warfare. The forward air controller would still be a mainstay--in the air and on the ground. Close air support tactics and techniques would be kept abreast of current and anticipated threats. In short the Air Force was girding to meet a challenge from any quarter.

In writing this study, the author had drawn deeply from the historical work of others. Their contributions are apparent in the sources cited. Special thanks are due those officers who gave generously of their time for interviews. The information gleaned has filled chinks in the written record and rounded out the study.

CONTENTS

Page

FOREWORD iii

PREFACE v

LIST OF ILLUSTRATIONS ix

MAP 61

I. INTRODUCTION AND BACKGROUND 1

II. EARLY INVOLVEMENT, 1961-1964 8

    Farm Gate Begins 8
    Introduction of Barn Door 11
    American Involvement Picks Up 14
    Early Ordnance and Weapons 16
    Control Net for Air Support Operations 19
    Early Day Tactics 25
    Night Operations 33
    Reevaluating Operations--1964 41
    The T-28 and B-26 Become War Weary 42
    The A-1E Tries Its Hand 45
    The Weapon Arsenal Expands 47
    The FC-47--A Friend in Need 49
    Summary 51

III. CLOSE AIR SUPPORT, 1965-1968 53

    Military Situation 53
    Coordinating Close Air Support 57
    Refining the Tactical Air Control System 59
    Close Air Support Aircraft 64
    Tactics 70
    Ground Controlled Radar Bombing 91
    Escort Tactics 93
    Supporting Special Forces 97

IV. NIGHT CLOSE AIR SUPPORT, 1965-1968 104

    Starlight Scope 106
    Strike Tactics 107
    The AC-47 Gunship 114
    The AC-130 (Gunship II) 119
    The AC-119 (Gunship III) 121
    Rocket Watch 125

V. THE FINAL YEARS, 1969-1973 128

    The Armed FAC in Close Air Support 129
    1970-1971 Operations 133
    1972 Operations 136
    The A-7D Makes Its Bow 139
    The End of American Combat 141

EPILOGUE 142

SOURCES AND NOTES 145

    Official Records 145
    Manuscript Histories 145
    Interviews 146
    Published Works 146

NOTES 148

GLOSSARY OF TERMS AND ABBREVIATIONS . . . .

ABSTRACT . . . .

ILLUSTRATIONS

No.		
1	Preplanned Air Request Net	21
2	Immediate Air Request Net	24
3	Marking Target Using Surprise (1963)	28
4	Normal Target Marking (1963)	29
5	Farm Gate Flare Pattern	36
6	B-26 Night Attack Pattern	38
7	Moving Figure Eight (Farm Gate)	43
8	Pulloff Variations (Farm Gate)	43
9	Tactical Air Control System	60
10	Military Assistance Command Vietnam Joint Air-Ground Operations System (JAGOS)	63
11	Steep and Close In Delivery	73
12	Turning Delivery	74
13	Outside Holding Pattern	76
14	Figure Eight Pattern	78
15	Inside Holding Pattern	79
16	Overhead Holding Pattern	81
17	Circular Attack Pattern	86
18	Attack by Elements	87
19	Floating Wheel Attack Pattern	89
20	Curvilinear Approach and Attack	90
21	Low-Altitude Helicopter Escort (A-1E)	94
22	A-1 Escort--Helicopters Medium to High Altitude	95
23	A-1E Convoy Escort	96
24	Night Airstrike Control--Outside Holding Pattern	109
25	Night Airstrike Control with Flareship	110
26	FAC/Gunship/Strike Procedure Pattern Night Tactics	111
27	155MM Howitzer Illumination for Air Strikes	112
28	Gunship Control Pattern	116
29	AC-130 Gunship II Special Equipment Arrangement	123
30	AC-119K Fuselage - General Arrangement	123
31	AC-119G Gunship	124

I. INTRODUCTION AND BACKGROUND

(U) During the first week of April 1972, three Communist divisions swept down from bases in Cambodia and hit key points in Bin Long Province,* South Vietnam. Major Viet Cong units seized Quan Loi airstrip on 5 April and the town of Loc Ninh 2 days later. A North Vietnamese division held Highway 13 (well to the south of the provincial capital of An Loc), sealing off allied road movements to and from Saigon. On 13 April, hard on the heels of a week's shelling of An Loc, more than two dozen enemy tanks spearheaded the attack in force. The ensuing 2-month battle--one of the most crucial of the war--threatened the very survival of the Saigon regime.

(U) Outnumbered, outgunned, and cut off except by air, the Army of the Republic of Vietnam (ARVN) escaped defeat at An Loc chiefly because of quick-reacting tactical air power. Airborne forward air controllers (FAC's) directed over 10,000 close air support sorties. Vietnamese and USAF tactical fighters pounded troops, tanks, and artillery positions--helping break the enemy's momentum. High-flying B-52's put heavy payloads as close as 300 meters to dug-in defenders; circling AC-130 gunships "hosed down" targets to within 30 meters. Air Force transports dropped much-needed supplies while evacuation helicopters shuttled in and out of the battered town. The Tactical Air Control Center (TACC) at Saigon tied all these actions into an efficient support operation.

(U) Gen. Frederick C. Weyand (USA), Commander, U.S. Military Assistance Command, Vietnam (COMUSMACV) praised "the magnificent job done by our airpower" in stopping the enemy at An Loc. "I can't see how anybody, in any service," he added, "could question the decisive role played by the fixed-wing gunships, tac air, and the B-52's in the successful defense of the key areas."[1] The success of close air support at An Loc typified its pivotal role during every step of the Southeast Asia war.

---

*Being the direct highway approach to Saigon from the north, Binh Long was often a battleground.

(U) The airplane's potential for supporting ground battles was virtually untapped at the outbreak of World War I. Within a year, however, tactics and systems of control started to take shape. In 1916, at the Battle of the Somme, the British Royal Flying Corps (RFC) for the first time massed its aircraft under a single commander to bomb German troops. Initial full-scale use of close air support came in November 1917 at the Battle of Cambrai. By 1918 the Royal Air Force (RAF)--successor to the RFC--was assigning an aircraft brigade headquarters (with attached air wing) to every field army. This let the RAF shift its few fighter and bomber squadrons between brigades as the military situation dictated.[2]

(U) When the American Expeditionary Force (AEF) entered the war in 1917, it adopted the air support tactics of its allies. Maj. William ("Billy") Mitchell, a rising young aviation officer,* believed air power should be more flexible. He therefore proposed to Gen. John J. Pershing (USA), AEF Commander in Chief, that the Air Service employ two distinct forces. One would consist of squadrons attached to ground armies, corps, and divisions and be controlled by ground commanders. The other would comprise "large aeronautical groups for strategical operations against enemy aircraft and materiel, at a distance from the actual line." Bombardment and pursuit squadrons of this force" would carry the war well into the enemy's country." General Pershing approved the tactical but not the strategic organization. Air operations and resources were centralized at field army level, the aircraft being allocated to corps and divisions as required.[3]

(U) Two competing outlooks arose to color development of the U.S. tactical air arm for years to come. Army commanders insisted on having units under their control. This meant either committing air units to specific ground commanders or merging them into the ground army. Air commanders argued that military aircraft had roles beyond close air support, citing the all-important one of achieving air superiority. They favored assigning theater air units to central headquarters, to be

---

* Mitchell rose to brigadier general during the war, becoming Chief of Air Service, First Army, and on 14 October 1918 chief of all Army aviation at the front.

apportioned by priority among the various users.[4]

(U) The Army viewpoint prevailed after the Armistice of 1918. Air Service units were assigned to domestic corps areas and overseas departments. Although General Mitchell and other air officers continued to advocate centralized control of air operations, they met with scant success.[5] On the other hand, the U.S. Marine Corps (USMC), which looked upon the air weapon purely as extra fire support for ground operations, made the most headway in refining close air support. The heart of the Marine method lay in tight control of air operations by the individual ground commander. During 1927 the Marine system was successfully used in strife-torn Nicaragua.[6]

(U) Early in World War II, Germany demonstrated great skill in fusing close air support with ground operations. Its blitzkriegs in Poland, the Low Countries, and France put to rest any doubt as to the potency of tactical air power. Seasoned Luftwaffe pilots, fitted with radios, rode in tanks and armored cars at the head of advancing columns, directing airstrikes by Stuka dive-bombers on targets immediately ahead. A reliable air request net linked army corps with tactical air forces.[7]

(U) Keenly impressed with the German air-ground system, the War Department directed the Air Corps to perfect its own close air support techniques. Tests followed in Louisiana and North Carolina during the first half of 1941. The results led to issuance of Training Regulation 52 on 29 August, which set up air-ground coordination parties (AGCP's) at army, corps, and division headquarters. Composed of Army Air Forces (AAF)* personnel, the AGCP's advised ground commanders and coordinated close air support.[8]

(U) In April 1942 the Army specified in Field Manual (FM) 31-35 that air support commanders serve as aviation advisers to ground commanders and assign attack sorties to meet "the needs of the ground units." This rendered air power more responsive to the local ground commander, but splintered and weakened overall tactical air operations. Some AAF

---

*The AAF was created on 20 June 1941.

officers complained that ground commanders misused and wasted aircraft (often against fleeting or unsuitable targets) while other priority requests "went begging."[9]

(U) On 8 November 1942, the Allies invaded North Africa. During the push into Tunisia, American and British tactical air units operated separately under the control of specific ground commanders, who demanded massive "umbrella" cover against German air attack. This left too few planes for other operations including the interdiction of enemy movements. As a result German ground and air units seized the offensive.[10]

(U) Gen. Dwight D. Eisenhower, commander of the North African invasion, countered in February 1943 by ordering all American and British air elements consolidated under a theater air commander. This removed the tactical air units from direct control of ground commanders and ended the umbrella air defense. Operating out of a joint air-ground headquarters, the theater air commander could now shift air power about and concentrate it where the tactical situation demanded.[11] Ground commanders nevertheless faulted the new setup as less responsive to their air support needs. On the other hand, the Army Air Forces considered its case proven by the outcome of the North African campaign. Lt. Gen. Sir Bernard L. Montgomery, British ground forces commander, and Air Chief Marshal Sir Arthur W. Tedder, attributed much of the "success of the drive from El Alamein to Tunisia to the system of centralized control" of air resources.[12]

(U) Operations in North Africa also introduced the forward air controller (FAC) as an integral part of Allied close air support. General Montgomery in March 1943 placed a FAC in a tank on high ground during an assault by his troops at the Mareth Line (the battle of El Hamma). This controller directed more than 400 airstrikes against enemy defensive positions, forcing the Germans to withdraw and allowing the Mareth Line to be turned. Later in the year, the U.S. Fifth Army used forward air controllers at Salerno during the invasion of Italy. Nicknamed "Rover Joes" after their British counterparts ("Rover Davids"), they soon became fixtures in the Fifth's battle plans.[13]

(U) These and other experiences shaped Field Manual 100-20, Command Employment of Airpower, 21 July 1943--the bible for close air support until the end of the war. Stressing that "land power and air power are co-equal and interdependent" forces, the manual pointed out that "the inherent flexibility of air power is the greatest asset" of a centralized control system. It accordingly ruled out attachment of air elements to individual ground units.[14]

(U) All the same, the Army by 1945 had built its own small "organic air arm" of 200-300 light planes apart from the Army Air Forces. Attached to the field armies, these planes were used for liaison duty as well as artillery and target spotting. When the United States Air Force became an independent service in 1947, the Army kept this tiny air force. It further pressed for a bigger role in visual reconnaissance (VR) and (under certain conditions) close-in air support.[15]

(U) The postwar version of Field Manual 31-35 mirrored many of the innovations and lessons learned in tactical air control. It preserved a joint operations center (JOC) at theater and command level. Tactical air control parties (TACP's)--replacing the AGCP's--were assigned to corps, division, and lower units as need be. Air liaison officers (ALO's), picked from experienced pilots, advised ground commanders on tactical air power. Besides a Tactical Air Control System (TACS) for controlling tactical aircraft, the manual provided for an Army Request Net (ARN), with radio centers at battalion through corps level to request air support.[16]

(U) After 1945, the U.S. tactical air arm shrank to a shadow of its massive wartime structure. This period was marked by a loss of skilled men, tight budgets, and a feeling in government circles that atomic weapons had made conventional forces obsolete. The post war Tactical Air Command (TAC) organized in March 1946, languished during the next 4 years as a planning headquarters under the newly formed Continental Air Command.[17] Little wonder the Communist invasion of South Korea on 25 June 1950 found the United States unprepared for the "conventional war" that ensued. The Fifth Air Force based in Japan, rushed the only two TACP's to the combat zone.* They operated

---

*Fortunately the two TACP's were in the Far East on a training exercise.

with World War II radio/personnel jeeps that often broke down under incessant pounding from the rough Korean terrain. The mountains also impeded efforts of these TACP ground FAC's to seek out the enemy and direct airstrikes against him. Fifth Air Force solved the problem with airborne "mosquito" forward air controllers, who flew borrowed Army L-17's until USAF T-6 aircraft arrived. *[18]

(U) TAC rose to major command status in August 1950 and at once reorganized. Within a month the Air-Ground Operations School (AGOS) at Fort Bragg, N.C., began training Army and Air Force officers in close air support tactics. At first the school couldn't keep up with early demands for air controllers, so the small FAC units in Korea turned to Army liaison pilots now and then for help. By July 1951, however, a centralized tactical air control system was in full swing, directing all air activity in Korea--including U.S. Marine air. The system put the limited air power when and where it was needed. Yet, both the Army and Marines objected to the absence of control over air support by local ground commanders.[19]

(U) The Army air arm went on expanding during the Korean war. A 1951 agreement with the Air Force let Army aircraft expedite and enhance ground command but not duplicate USAF close air support. They could likewise do aerial observation and control ground forces. A second agreement in 1952 restricted the weight of Army planes except rotary-wing aircraft. This spurred use of helicopters for battlefield observation and operations. Consequently, the Army's inventory rose to over 3,500 aircraft of all sorts by 1953.[20]

(U) After the war the Air Force again shifted priorities in line with President Eisenhower's "New Look" defense program. He said the United States would not be caught using "the same policies and resources to fight another war as were used in the Korean conflict." He added that the United States couldn't afford to waste "manpower in costly small wars" that achieved no clear-cut results. To do so only played into the hands of a potential enemy whose manpower reserves were endless. The United States, he declared, would not allow such a foe to enjoy sanctuaries as had been the case in Korea. Instead America would be ready to strike at the heart of enemy power with "means of our own choosing."[21]

---

* Nicknamed Mosquitos after their first tactical call sign, these airborne FAC's were known as tactical air coordinators during the Korean War.

(U) New Look's dependence on nuclear air power to deter Communist aggression again pared TAC's funds and sharply curtailed close air support. The Air Force retired the T-6 as a FAC aircraft. It also transferred the remaining liaison aircraft to the Army, which added L-19's for air observation and artillery spotting.* In 1956 the Army took over training of its fixed-and rotary-wing pilots from the Air Force, putting the program at Fort Rucker, Ala. [22]

(U) Noting the decline of USAF close air support preparedness, Secretary of Defense Charles E. Wilson issued Directive 5160.22 on 18 March 1957. It limited any greater involvement of Army aviation on close air support missions, and instructed the Air Force to expand support to the Army from the means at hand. [23] TAC and Continental Army Command (CONARC) held several joint exercises a short time later, coming up in September with a new Joint Air-Ground Operations Manual. It came closer to Air Force concepts of centralized control of air resources, but displeased ground commanders by loosening their hold over local air assets. [24] The manual nevertheless paved the way for better coordination.

(U) The 1958 Lebanon and Quemoy crises led the Eisenhower administration to reevaluate national and military strategy. The study concluded that nuclear deterrence couldn"t check crises "at the lower levels of the warfare spectrum." The Air Force thereupon turned to conventional munitions. Again getting approval to beef up its aviation force, the Army bought the CV-2B Caribou transport and the OV-1 Mohawk-- a twin engine aircraft suitable for forward air control and light attack roles. [25]

(U) In March 1961 President John F. Kennedy requested the Joint Chiefs of Staff (JCS) to develop a unified force that could swiftly react to conventional wars anywhere in the world. The U.S. Strike Command resulted, formed from elements of Tactical Air Command and Strategic Army Command. [26] One of its first tasks was to overhaul the close air support control system to make it more responsive. Before this could be done, however, American involvement in South Vietnam swelled. Thus, USAF units arrived there during late 1961 and early 1962 with an incomplete and undermanned system that had to make do with worn-out and obsolete equipment.

---

* The L-19 was later renamed 0-1 Bird Dog.

II. EARLY INVOLVEMENT, 1961-1964

Farm Gate Begins

In April 1961--even before creation of Strike Command--the Air Force activated the 4400th Combat Crew Training (CCT) Squadron at Eglin Air Force Base (AFB), Fla. Manned entirely by handpicked volunteers, the unit (code name Jungle Jim) was designed to react to small brushfire incidents in any part of the world.*[1] Self-sufficiency was stressed, since the squadron was expected to operate in every climate and terrain, with little or no outside support. Hence, the latest in USAF hardware was bypassed in favor of the simpler and older-- the choice of B-26, C-47, and T-28 aircraft being a case in point.[2] Working closely with the U.S. Army Center at Fort Bragg, N.C., Jungle Jim pilots practiced operating from primitive airstrips and trained in close air support bombing/gunnery tactics. They learned to pump gas from 55-gallon drums, draw up their own local security plans, become proficient with firearms, and get themselves into top physical trim.[3]

Meanwhile, President Kennedy tried to shore up South Vietnam's sagging strength to counter North Vietnamese aggression. / On 29 April 1961 he made a series of economic and military moves. One expanded the U.S. Military Assistance Advisory Group (MAAG) to help train Saigon's swelling armed forces. Ordered to Hawaii during the summer, Colonel King briefed the Commander in Chief, Pacific Command (CINCPAC) on Jungle Jim's progress. He moved on to Saigon for similar talks with the Air Force MAAG Section. When King returned to Eglin, Gen. Curtis E. LeMay, Air Force Chief, told him to get his squadron combat ready and be prepared to move out on short notice.[4]

---

*Lt Col. Benjamin H. King was Jungle Jim's first commander. As a cover for its true mission, the squadron developed a curriculm for training foreign nationals.

/ In doing this he had to walk a fine line, if the 1954 Geneva Accords were not to be violated.

Other plans also jelled. At a 5 September meeting with his deputies, Secretary of Defense Robert S. McNamara favored dispatching experimental units to South Vietnam to refine counterinsurgency (COIN) tactics. His idea took in a tactical air control system for coordinating air-ground operations, dovetailed to Vietnamese needs. A few days later, a small team of air-ground operations specialists arrived in Da Nang to see what such a system might entail. Following the team's report, Secretary McNamara decided to send in a control and reporting post (CRP) to give radar coverage for South Vietnam, and to train VNAF in the basics of TACS operations. The CRP left Shaw AFB, S. C., on 26 September and reached Tan Son Nhut on 1 October. Expanded to a control and reporting center (CRC), it was in full operation 4 days later.[5]

On 11 October the Air Staff got the go-ahead to deploy Detachment 2A of the 4400th CCT Squadron to South Vietnam.[6] The Joint Chiefs of Staff issued orders on 14 November and by the 16th the 154-man unit was in place at Bien Hoa. Detachment 2A (code name Farm Gate) brought along four B-26's (picked up at Okinawa),* four SC-47 cargo/flareships, and eight T-28's--all carrying the Vietnamese Air Force (VNAF) insignia. 2d Advanced Echelon (ADVON), ǂ the USAF headquarters set up at Saigon by Thirteenth Air Force, controlled Farm Gate operations. On VNAF training matters, however, Detachment 2A reported direct to the Chief, Air Force Section, MAAG.[7]

Although none of the original Farm Gate aircraft were suited to counterinsurgency operations, they did an adequate job.[8] The T-28

---

*The Geneva Accords ruled out tactical bombers in South Vietnam, so the B-26 was redesignated RB-26 to imply a reconnaissance role.

ǂ Originally Advanced Echelon, Thirteenth Air Force. On 15 November 1961, Pacific Air Forces (PACAF) had Thirteenth Air Force set up Detachments 7, 8, 9, and 10 at Saigon, Tan Son Nhut, Bien Hoa, and Don Muang. These were part of "2d ADVON" (at first a meaningless cover designation). But on 7 June 1972, Detachments 8, 9, and 10 were closed out and Detachment 7 publicly designated 2d ADVON. The 2d ADVON became 2d Air Division in October 1962, then Seventh Air Force in April 1966.

Trojan (designed and built by North American) served as the Air Force's basic pilot trainer in the late 1940's and 1950's. Now, a bigger engine, toughened wings, and six ordnance stations resulted in a light tactical attack aircraft. The Trojan took the poor airstrips and austere maintenance in stride, but slow airspeed and thin armor-plate bared it to the quickening enemy ground fire.[9]

A veteran of World War II and Korea, the Douglas B-26 Invader seemed suitable for duty in Southeast Asia (SEA). Each of eight nose-mounted .50-cal machineguns packed 350 rounds--a deadly array against troop concentrations. The Invader could further deliver a 4,000-lb bombload plus the extra ordnance hung on outside wing racks. Powered by two reciprocating engines, the aircraft was fairly slow but economical to operate and able to use short tactical airstrips. Also, by converting the solid nose to a glass one, the B-26 could switch over to photo reconnaissance.[10]

Service of the C-47 Skytrain, the oldest Farm Gate aircraft, dated before World War II. The "SC"* models sent to SEA had already been beefed-up for Strategic Air Command (SAC) aircrew recovery operations. The plane featured twice normal fuel capacity, reinforced landing gears for cushioning the jolts of dirt strips, jet-assisted takeoff (JATO) to cope with short runways, and a loudspeaker system for psychological operations (PSYOP).[11] During the Korean War, the C-47 had hooked up with the B-26 to forge a powerful night attack team. The Skytrain crew dropped flares out the rear cargo door; as they ignited the B-26 moved in to strike enemy targets. Soon the North Vietnamese began breaking off attack the moment a descending flare blossomed--a reaction later repeated by the Communists in South Vietnam.[12]

Farm Gate flew its first armed reconnaissance mission in late November 1961. Four T-28's (a USAF pilot in each front seat and a VNAF

---

*Later reference to Farm Gate aircraft will be to the "T-28," "C-47" in lieu of "SC-47," and "B-26" rather than "RB-26."

member in the rear) reconnoitered a rail link between Bien Hoa and NHA Trang at night. Two of the Trojans flew a mile ahead of and 500 feet below the others. Once in the target area, the lead T-28's flared * while the higher ones dove in on the attack. The pairs next reversed positions and continued the strikes.[13] A few days later, the B-26's carried out their initial recon sorties.

To reduce the risk of world censure, USAF orders barred 2d ADVON pilots from combat operations unless VNAF crew members were on board to receive "training." Farm Gate crews would fly only when the VNAF couldn't, clearing such missions through 2d ADVON. During December, however, the upsurge in enemy activity (chiefly at night) forced an expansion of Farm Gate flights.†[14]

Introduction of Barn Door

As noted earlier, a control and reporting center had begun operation at Tan Son Nhut on 5 October 1961. Later in the month, several members of the AGOS specialist team went back to South Vietnam and picked sites for elements of an enlarged manual tactical air control system.‡ CINCPAC approved the larger TACS in November, and PACAF ordered Thirteenth Air Force to prepare the operations plan for the system's deployment.[15]

The operations plan (code name Barn Door I) set forth a Tactical Air Control System tailored on the lines taught by the AGOS at Keesler AFB, Miss. The system sought to give the COMUSMACV, Air Force, and VNAF an efficient, quick-reacting means to direct, coordinate, and control close air support. As proposed, an Air Operations Center (AOC) and two Air Support Operations Centers (ASOC's) received and filled air strike requests.

---

* Dispensed flares.

† Very few VNAF pilots were qualified to fly night combat sorties.

‡ The choice of a manual system reflected the thinking of Mr. McNamara and Army MAAG officers in South Vietnam. They viewed the conflict as basically a ground war in which tactical air power would have no major part.

A Control and Reporting Center plus two Control and Reporting Posts performed radar surveillance and controlled military air traffic. Rounding out the system were experienced air liaison officers and forward air controllers.[16]

The Air Operations Center* opened for business at Tan Son Nhut on 2 January 1962, serving as command post for the VNAF and 2d ADVON. In line with joint training policy, a VNAF officer headed the Center. His deputy, an American, directed all USAF operations in support of the VNAF. This dual arrangement, geared to speed up Vietnamese training, rippled down through the lower elements of the TACS. The AOC also coordinated activities of the two air forces and acted as a liaison point for Army and and Navy air operations.[17]

Two divisions discharged the duties of the Air Operations Center. Combat Operations supervised current air operations and handled immediate requests for close air support or tactical reconnaissance. Combat Plans took care of all air operations occurring more than 3 hours after the AOC got a support request.[18]

Barn Door I put Air Support Operations Centers at the headquarters of I Corps (Da Nang) and II Corps (Pleiku). The Air Operations Centers doubled as an ASOC for III Corps, and a "floating" ASOC handled special operations requests.† As extended fingers of the AOC, the Air Support Operations controlled close air support and tactical reconnaissance within their areas. They obtained air sorties daily from the AOC and parceled them out as ground operations dictated.[19]

---

*Under Barn Door I the AOC was known as the Joint Operations Center. Between 1962 and 1965 it became known as the Air Operations Center and later as the Tactical Air Control Center.

† The Government of South Vietnam (GVN) approved Barn Door I on 31 December 1961. Barn Door II replaced Barn Door I in June 1962 (retroactive to January), extending the TACS to embrace IV Corps and retaining the floating ASOC.

The Control and Reporting Center stayed at Tan Son Nhut, next door to the Air Operations Center. From there it monitored radar coverage of South Vietnam through the Control and Reporting Posts at Da Nang and Pleiku. In addition, the CRC and CRP's trained VNAF personnel in air traffic control.[20]

Barn Door assigned air liaison officers to the ground commands at Bien Hoa--III Corps Tactical Operations Center (CTOC) and ARVIN Field Command. Others went to ground units as needed. Additionally, the Air Operations Center secured authority to form a 5-man FAC pool for accompanying ground forces expected to clash with the enemy. These controllers, all experienced tactical fighter pilots, could train their VNAF counterparts in strike control techniques. They were not allowed, however, to direct airstrikes or mark targets. South Vietnam's President Ngo Dinh Diem reserved those duties for rated VNAF observers.[21]

In January 1962 Fifth Air Force sent five forward air controllers on 90-day tours to South Vietnam under the Barn Door plan. These controllers did duty in the Offensive Air Section of the AOC, but looked for early involvement in training and combat. Instead, they found the VNAF with no formal FAC organization and but mild interest at the AOC to create one. What's more, Vietnamese ground commanders were for the most part unfamiliar with air power and skeptical of it.[22]

Two of the controllers, Captains Thomas N. Cairney and Douglas K. Evans, spent off-duty time selling the merits of the TACS and nailing down the need for a VNAF FAC training program. To promote a clearer understanding of what the TACS and FAC could do, Cairney and Evans paid visits to the Farm Gate detachment and VNAF's 1st Fighter Squadron at Bien Hoa. They made orientation flights on Farm Gate aircraft, studies VNAF strike and control methods, rode with Army helicopter crews, and took part in joint air/ground training exercises. The two officers went to Vietnamese outposts and villages to discuss air-ground operations with local chiefs. Finally, they held many meetings with U.S. Army, ARVN, and VNAF personnel to go over close air support procedures.[23]

From their spadework Cairney and Evans built solid proposals. They suggested to the AOC Deputy Director that training programs be formed for VNAF forward air controllers and ARVN forward air guides (FAG's). To lick the problems in pinpointing targets, they pressed for Farm Gate T-28's in an airborne FAC role, but none could be spared from strike and training duty. Attempts to borrow U.S. Army L-19's likewise fizzled. The two controllers did secure approval to fly as instructors in operational VNAF L-19's--fitted with rocket rails to aid target marking.[24]

Although the Barn Door package became "operational" on 14 January 1962, it didn't really function as a TACS until late February when more elements were in place. Even then, operations remained primitive. Capt. David M. Murane, Duty Officer for II Air Support Operations Center at Pleiku in 1962, depicted conditions there. The high frequency (HF) radio transmitter--the sole link with the AOC in Saigon--was more than a quarter-of-a-mile from the ASOC. Moreover, the absence of phones in their quarters cut off the USAF advisers from the Center; when they were needed, someone had to come for them. What's more, the advisers' only contacts with forward air controllers or Farm Gate crews took place when they happened to land at the ASOC to iron out current procedures.[25]

American Involvement Picks Up

The enemy greeted the coming of Farm Gate and Barn Door with stepped-up attacks on South Vietnamese hamlets and outposts. The Viet Cong's hardcore cadre, estimated at 12,000 in the summer of 1961, rose to about 17,000 in December. The climb continued through January then tapered off to between 20,000 and 25,000 men. This level held until September 1962, in spite of an estimated loss rate of nearly 2,000 men a month.[26] The feverish pace of operations severely strained air resources, forcing Barn Door and Farm Gate to expand. By December 1962 the Barn Door FAC force jumped to 32 pilots, and Farm Gate aircraft grew to 24 (8 T-28's, 4 C-47's, 8 B-26's, and 4 U-10B's).[24]

During 1963 enemy operations again spiraled upward, fueled by swelling infiltration of men and supplies from North Vietnam. The Air Force responded by sending the 19th Tactical Air Support Squadron (TASSq) to South Vietnam in June. The squadron not only boosted the overall FAC total from 32 to 75, but brought along 22 0-1's acquired from the Army. In addition the Farm Gate detachment increased to 275 men and 41 aircraft.*[28]

---

*Included were 18 B-26's, 13 T-28's, 6 C-47's, and 4 U-10B's. Farm Gate attack sorties went from 200-250 per month in early 1962 to over 1,500 in June 1963.

USAF air liaison officers at ARVN corps and divisions had a hard time convincing ground commanders that air power--properly used--could spell the difference between victory and defeat. One drawback was that ALO's required 2d ADVON approval to commit aircraft, and the support didn't always get there on time. This contrasted sharply with U.S. army advisers who often had aviation permanently assigned--to offer or withdraw on the spot. ARVN commanders naturally preferred Army air support because it was right at hand. Nevertheless, the ALO's persuaded them to call for more USAF strike and FAC support, thereby upping Farm Gate's workload.[29]

As Farm Gate crews took over a bigger chunk of the air war, VNAF efforts dwindled. Being used to far simpler tools of war, the South Vietnamese were bewildered by U.S. firepower and technology. They doubted their ability to master modern warfare methods, and readily stepped aside to let the more experienced Americans carry on. Furthermore, VNAF training failed to turn out first-rate crewmembers. The 14-hour observer flying course, for example, hardly got trainees used to the air, let along prepare them to control airstrikes. By the same token, VNAF pilot training barely fitted pilots to fly solo.[30]

The decline in South Vietnam's fighting activity caused Secretary McNamara to closely question the quality of American help and training. At a May 1963 conference with U.S. military assistance commanders, he pointed out that the VNAF's war effort hadn't increased from the past year. He therefore urged that USAF pilots perform less combat flying and encouraged VNAF crews to do more.[31] Still, the VNAF was not ready to take charge of the air war, so the Air Force continued to shoulder a heavier load.

(U) One of the key factors influencing USAF close air support operations in South Vietnam was topography. Its landscape ranged from dense tropical rain forests, to the scattered trees and grass of savannas, to cleared areas.* Numerous mountain chains crisscrossed the peninsula, each cut by many deep, river-gouged valleys.[32] Most of the forests contained three canopies. Trees of the top layer towered 80-100 feet, those of the middle rose 50-60 feet, while the seedlings and sapling jutted just 20-30 feet from the jungle floor. This ground seldom saw the sun and was fairly free of undergrowth,

---

*The forests made up roughly 40 percent of the region; savannas, 45; and cleared areas, 15.

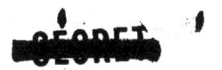

save in the marshlands of the Delta and coastal flats. Pilots found picking out targets through the dense carpet of green virtually impossible. What's more, few weapons could penetrate the layers to hit the enemy beneath. On his part, the enemy considered the forest floor ideal as a footpath or even a roadway. The high grass, shrubs, and small trees of the burnt-out savannas afforded him easier travel but less cover. To avoid airstrikes he rarely ventured into open farming areas by day.[33]

Early Ordnance and Weapons

Air Force testing after the Korean War Dealt chiefly with nuclear rather than nonnuclear weapons.[34] Consequently, the supply of conventional air munitions (especially iron bombs) shrank as allied nations bought them up. Iron bombs became so scarce that for a time the United States tried to buy some of them back.[35] The Air Force did have stocks of special purpose ordnance--cluster and fragmentation bombs as well as napalm and incendiaries--but the specter of world censure limited their use. Hence, to arm Farm Gate aircraft, 2d ADVON had to borrow from the South Vietnamese armed forces. This in turn spawned a "hodgepodge of conventional munitions" of which USAF weapon crews knew next to nothing, having been trained mostly for nuclear armament.*[36]

By March 1962 Farm Gate crews had experimented enough to know what weapons worked best for various tasks. General purpose (GP) bombs, especially the bigger ones--could blast holes in the jungle canopy, carve out helicopter landing zones, and drive troops from hiding. † They could also be dropped from altitudes above the range of ground fire. On the minus side, GP bombs needed to land on target to do much damage. Now and then they exploded in the air, uncomfortably close to the aircraft. At other times they burrowed into the ground before going off. ‡

---

*Recalling his armament officer duty at Farm Gate in 1961-1962, Col. Ira L. Kimes said Vietnamese storage was so poor that at times old iron bombs had to be dug out of the mud and scrubbed up before use.

† GP bombs came in sizes of 100, 250, 750, 1,000, and 2,000 pounds.

‡ A variable fuze solved this problem by detonating the bombs just above the ground or on impact.

Fragmentation (frag) bombs proved deadly against troops in the open. When detonated slightly above the ground, their lethal fragments scattered widely. The bulk of Farm Gate's frag bombs were the small 20-pounders. The crews therefore liked to strap six of them together for dropping at altitudes of 2,500 to 3,000 feet.* On the way down, the clamps on each cluster broke open to allow the bombs to fall free. Fragmentation bombs well nigh lost their punch against troops shielded by heavy tree overhangs--usually exploding harmlessly among the branches, "killing only leaves."[38]

Incendiary clusters, napalm, and smoke bombs likewise found favor with Farm Gate crews. Carried on wing racks, the incendiary cluster consisted of a case packed with bomblets. These small weapons held a mixture of magnesium, gasoline, other oil derivatives, and a thickener. Ejected shortly after the case left the aircraft, the bomblets spread out and exploded close to the ground. They stuck fast to whatever they hit, burning intensely for 5-10 minutes. The clusters did well in open areas and against massed troops, but in forests the lightness of the bomblets kept most of them from reaching the ground.[39]

Of all weapons faced during 1962-63, the Viet Cong feared napalm most. At first this firebomb was used sparingly in Southeast Asia since world opinion deemed it a "terror weapon." The first "nape" consisted of light aluminum cases filled with a flammable mixture of soap and gasoline. Unfortunately, lengthy storage caused the gas and soap to separate, yielding a napalm that would flare into a vertical fireball with little spreading action. To prevent this, crewmembers tried adding such items as charcoal and bits of rubber to the mix, but prompt use seemed the best answer.✝[40]

---

* Early drops of 20-pound frag bombs from C-47's turned out poorly. The frags tended to erupt safely in the trees. In addition the crews couldn't drop them accurately.

✝ This mix was replaced by Napalm B, a sticky substance of honey consistency. Made of JP-4 fuel, plystyrene, and benzene, "Nape B" spread better and had a longer shelf life. To save time and money, the new nape was put in cannisters and shipped as a single unit from the United States to South Vietnam.

Napalm often flamed so fiercely as to suck oxygen from the surrounding air. It accordingly became popular for flushing Communists out of their tunnel complexes. Like the incendiary cluster, nape worked well in open areas, but spread and ignited treetops when dropped over woods. Farm Gate pilots consequently dispensed two cans of napalm together--one to burn a hole in the forest canopy for the other to pass through to the enemy beneath.[41]

In June 1962 Farm Gate tried C-47's on napalm runs. The aircraft would take off loaded with barrels of the mix, fly over the target area at 50-100 feet, and drop them one at a time. Their weight usually sent the barrels crashing through the trees to erupt on the ground. Even so, this low-level tactic made it hard for the pilot to spot the target and exposed the vulnerable old Gooney Bird * to ground fire. Hence, Farm Gate ended these missions almost as soon as they began, relying on T-28's and B-26's for nape delivery.[42]

The white phosphorous (WP) bomb--mainly the M-47--soon emerged as a key Farm Gate weapon.† Besides being in good supply, these bombs could be carried by the T-28's, and B-26's, and (later) the A-1E's. Willy Pete could penetrate jungle canopies before detonating. Burning with an intensity comparable to napalm and the incendiary cluster, it proved potent against troops and combustible materials. Its dense persistent column of smoke served as a target marker. If a long smoke mark was needed, WP could be dropped safe.‡ Then the case ruptured on impact and the slowly oxidizing contents smoked for several hours. The M-47 could be dropped from fairly low altitudes without endangering the aircrew, so it was in demand for close air support missions during marginal weather. Lastly, this bomb could be released from moderate to steep dive angles, giving strike pilots an added safety margin.[43]

---

* Gooney Bird was the C-47's nickname.

† WP was also called "Willey Peter" or "Willy Pete."

‡ "Safe" means the bomb "won't explode" or "will not fire."

Supplies of .50-cal ammunition, rockets, and smoke grenades supplemented Farm Gate's bomb inventory.* Because the .50-cal rounds were old, they often malfunctioned during strafing attacks and sometimes exploded in the gun barrel. Their poor penetration and short range forced pilots to fly into the Viet Cong's ground-fire zone to be effective. In addition, the flash of the guns at night tended to give the plane's position away. Nonetheless, when good judgment rules, the strafing hindered enemy movement. 44

Farm Gate crews frequently employed the 2.75-inch folding fin aircraft rocket (FLAR). The FLAR's did have drawbacks however. They destroyed or damaged ground targets only by a direct hit. Also, they were apt to pass clean through soft targets such as thatch-roofed huts and sampans--bursting harmlessly in the dirt or water. In swampy areas their fuzes usually smothered out before detonating the explosive charge. When fired into forested regions the rockets often burst ineffectively in the tree-tops. Fitted with WP warheads, however, the rockets made excellent target markers. From heights beyond the range of small-arms fire, the forward air controller could fire them more accurately than smoke grenades and leave a larger smoke column for identification. 45

Control Net for Air Support Operations

Early in the war, Farm Gate got word of upcoming combat strike missions through the State Department's Combined Studies Division (CSD)/ in Saigon. As the crews filed flight plans, warmed up their aircraft, and

---

* The machineguns of the T-28's and B-26's took .50-cal ammunition. The Air Force also furnished 20-mm rounds for the A-1H's of the Vietnamese Air Force.

/ The Combined Studies Division's staff came from the State Department, U.S. Army Special Forces, and Farm Gate. Attached to the U.S. Embassy in Saigon, the CSD operated from the basement of the MAAG building. Its radio center monitored all traffic around the clock and could communicate direct with most of the strategic hamlets and outposts. Often receiving notice of strike requests before they arrived at the AOC, the CSD alerted the Farm Gate command post to get aircraft ready, while it cleared the mission through 2d ADVON. These CSD functions were absorbed by the AOC in March 1963.

taxied to the end of the runway, the CSD sought strike approval from 2d ADVON and the AOC. Thus the pilots had the green light by the time they were ready to take off. The CSD function waned when the TACS went into full operation, but continued on until March 1963 for Special Forces (SF) strike request clearances.[46]

Almost without exception strike pilots were directed by a forward air controller--always when supporting troops-in-contact (TIC). Only VNAF FAC's (nonpilot air observers) had authority to control airstrikes. Since many of them could not speak English, the Farm Gate pilot had to rely on his "trainee" in the backseat as interpreter. What's more, when the VNAF controller could not find a pilot to fly him, he did not show up. This forced the Farm Gate crew to abort the strike mission or switch to armed reconnaissance which required no FAC.[47] The picture brightened as more USAF forward air controllers arrived in SEA. By mid-1962 Americans piloted many O-1's, coordinating with Farm Gate pilots while at the same time "instructing" VNAF FAC's in airstrike control.[48]

Air-ground communications also drew Air Force attention. The lack of FM radios in the first O-1's to fly in South Vietnam kept forward air controllers from talking with ground troops. The FAC's took to strapping PRC-10 FM ground packs (of World War II vintage) to the back of the pilot's seat in their aircraft. This set's short range, however, compelled the controller to fly almost directly over the ground commander to speak with him. In the summer of 1962 the problem eased as all O-1's began receiving the AN/ARC-44 (FM) radio.[49]

In 1962 the Army Air Request Net resembled the Air-Ground Operations School system, shaped to South Vietnam's needs. The AARN processed two types of air support requests--preplanned and immediate. Each demanded different handling. Preplanned air requests assumed that aircraft would be over the target 3 or more hours after the Air Support Operations Center got the request. (See Fig. 1.) Since the division planned nearly all ARVN operations, preplanned requests usually started off there. Yet the point of origin could be any command level down to battalion. A preplanned request from a battalion commander passed through the S-3 (Operations) to regiment S-3 who informed to ARVN regimental commander. If he couldn't take care of the request with artillery or organic air, it moved up to division and corps for similar screening. When not killed along the way

PREPLANNED AIR REQUEST NET

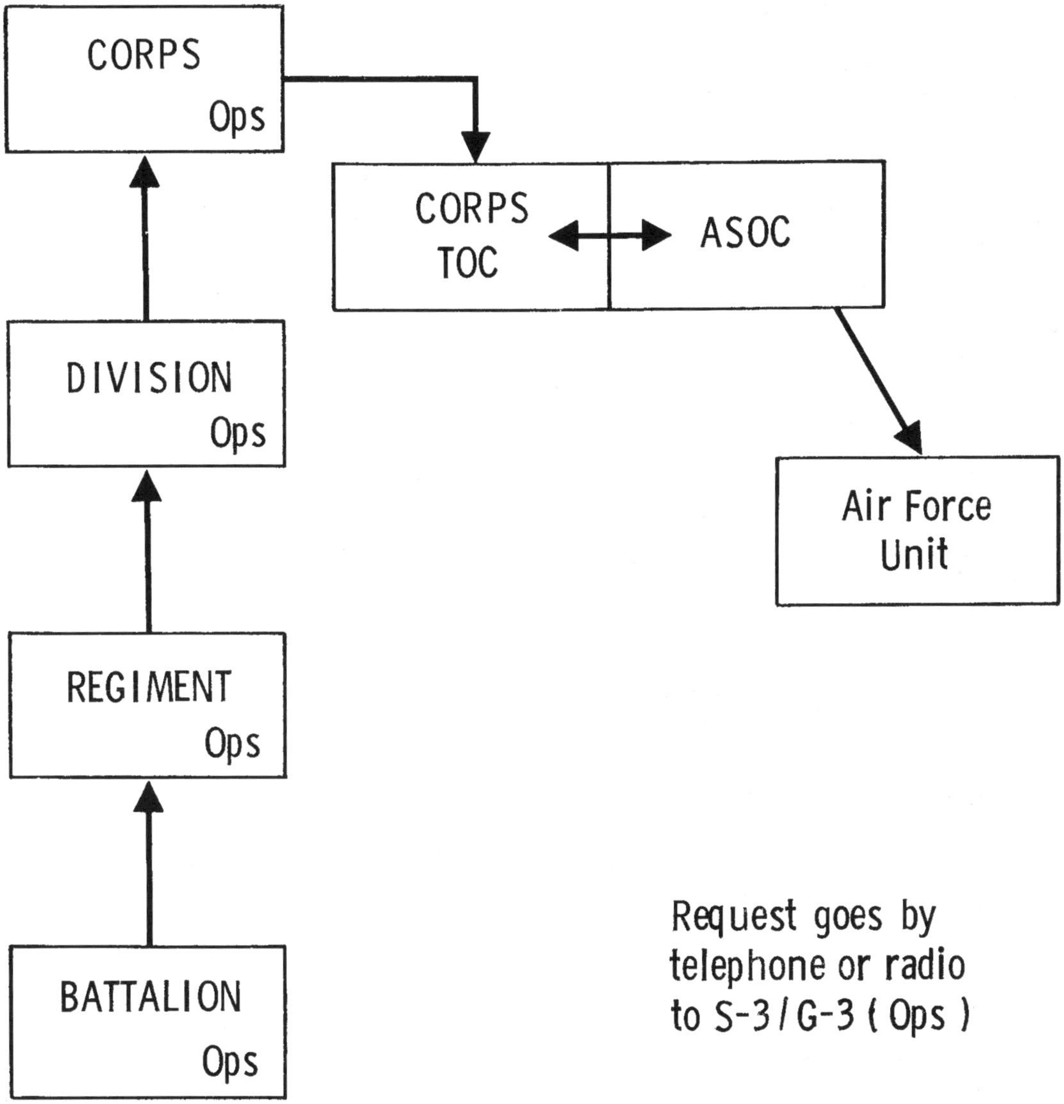

Request goes by telephone or radio to S-3/G-3 (Ops)

Figure 1 (U)

(This page Unclassified)

for political* or operational reasons, the request ended up for action at the Corps Tactical Operations Center and its collocated VNAF Air Support Operations Center. ╪50

The immediate air request traveled a faster route. If an infantry company commander required prompt artillery fire or airstrikes to beat back the enemy, he would notify the S-3 (Air) normally located at the battalion Fire Support Coordination Center (FSCC). The immediate request then underwent the same decision-making process as the preplanned. If airstrikes were opted for, it was sent on to regimental headquarters. Until 1 May 1963 the regiment had to have division approval before forwarding the request to corps. After that date, however, routing became direct to the CTOC╪-- bypassing division which now could only monitor but not disapprove. Response to "immediates" normally took from 15 minutes to 3 hours. The amount of time hinged on the number of FAC's and strike aircraft available to the ASOC and the length of the delay in obtaining approval of the Vietnamese authorities. @51

---

* The ARVN military commander and the province chief were often the same man. Hence, he might turn down a request because approval might not sit well with his government superiors.

╪ Situated side by side, members of the CTOC and ASOC coordinated informally. Arrival of an air support request triggered a flurry of activity. Typewritten message in hand, an ARVN officer on the CTOC side went to the board and began plotting. His VNAF counterpart from the ASOC side joined him and talked over the requirement. After determining what was needed, he returned and had an enlisted man type up the information into a so-called frag order. At Pleiku the ASOC often called in the VNAF pilots and briefed them on the spot, after which they went out and flew the mission. [Murane intvw (S), 26 Nov 73.]

╪ The U.S. Army abandoned the regimental structure in South Vietnam, so the battalion fell directly under the division. Hence, when Army troops entered combat in 1965, their immediate air requests direct from battalion to corps.

@ Preplanned and immediate requests also differed in that immediates were not encoded, the gravity of the situation outweighing the need for caution.

The latter severely impeded any speedup in responsiveness to immediate air requests. The root cause was the Saigon Government's policy of stiff penalties for those approving airstrikes that resulted in friendly casualties. ARVN commanders therefore hesitated to delegate this authority to duty officers. They did not always know whom to trust within their own commands, and such power in the hands of Viet Cong sympathizers could prove disastrous. In I Corps, for example, just the corps commander, chief of staff, and assistant chief of staff sanctioned airstrikes. When none of these officers were at hand, an air request (no matter how critical) went begging.[52]

Delayed responses to air requests struck hardest at isolated Special Forces posts. Often their very survival rested on the swift arrival of strike aircraft. So Special Forces set up a "quasi-request net," enabling a unit or outpost in trouble to send its air request straight to the CSD Operations Center in the U.S. Embassy. Besides routing the request to the proper CTOC and ASOC for approval, the CSD alerted Farm Gate to ready crews for takeoff.[53]

In late 1962 the Air Force took a fresh look at the overall request system. One of several options was to adopt Strike Command's way of handling immediate air requests. That is, each request originated with the ground commander in trouble. His air liaison officer radioed the Air Support Operations Center direct for air support, while ALO's at intermediate army levels monitored and told their ground commanders of progress. If an intermediate commander wanted to fill the request with his artillery or air, he had 5 minutes to let the CTOC know. Otherwise, the request received automatic approval and strike aircraft responded. Despite the good points of such a system, a shortage of single-sideband (SSB) radios put off its adoption in South Vietnam for nearly 2 years.[54]

Even so, air liaison officers began at once to minotor the radios for immediate air requests. When they picked one up, they unofficially alerted their ASOC's by phone or radio as the request worked its way up ARVN channels. In addition, ARVN commanders reluctantly agreed to give immediate air requests priority over other close air support missions. This meant that the ASOC could divert strike aircraft already committed to preplanned sorties.[55]

AIR FORCE IMMEDIATE AIR REQUEST NET

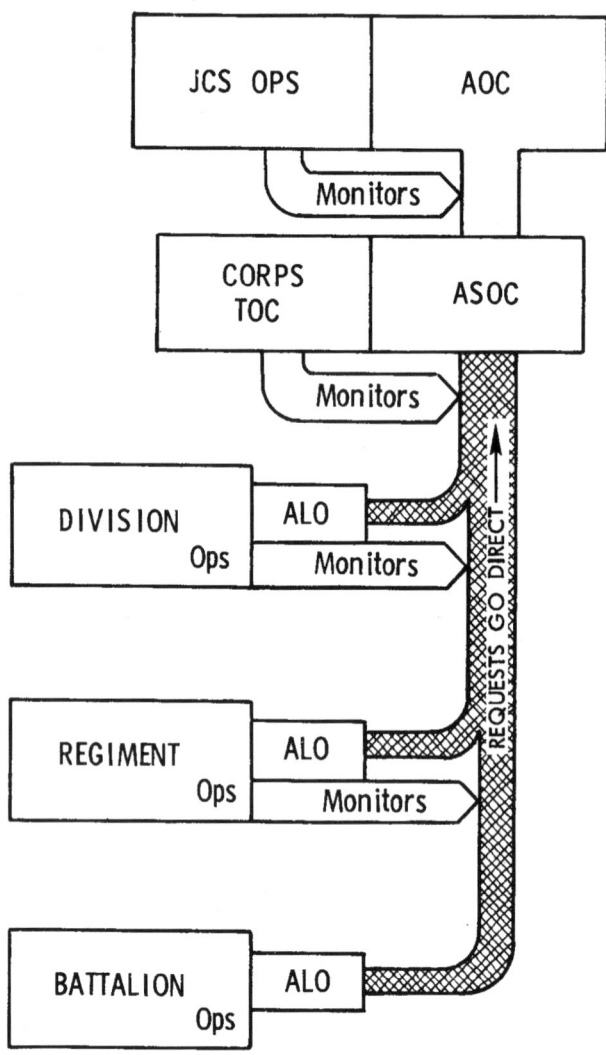

FEATURES: 1. REQUESTS GO DIRECT TO ASOC
2. INTERVENING ECHELONS MONITOR
3. IF NO DISAPPROVALS ARE HEARD IN 5 MINUTES, REQUEST IS CONSIDERED APPROVED.

Figure 2 (U)

(This page Unclassified)

On 15 May 1964 Lt. Gen. Joseph H. Moore, 2d Air Division Commander, set up a new VNAF air request net patterned after Strike Command's. (See Fig. 2.) Integrated into the Tactical Air Control System, it worked closely with the Army request net. The new system featured jointly manned USAF and VNAF tactical air control parties assigned to every regimental and battaltion command post in the field. Each TACP had the new SSB radio for dealing direct with the Air Support Operations Center. This in turn allowed the ASOC to get aircraft airborne almost as soon as the immediate air requests were sent and approved.[56]

Early Day Tactics

Rendezvous and Target Marking

As a rule, forward air controllers and strike crews got the word on preplanned close air support missions from a frag order the night preceding the scheduled airstrike. This let them plan the flight and check the latest intelligence on the target areas. When time permitted, VNAF FAC's and their USAF "instructors" also dropped by division headquarters for G-3 (Air) briefings before flying to the rendezvous area. Base operations gave strike crews final instructions.[57]

Immediate air requests seldom allowed time for flight planning. Controllers and strike pilots were often alerted a few minutes before take-off or while flying another mission. Coordination of details took place on the way to the target area. Upon arrival final preparations were firmed up with the ground commander. Whether immediate or preplanned strike, enroute and rendezvous techniques were essentially the same.

Following takeoff, the FAC told the control tower and the ASOC he was enroute to the target area, then verified rendezvous point and procedures. Once in the vicinity of the target, the controller radioed the ground commander to talk over the tactical situation. He noted prominent terrain features, high ground, distances between friendly and Communist troops, and desirable attack headings. Afterwards he flew to the rendezvous point.[58]

Meanwhile, the strike crews took off and instantly contacted the control tower.* They received vectors to the rendezvous point and handoff to a control and reporting center for flight following. Depending on the

---

* They usually flew in 2-ship cells.

weather and ground-fire threat, the pilots skimmed the tree tops or climbed as high as 2,500 feet above ground level (AGL). For navigation they turned to dead reckoning (DR)* or ultra high frequency (UHF) omnigrange./ 59

Since the forward air controller had no TACAN (tactical air navigation),/ the rendezvous point was usually a set of coordinates. These were located far enough from the target to maintain the element of surprise and also be safe from enemy ground fire. To hasten join-up with the fighter crews, the controller would call off obvious landmarks, dip his wings, or drop a smoke cannister. After rendezvous FAC and fighters headed for the target area, all the while going over strike information and tactics as well as deciding on attack headings @ and ordnance drop sequence. The controller cleared with the ground commander before the strike began. 60 Dispensing both napalm and general purpose bombs demanded special care. If possible the strike aircraft swept in low and dropped nape first. Then they climbed to higher altitude before releasing GP bombs because the blast could damage low-flying planes. Nor could these bombs land close-in to friendlies--a 500-pounder could kill or injure up to 500 feet from the impact point. Hence, the ground commander had the final say on such strikes. 61

---

* Finding one's position by means of a compass and calculations based on speed, time elapsed, effect of wind, and direction from a known position.

/ "Omni" is a radio aid to air navigation that creates an endless number of paths through space through 360° of azimuth. The first Farm Gate planes lacked some of the navigation (nav) aids found on later strike aircraft.

/ A system consisting of short-range UHF radio stations. In the form of a readout on the instrument panel the pilot continuously receives accurate distance and bearing information from a particular station tuned.

@ The FAC had to be certain the attack heading didn't run the strike aircraft into a hillside or box canyon, nor over friendly positions.

Before mounting a close air support attack, the USAF forward air controller identified the friendly position. The ground commander then helped him find the enemy's location. The FAC pinpointed the target to make sure the strike pilots knew exactly where to put their ordnance. Early in the war, he did this by dropping smoke grenades out the O-1's window. The method proved highly inaccurate, however, unless he flew on the deck (below 50 feet AGL) to release. As an alternate, the controller could ask the ground commander to fire smoke rounds, but the Viet Cong easily duplicated the tactic and it was seldom used. There was an emergency technique employed. The controller instructed the strike pilots to watch the shadow of his aircraft on the ground. Upon passing directly over the target, he called off its location in relation to the shadow's position. The strike crews had to be right above the FAC aircraft at the time or their perspective would be thrown off.[62]

Pressing the search for a better target marker, USAF and VNAF officers considered and rejected 60-mm rounds and rifle-launched smoke grenades. They elected instead to equip the O-1's with rocket launchers and make do with the 2.75-inch WP rocket. This weapon sharpened marking accuracy but had drawbacks. Its smoke often became trapped under the jungle canopy and couldn't be seen from the air. Falling in mud or water, the rocket usually failed to go off. If detonated above the trees, its smoke faded too fast. Notwithstanding, it was the best marker available through 1964.*[63]

To mark the target the forward air controller dropped to an altitude of 150 to 800 feet AGL, depending on the weather and ground threat. The two strike aircraft stayed in orbit at rendezvous level--one at 4,500-5,000 feet, the other 500-1,000 feet higher to cover against possible antiaircraft (AA) fire. As the controller worked his way to the enemy position, he used trees, hills, valleys, or other terrain features to screen his approach. He made one last check of target location with the ground commander and received final approval for the strike.[64]

---

*In that year the Commander, 19th TASSq, described the ideal marker. It would be a flare that trailed smoke on the way down, floated in water, and went on burning for up to 10 minutes after sinking. Such a marker didn't exist at the time, but the MK-6 parachute flare underwent testing. Released from the O-1, the MK-6 deployed by parachute to treetop level before igniting by a preset fuze. The flare's thick pillar of smoke and brilliant light lasted about 3 minutes and could be seen from 5 miles away. Inaccuracy ruled out use of this flare however.

() To retain the element of surprise, the FAC flew alongside and past the target, pulled a tight 270° turn and darted back across. He dropped the marker and broke out into an orbit over friendly troops opposite the strike aircraft's pattern.[65]

MARKING TARGET USING SURPRISE (1963)

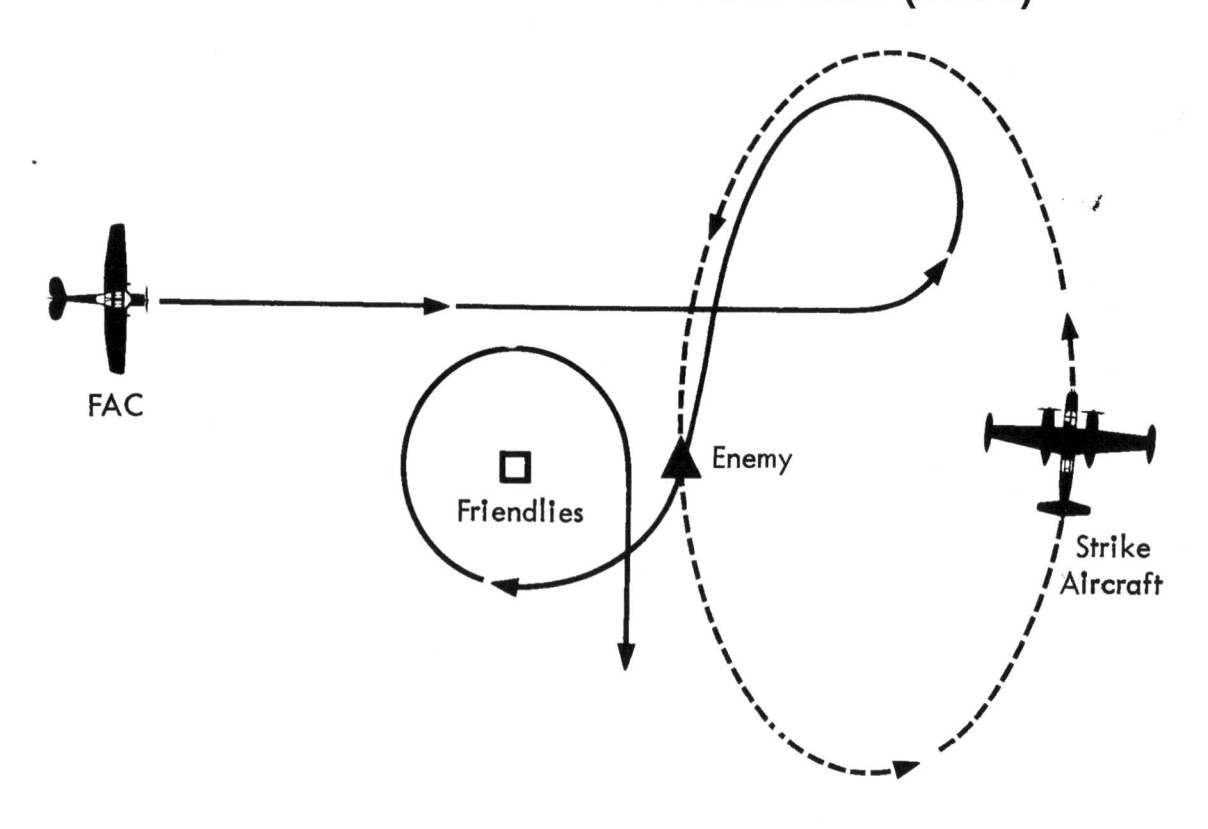

Figure 3 (U)

(This page Unclassified)

(S) Whenever the Viet Cong knew of the impending attack, the controller didn't try for surprise. He set up his marking pass on the desired strike heading, flew abreast of the target, and entered a slight diving turn. Upon leveling out, he lined up on the target--sighting it in from a grease mark on the O-1's windshield (or using the cowling as a reference)--and released his marker. As he turned-off-target, the FAC kept the impact point in sight, established his orbit (as in surprise marking), and adjusted follow-on strikes as necessary.[66]

NORMAL TARGET MARKING (1963)

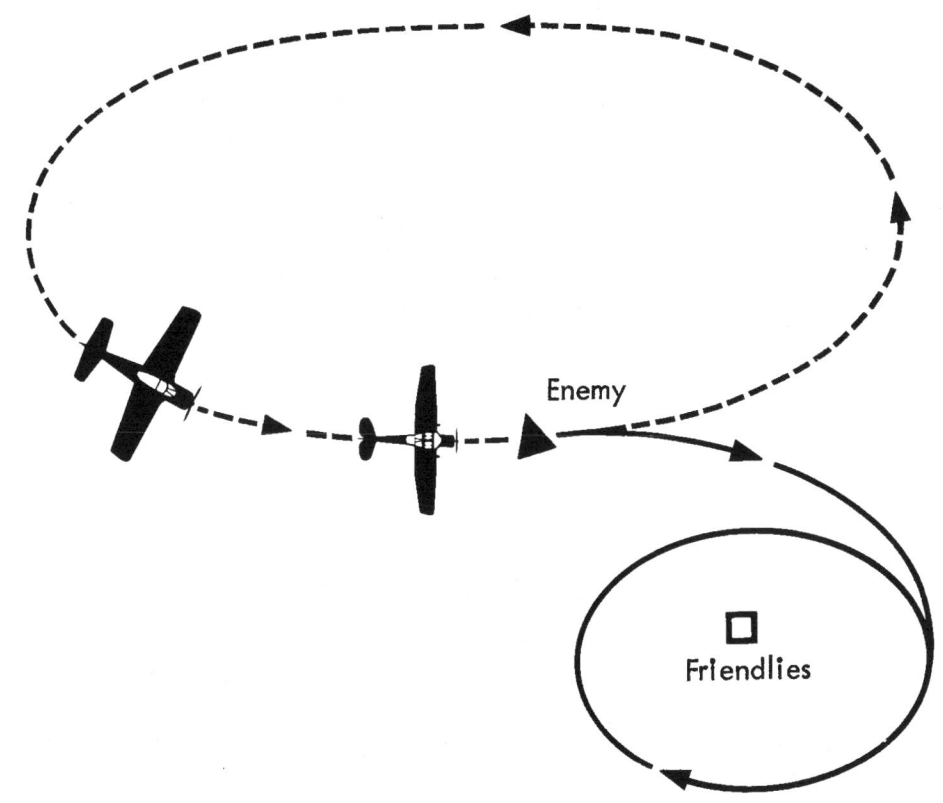

Figure 4 (U)

(This page Unclassified)

The Airstrike

T-28 crews most often used a rectangular strike orbit (see Fig. 4). One fighter remained high. The other took up the controller's final heading to the target, completed the bomb run, pulled off-target, and started climbing to altitude. At this point, the other aircraft descended and maneuvered for its bombing pass on the same attack heading. When general purpose bombs were dropped, the orbit altitude varied from 3,500 to 4,000 feet AGL.* As the strike pilot came around to his final approach, he set up a steep dive (30°-45°) and accelerated to 250-275 KIAS (knots, indicated airspeed). Upon approaching 1,200 feet, the pilot pickled † his bombs (usually one at a time) and began recovery so as to round out at 900-1,000 feet. This kept the aircraft free of the bomb blasts.‡[67]

On strafing runs, the T-28 pilot dropped out of orbit to 1,200 feet feet AGL. During final approach he executed a shallow dive (10°) and stepped up to 220KIAS. Nearing 100 feet he commenced firing quick short bursts from two .50-cal machineguns. He pulled out of the dive around 50 feet and flew on the deck for another 1/2 mile, using terrain as a screen from ground fire. Next he gunned to orbit altitude in a climbing turn.[68]

T-28 napalm tactics resembled those for strafing runs. Rolling in on "final" at 1,200 feet AGL, the pilot made a shallow dive toward the target. He leveled out at 50-75 feet, held the attack heading, and dropped the nape. He moved off-target like in strafing, climbing back to orbit altitude in time to cover the other T-28 during its bomb run. When AA fire heated up, the pilot steepened the dive angle and strafed up to the moment of bomb release.[69]

---

*The T-28 generally carried two 50 - or 100-pound bombs on the outboard wing racks and a couple of 500-pounders on the two inboard points. The bombload had to be reduced when the aircraft hauled the 19-rocket LAU-3A pods. Moreover, heavy bombs couldn't be conveyed on the outboard racks because the wings would twist and bend during taxiing, making the plane hard to steer.

† To release a bomb or expend ordnance by depressing a button (pickle).

‡ The FAC and strike crews were constantly alert to bombs hitting too close to friendly positions. If the danger appeared likely, the bombing pass was aborted.

(U) Napalm drops proved more accurate than bombing because they took place at low altitude. Lacking the strong blast of bombs, nape could be delivered to within 50-100 feet of friendly positions. However, to escape the searing heat, the troops had to be dug-in or otherwise well-covered.[70]

Farm Gate B-26's carried a 3-man crew--a pilot and navigator seated side by side and a VNAF observer in the jump seat behind the nav. Close air support tactics, fashioned by the crews during training at Eglin, were fitted to South Vietnam needs. Besides conveying 6,000 pounds of bombs on the wing racks and in the 2 bomb bays, the Invader could store 3,200 .50-cal rounds for its 8 noseguns.*[71]

In carrying out an airstrike, the B-26 pilot penetrated the target area at 3,000-6,000 feet AGL. He descended to remain at least 500 feet above the FAC's altitude, which ranged between 1,500-4,500 feet according to the ground threat. He took up an egg-shaped orbit on the opposite side of the target from the forward air controller./ While the latter marked the target, the B-26 turned on base leg ǂ and continued on around to the strike heading. The crew at this point got final instructions and target adjustments from the controller. While the pilot lined up on the target, the navigator set the bombing switches, armed the machineguns, and monitored the aircraft instruments. Napalm on the wing racks went first, so the pilot started a shallow dive (5°-15°) at 2,500 feet. He jinked @ if necessary as airspeed built to 240 knots and the aircraft approached 50-75 feet AGL. Leveling out around 1/2 mile in front of the target, he zeroed in and dropped the nape. He kept going straight ahead for several seconds before returning to altitude in a left-hand climbing turn.[72]

---

* At first B-26's hauled mixed loads of napalm and GP on their wing racks. This posed the danger of weapon release from the wrong height--for example, bombs from napalm altitude. Consequently, the wing racks and each of the bomb bays were confined to one type weapon.

/ Seated in the left seat, the pilot always tended to fly a lefthand pattern-- a dangerous practice. Hence, he had to force himself to alter his orbit.

ǂ The heading flown just prior to the attack heading.

@ Jinking is a series of rapid turn reversals and abrupt changes of roll and/or pitch attitude at random intervals. It prevents an enemy gunner from tracking the aircraft.

Next the B-26 pilot set up to deliver general purpose bombs. He took the aircraft to 3,500-4,500 feet AGL and swung around to the attack heading. He nosed down steeply (30°-45°) and let the speed rise to about 260 KIAS. Just before reaching the 1,000-foot pullup altitude, the pilot released the bombs one at a time or rippled them off in sets of three across the target. He maneuvered off the target either right or left (away from friendly positions) into a 90° then a 270° climbing turn back to altitude. This positioned him for a follow-on attack from the opposite direction. *73

B-26 crews used the basic napalm pattern for strafing, but with a 10°-20° rather than a 5°-15° angle. To shorten the strafing pattern, the pilot steepened his dive to 30°. He shallowed it to 5° for a longer run. 74 Rocket delivery resembled high-angle dive-bombing. Executing his dive from 4,000-5,000 feet AGL, the pilot fired the rockets singly or in salvo ⟋ a moment previous to leveling off at 1,000 feet. 75

Air Cover

Beginning in 1962, lightly defended ARVN truck and train convoys became favorite Viet Cong targets. Farm Gate and the VNAF countered with air cover missions by 0-1 controllers and T-28 crews. The FAC as a rule flew at 100-150 feet AGL and 1-1 1/2 miles in front of the convoy, weaving back and forth. He swung behind the convoy now and then to check on possible Communist attack from the rear. Meantime, two T-28's stayed at 1,500 feet in a pattern that sent them 1-2 miles ahead of the convoy and 3/4 mile behind. The two fighters kept opposite each other so one would always be set to roll in for an attack. ⟋ 76

---

* Bombing a hill demanded an adjustment in tactics. Downhill, the pilot dropped the bombs short; uphill, he released them late.

⟋ A salvo is the release of several bombs or rockets simultaneously (or in close train) from one or more aircraft at a single target.

⟋ For cover duty the T-28's commonly carried incendiaries and fragmentation bombs.

To cover ground force sweep operations*, the controller flew a bit ahead of the advancing troops at 800-900 feet AGL. He crossed from side to side seeking out retreating enemy soldiers. Upon spotting the Communists, the FAC sought to stop them by dropping grenades, buzzing, or firing marker rockets. If this failed or the force looked too large for the sweep to handle, he called in the T-28's standing by at higher altitude.[77]

In covering helicopters, a pair of Farm Gate T-28's waited at 1,000 feet AGL as the choppers whirled from their pads and formed up at 700-foot cruise altitude. The first Trojan dropped to around 200 feet and began sweeping ahead of the lead copter in slow S-turns. The second Trojan orbited higher, poised for an instant firing pass should trouble be spotted.[78] When the choppers flew low along the terrain's contours, both fighters stayed 800 feet above them in the same S-maneuver.[79] As the helicopters approached their landing zone, they closed in tight trail. † The T-28's descended and flew one on each side of the formation--keeping high enough to make immediate strikes in any direction.[80]

Night Operations

(C) The Government of South Vietnam's efforts to win the support of its rural people centered around the development of strategic hamlets and Special Forces outposts. The SF outposts, or camps, served as visual remainders of the government's will to defend its outlying areas. ‡ In addition, special reconnaissance teams set out from the camps to spy on enemy movements.[81]

(U) The Communists well knew what the hamlets and outposts stood for. They focused on wiping them out, attacking chiefly at night when defenses were weakest. Moreover, in 1961 the tactics and equipment for detecting enemy movements under cover of darkness hadn't yet been perfected. The Farm Gate detachment took pioneer steps in November, a few days after arriving at Bien Hoa AB, South Vietnam.

---

* In sweeps the troops searched out and cleared the enemy from a specific area.

† Directly behind one another and spaced fairly close.

‡ SF teams with American advisers went to the hamlets and helped build defensive works. They also taught the villagers combat tactics for fighting off attacks.

An enterprising Farm Gate C-47 crew borrowed flares from the VNAF, found out how they worked, then took off to test them. After reaching what the pilot deemed a reasonable altitude, the crewchief began throwing flares out the cargo door. The blossoming light caused a stir among the crews on the ground. Several pilots scrambled into their T-28's and under the flarelight simulated bombing passes over the field. The next day, Col. Benjamin H. King, Farm Gate Commander, told 2d Advanced Echelon his men were ready for night operations.[82]

Farm Gate experiments quickened over the next few months. The crews tried many flare techniques before settling on the best drop intervals, dispensing altitudes, and flare and strike patterns. They learned that airstrikes couldn't be made in the shadows cast by flarelight, because the target grew dim and hard to identify. Again, flares dispensed on attack headings tended to blind and disorient the strike crews, and increased the risk of air collision. Hence, the flareship pilot flew offset on a heading paralleling the strike track and dropped his flares opposite the target. This let the strike pilot attack without facing straight into the flarelight. He could also use the flare as a reference point.[83]

Flareship crews at first attached ignition lanyards to the flares and dropped them by hand out the cargo door. This method, however, resulted in preignition and uneven flare patterns. What's more, the slipstream whipping around the open door sometimes slammed the flares against the aircraft or even back into it. Crews solved the problem by building a wooden flare dispenser having five parallel chutes. First used in C-123 flareships during late 1962, the dispenser got the flares out beyond the slipstream. After loading the chutes, the operator would move a lever that dispensed the flares and pulled the ignition lanyards.[84]

VNAF C-47's by February 1962 had joined the regular flare and strike missions in support of hamlets and outposts. A few weeks later, Farm Gate put a loaded flareship on alert nightly from dusk to dawn. When the Air Operations Center got word of a hamlet under attack, this flareship and fighters would lift off and be over the combat area inside of 20-30 minutes. As Viet Cong attacks multiplied, Farm Gate flareships also flew airborne alert over certain areas.[85]

When an air support request came in, the AOC obtained necessary clearances and alerted the C-47 flareship standing by at Bien Hoa. The C-47 stopped at Tan Son Nhut AB on the way to the target area. It picked up a VNAF navigator (preferably one who spoke English) and an FM radio for air-ground communications. Farm Gate T-28's (sometimes B-26's) got to the rendezvous point at the same time or shortly after the flareship.[86]

Flareship and fighters showed their outside lights for an easier join-up. They pushed on together to the target area with FM radios tuned to the hamlet's frequencies. Five minutes before arrival, the C-47 co-pilot contacted the ground commander for weather, terrain layout, and enemy location. The pilot picked the strike heading and altitude and instructed the fighter crews.* Before the strike could get under way, all crews had to positively identify the target. They did this either by radio using visual reference points or fire arrows on the ground.† In addition they needed to be sure of friendly positions and have reliable radio contact. Throughout the strike, the crews kept navigation lights on unless ground fire heated up.[87]

Although C-47 flareships as a rule orbited at about 2,500 feet AGL, they went as low as 1,000 feet if need be. The basic pattern was a right-hand orbit of 15-second legs and 1-minute turns, bringing the aircraft over the target every 2 1/2 - 3 minutes to re-flare (see Fig. 5). The loadmaster served as kicker,‡ aided now and then by other crewmembers. Before the flare dispenser came along, the kicker (in safety harness) sat on the floor or stood in the door, pushing out flares at the pilot's command. He would drop two MK-6's upwind at 7-second interval (5-second intervals for the weaker MK-5's). The fuze setting delayed ignition until the flare was 300 feet below the aircraft. If all went well, the two flares drifted over the target, bracketed it at the midpoint of their descent, and spread maximum shadow-free light.[88]

---

* The rules of engagement required no forward air controller for night strike missions supporting hamlets under attack--provided the flareship could maintain radio contact with both the fighters and the ground. However, a FAC had to be present if the support was for friendly troops in the field.

† The fire arrows often consisted of metal cans filled with fuel-soaked sand. The flareship and fighters could clearly see them blazing at night--pointing toward the enemy position. Hamlet defenders gave the Communist location to the aircraft with reference to the arrows.

‡ The flareship/gunship crewmember charged with dropping the flares.

FARM GATE FLARE PATTERN

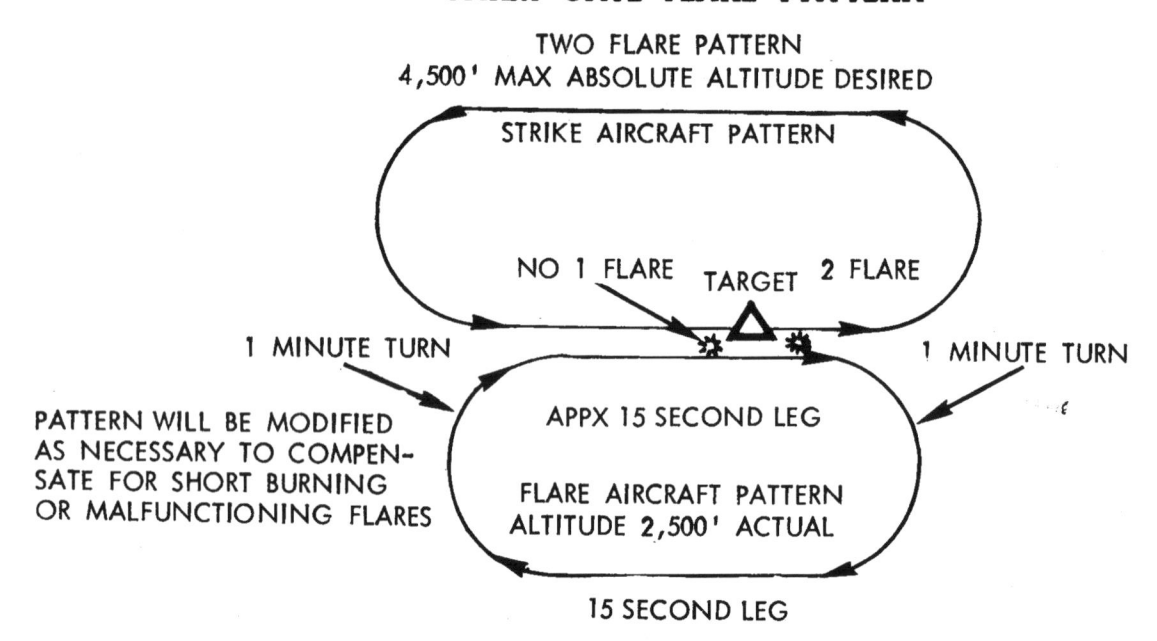

TWO FLARE PATTERN
4,500' MAX ABSOLUTE ALTITUDE DESIRED

STRIKE AIRCRAFT PATTERN

NO 1 FLARE   TARGET   2 FLARE

1 MINUTE TURN   1 MINUTE TURN

PATTERN WILL BE MODIFIED
AS NECESSARY TO COMPEN-
SATE FOR SHORT BURNING
OR MALFUNCTIONING FLARES

APPX 15 SECOND LEG

FLARE AIRCRAFT PATTERN
ALTITUDE 2,500' ACTUAL

15 SECOND LEG

WIND FROM RIGHT, FLARES DRIFT LEFT

EXAMPLE: RELEASE ALTITUDE 2500'
DEPLOY AND IGNITE
2200' ABOVE TERRAIN

Figure 5 (U)

(This page Unclassified)

After forming his flare pattern, the C-47 pilot rechecked to insure the strike crews knew the target's exact location. The two T-28's next set up a standard rectangular left-hand orbit at about 4,500 feet AGL. This pattern--slightly longer than and opposite to the flareship's--enclosed the friendly position to protect it against accidental attack (see Fig. 5). To compensate for the difficulty in seeing at night, all attack angles were shallowed 5°-15°. Each fighter pilot in turn dove below the flares, bombed or strafed, and recovered in a left climbing turn back to orbit altitude. During ascent he kept tabs on the positions of the other aircraft. [89]

If four T-28's took part in an airstrike, they orbited nearly 500 feet beneath the flareship in a box or touch-and-go pattern. As the flight leader turned in toward the target, the other three fighters peeled off behind him at fixed intervals. This gave them proper spacing behind one another and a view of the flareship at all times. Each pilot called out his position upon turning, for example, "Number one on base," "Number two turning downwind." This tactic trimmed the chances of mid-air collision with other strike aircraft or the flareship. [90]

The T-28's sometimes got to the target area ahead of the flareship. They contacted the ground commander and, if the situation was critical, attacked under their own flarelight. With lights out the lead pilot started a shallow dive toward the target, dropping napalm if he had it. Recovering on the upwind side, he dispensed a delayed-fuze flare. The second pilot by this time was turning on the attack heading. So if timing was right, just as he pulled off the target the flare lit up--spreading light for the next bomb run. After the lead T-28 had used up all its flares, the fighters traded places and the strike went on. [91]

The B-26 proved safer for night operations than the T-28. It had better range, higher cruise speed, longer endurance, and greater firepower. Moreover, the side-by-side seating for USAF members of the 3-man crew bolstered teamwork. The navigator kept track of the Invader's position and altitude, freeing the pilot to pinpoint the target and carry out the bomb run. [92]

B-26 night tactics for the most part matched those of the T-28. However, as noted earlier, the pilot favored a left-hand orbit because he found it hard to see out the right side of the aircraft. Established at 4,500 feet AGL, the orbit usually circled the hamlet or other friendly position. The Invader dipped through the flareship's altitude during the bomb run. Hence, the crew kept an eye out for the C-47 to make sure the B-26 didn't come too close.[93]

B-26 NIGHT ATTACK PATTERN

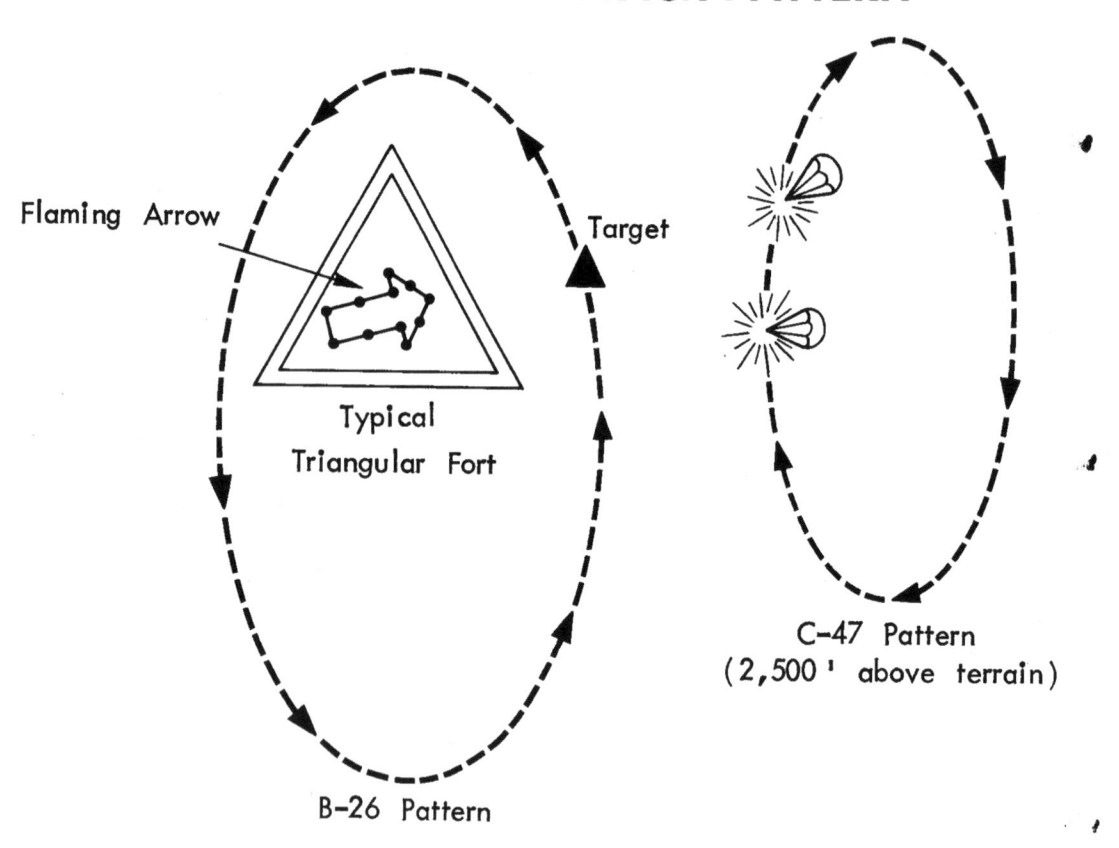

Flaming Arrow

Target

Typical Triangular Fort

B-26 Pattern

C-47 Pattern (2,500' above terrain)

Figure 6 (U)

During 1962 and most of 1963, Farm Gate and VNAF C-47's handled the lion's share of the night flaredrops in close air support operations. The steady rise in Communist nighttime attacks, however, stretched C-47 flareship capability to the breaking point. So in August 1962, Mule Train C-123's* of the 315th Troop Carrier Group joined in ground flare alert. The Provider carried twice the flares of the C-47 and surpassed it in endurance time. Little by little, Farm Gate turned over its flare duties to Mule Train and the VNAF. By September 1963 the C-123's pulled air/ground flareship alert and flew 5-hour night flare missions out of Tan Son Nhut. A year later, the Providers were making more than half of all night flaredrops. [94]

C-123 and C-47 crews faced similar flare-dispensing problems. As mentioned above, the C-123 was first to use the 5-chute flare dispenser. The crew strapped it to the outer edge of the ramp then lowered the cargo door partway from the top. This cut down the chances of the slipstream sweeping a flare back into the aircraft. Accidental fires within the cabin caused by faulty flares posed another danger--the burning magnesium could melt steel. As a precaution, special containers were built. The crew set these boxes on roller conveyors and strapped them to the floor directly across from the flare dispenser. A flare igniting too soon could be dumped into the container, the straps cut, cargo door and ramp opened, and the whole box dropped from the plane. [95]

Mule Train adopted Farm Gate flare tactics. The C-123 crew, after being alerted by the Air Operations Center, picked up a VNAF navigator and flew on to the trouble spot, navigating by mapreading or low-frequency radio. If possible, the flareship met the fighters enroute and rendezvoused in the same way as FAC/strike aircraft. Once within radio range of the hamlet, the VNAF navigator got a rundown from the ground commander and passed it to the fighter crews. / [96]

---

* The Fairchild C-123 Provider entered USAF service in July 1955 as a troop carrier and cargo plane. Powered by two 2,300-housepower engines, the aircraft had a top airspeed of 245 mph and a cruise speed of 205 mph. It also had over 7 hours endurance time and a range of 1,470 miles. The original mission of the Mule Train C-123's in South Vietnam was to furnish supplemental tactical airlift for the Vietnamese armed forces.

/ The language barrier commonly blocked clear communication between VNAF and American crewmembers. The C-123 copilot often needed to relay the information to the fighters. Many crews used point-and-talk sheets with Vietnamese instructions on one side and English on the other.

(U) Before entering the target area, the C-123 pilot dropped to between 2,500 and 4,000 feet AGL, dimmed inside lights, and firmed up final details. The loadmaster and his two kickers (often ARVN soldiers) fixed the flare fuzes for the desired illumination altitude. They raised the cargo door, shoved the dispenser in place, and set the injection timer-- normally for 5-second intervals. The pilot and copilot checked weather, terrain hazards, and target information. After choosing the correct orbit pattern for lighting the target evenly, they went over delivery tactics with the strike crews. They put the navigation lights and rotating beacons on bright-flash, to help the fighters keep the flareship in view.[97] Once in the target area, the Provider took up a right-hand racetrack pattern, and as a rule dropped two flares during the first pass by the target. The orbit was then altered for wind drift so flares could be dropped every 3 minutes. Each strike pilot made his bombing or strafing run in turn. He broke left off-target and climbed to an orbit on the opposite side of the target from the C-123.[98]

Although the C-123's proved a boon to the flareship force, 2d ADVON was still hard put to fill all support requests. The flareships nevertheless made themselves felt. For example, the Viet Cong often broke off attack at the first sign of their approach. On many other occasions, the dropping of flares alone turned the enemy back.[99]

Late 1963 saw Viet Cong attacks on outposts and hamlets soar, spurring the demand for night close air support. At the same time, the VNAF shifted its C-47's from night airborne flare alert to other support duty. This induced 2d ADVON to boost the number of C-123's on flare alert to five at Tan Son Nhut and two at Nha Trang.[100] Enemy AA fire also mounted alarmingly, the gunners sharpening accuracy with barrage fire along the expected flight paths. Strike and flare aircraft of necessity departed from fixed orbit patterns and standard strike headings.*[101] The accepted flare-dispensing altitude of 2,500 feet AGL likewise went by the board. Flare-drops from 4,000 feet became the rule with some loss in accuracy. When the MK-6 didn't burn brightly enough at higher altitudes, tests of the new MK-24 got under way. These disclosed that the flare was harder to set up for dispensing and had a higher dud rate (up to 23 percent). Consequently, the MK-6 continued as the chief flare until the bugs were worked out of the MK-24.[102]

---

* Because strike pilots found it difficult to judge distance and rate of closure at night, they reduced airspeed and shallowed their attack angles. These changes worked to the advantage of enemy gunners.

Reevaluating Operations--1964

The quickening tempo of the war in South Vietnam dictated further changes in tactics. On 8 July 1963, Farm Gate (Detachment 2A) had merged with the newly created 1st Air Commando Squadron of the 34th Tactical Group (TGp). Moreover, by 1964 it was clear the Vietnamese Air Force couldn't possibly produce all air support needed by ground troops. The rules of engagement were accordingly relaxed to extend the Air Force's role in combat operations. VNAF observers, for example, no longer had to be aboard USAF strike aircraft supporting hamlets or villages at night. Similarly, enlisted men* could fill in for pilots as the VNAF crewmember required on air commando aircraft flying other than close air support missions.[103]

The Viet Cong adapted very well to the stepped-up bombing and strafing. During attacks they captured thousands of handguns, hundreds of automatic rifles, and dozens of .30- and .50-caliber machineguns--turning them against their original owners. For firing on low-flying planes, the Communists placed captured .50-caliber guns on homemade mounts that tilted up to 43°. They linked a pair of fifties for 2-man use. One operator tracked the aircraft, the other did the firing.[104]

Deadly enemy ground fire below 3,500 feet † forced strike pilots to switch attack headings for follow-on passes. They further shunned low-altitude pullouts and one-in-at-a-time tactics. Shallow dives and on-the-deck delivery, used with napalm and other incendiaries, gave way to steeper dives and use of frag bombs, dropped from above small-arms range.[105]

To keep enemy gunners guessing, Air Commando crews made second and third bomb runs 30° or more off the first attack heading. They also took to flying a "moving figure 8" pattern. (See Fig. 7.) From a steep dive, the pilot pickled his bombs in time to level off at or around 1,500 feet AGL,

---

* These airmen for the most part stood by in the squadron operations room. A VNAF noncommissioned officer scheduled them.

† .30-caliber weapons were lethal up to 1,400 feet; .50-caliber, to 3,500 feet.

then zoom back to altitude. He varied pulloff direction on each of the three passes--right, left, or straight ahead to let terrain shield the aircraft. (See Fig. 8.).[106]

When low-level delivery was a must (e.g., for napalm), the pilot dove from the higher altitude to pick up all possible speed. He pulled out on the deck at least 3,500 feet from the target, moved in, dropped the nape, and kept low for another 1/2 mile or so before pulling up. When the terrain ruled out a long low-altitude run-in, the strike pilot came in closer, dove more steeply, and strafed the target on his way down. This generally kept the enemy under cover long enough for the fighter to drop the napalm and get off-target.*[107]

The T-28 and B-26 Become War Weary

Hard usage of the T-28 and B-26 in the first 3 years of the war took its toll and spotlighted their shortcomings. Even with a beefed-up engine, the T-28 hadn't the speed to get in and off a target quickly. Its thin armorplating could stop only light small-arms fire.[108] The aircraft's gunsight--the old F-86 sight minus the gyro--was mounted above the instrument panel. To peer through it, the pilot needed to crame his neck forward as far as he could. But in this position he couldn't read the top instruments--critical during a dive. So he sat back to read them then stretched forward again to reacquire the target. It took a seasoned pilot to master this rocking motion during an airstrike when each second counted.[109]

The B-26, termed a "maintenance nightmare," had weathered two rigorous wars and returned to mothballs each time in doubtful shape. A great deal of its old, moisture-cracked, and frayed wiring had been disconnected or led nowhere. Furthermore, no two Invaders were wired the same. Maintenance crews found the engines complex and cumbersome to work on in the field and sometimes hard to get parts for. What's more, the huge, jutting engine nacelles shut off most of the view on either side of the aircraft. Finally, the B-26's age and stress limits supposedly confined it to fairly shallow dives.[110]

---

* The strike pilot adjusted a high-angle strafing run for recovery at or above 1,500 feet and a zoon back to altitude. This was not so accurate as a low-angle run but a lot safer. During low-angle strafing (under 1,500 feet) the pilot attacked at treetop level and held off recovery until at least 3,500 feet past the target.

MOVING FIGURE EIGHT (FARM GATE)

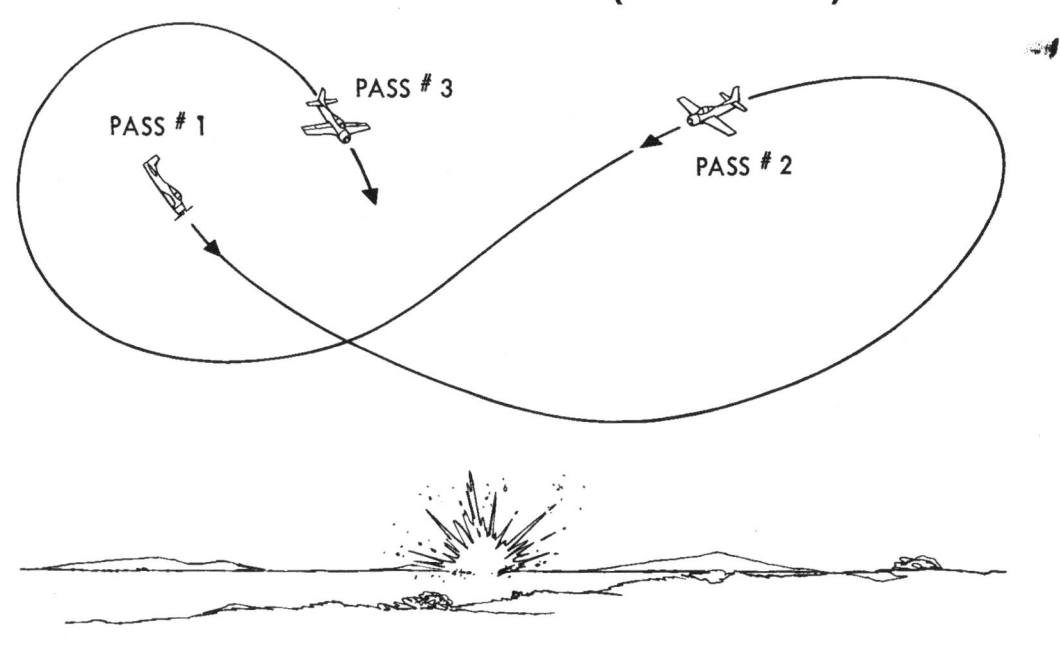

Figure 7 (U)

PULLOFF VARIATIONS (FARM GATE)

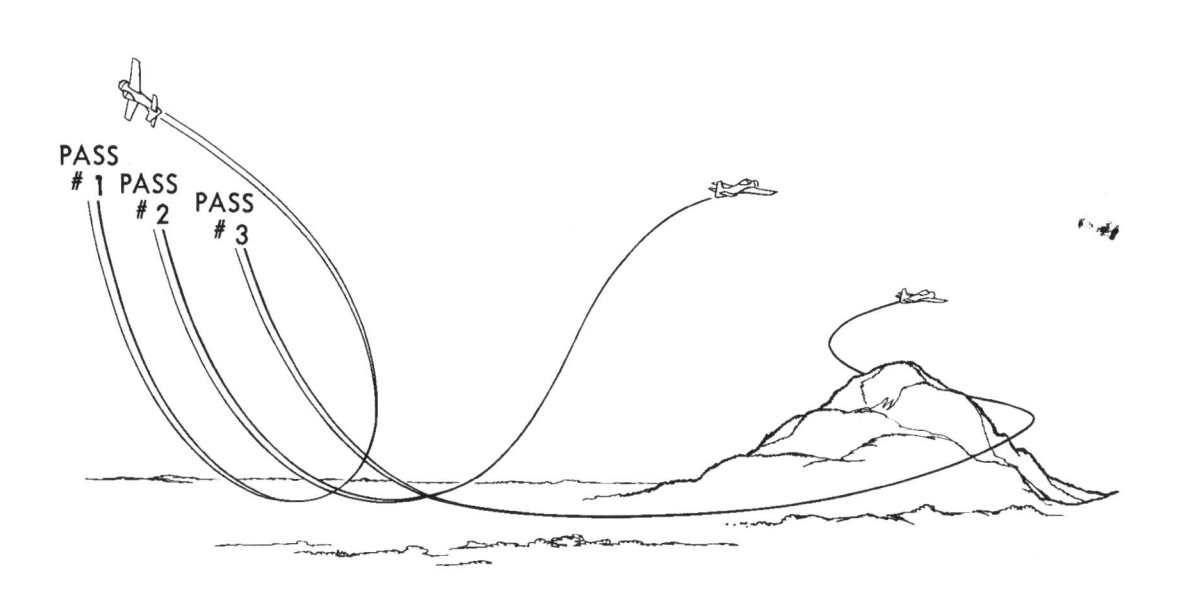

Figure 8 (U)

(This page Unclassified)

The Air Force had taken into account the age and condition of the B-26 and T-28 before turning them over to Farm Gate in 1961. Training and combat tactics were built around what these aircraft could or could not do. Still, the tactical situation in South Vietnam and young pilots tasting "live combat" for the first time soon thrust aside "standard tactics" in favor of "more realistic" ones. Then, too, the type of terrain and targets often demanded evasive actions that put undue stress on the aircraft. Also, pilots threw speed restrictions to the wind when they struggled to work free of the deadly ground fire.[111] A few days after assuming command of the 34th Tactical Group in February 1964, Col. Benjamin S. Preston, Jr., criticized the use of the B-26

> as a straight fighter/bomber aircraft, with 40 degree dive angles, hard pullouts, and rolling pullouts. It was being thrown around with full aileron deflection at high speeds in clover-leaf gunnery patterns that went from the deck up to wingover around 2000 feet. The B-26 and T-28 both were being used to make rocket and machine gun attacks flat out on the deck, kicking up and flying through the clods of mud and debris. The leading edges of the T-28 wings in particular looked as though they had been hammered in with sledge hammers.[112]

Colonel Preston instantly directed a return to proven tactics that stayed within T-28/B-26 strain limitations. He set acceleration limits and instructed pilots to keep to the lowest G-force "consistent with effective weapons delivery and evasive" techniques. Preston prescribed a 1,000-foot minimum altitude for all strike passes and restricted ordnance weight on strike aircraft.*[113]

This tightening-up was overdue. In January 1964 a B-26 had been lost on a combat mission, apparently because of structural failure. At Hurlburt Field in February, another Invader lost a wing and crashed during a firepower display. The upshot was grounding of all B-26's in South Vietnam--inspections disclosing numerous cracked stress plates and loose wing rivets. Back in combat after repairs, the Invaders were confined to straight-and-level bomb runs, lighter loads, and a top stress of 2.5 G's. Structural weaknesses cropped up anew, however, and the Air Force removed all B-26's from combat service. The Invaders were cleared on 19 March for a one-way flight to the Naval Air Station at Subic Point in the Philippines.[114]

---

*He held the T-28 to 260 pounds on each of the intermediate stations and 100-120 pounds on the outboard ones.

On 24 March a T-28 crashed in combat, another apparent victim to structural failure. Over the next 4 weeks, two more Trojans lost wings during bomb runs. These losses and the B-26 phaseout sapped 2d ADVON's strike capability and prompted the Air Force to replace all T-28's with A-1 Skyraiders. In May all Trojans went into areas off the parking ramp at Bien Hoa to await shipment back to the United States.*[115] By 30 June the first 15 of 50 A-1E's had funneled into the 1st Air Commando Squadron and the 602d Fighter Squadron (Commando), both part of the 34th Tactical Group.[116]

The A-1E Tries Its Hand

The Skyraider had been built by the Douglas Aircraft Company and turned over to the U.S. Navy (USN) as the AD-5 in 1945, too late to see action in World War II. A versatile attack bomber, the Skyraider carried more than 6,000 pounds of bombs and/or rockets on 15 external stations, plus 800 rounds for 4 wing-mounted 20-mm cannon. After the Korean War the AD-5 wound up in mothballs at Litchfield Park, Ariz. In 1964 the Air Force got Navy's approval to draw the aircraft out and to modify them into the A-1E.[117]

The 2-seat, prop-driven, A-1E featured communications and navigation gear for day-and-night operations, armorplating, dual-ejection seats, and a reticle ǂ gunsight. Dubbed Old Reliable by the Navy, the Skyraider had long loiter time, supurb flying qualities, and controls that responded smoothly to the touch. In addition, the aircraft could operate from airstrips of 4,000-4,500 feet and fly under low ceilings. Its fairly

---

* A vastly improved T-28 and B-26 later rejoined the war. During 1964-65, for example, the On Mark Engineering Company extensively modified and rehabilitated 40 B-26's. Renamed A-26K's, they reached SEA in 1966, flew interdiction in Laos, and became one of the deadliest truck killers around. Vulnerability, age, and support problems forced them to retire in November 1969.

ǂ A system of lines, dots, crosshairs, or wires in the focus of an optical instrument.

slow speed--just 30 KIAS over the T-28's--let it bomb with finer accuracy than the other attack aircraft (until the jets began using the laser-guided bomb). On the minus side, the Skyraider's slowness exposed it to enemy AA fire longer. When fully loaded it maneuvered sluggishly--top speed dropped to 155 KIAS, turn radius nearly tripled, and climb rate sank to 200-300 feet-per-minute.*[118] All in all, however, the A-1E ranked with the best close air support aircraft of the war.

The Skyraiders hurried into combat after arrival in South Vietnam. Each A-1E flight as a rule consisted of four aircraft during day operations and no fewer than two on night missions. In the 4-ship flight, one pair of E's carried general purpose bombs while the other hauled napalm. When attacking the target, two crews stood by to suppress ground fire as the others made their bomb runs. The pairs then traded places and repeated the procedure.[119]

Skyraider methods of mission planning, takeoff, and rendezvous matched those of the former Farm Gate B-26's and T-28's. The A-1E pilots navigated by TACAN or omni to the join-up area. Following rendezvous with the FAC, they reviewed the ground situation and desired strike tactics with him. Afterwards, they took up orbits that didn't overfly friendly positions.[120]

The two A-1E's bearing GP bombs attacked first, so that they would be free to strafe for the low-level napalm runs. The pilot turned into final heading from a rectangular orbit at 3,500-4,500 feet AGL. He dove steeply and let airspeed build to 280 KIAS. Just before leveling out a 1,500 feet, he released the bombs (one or more at a time), and zoomed back to altitude in a climbing turn. After expending all bombs, the pair pinned

---

* The single-seat A-1H (a modified AD-6) arrived in Southeast Asia ahead of the A-1E. The U.S. Military Assistance Program (MAP) in 1960 had picked it to replace the VNAF's aging World War II planes. The VNAF had 75 H's on 31 December 1974 and over 150 a year later. As for the A-1E, its extra seat came in handy for Air Force pilots checking out VNAF trainees. The number of USAF E's peaked in 1969 at about 100, operating in- and out-country. The Skyraiders began to feel the pinch of old age during 1970-71. Parts became hard to find and replacement aircraft stopped coming.

down the enemy with high-angle strafing.* The two Skyraiders carrying napalm struck swiftly before the foe could recover. Using a lower dive angle and 260 KIAS, the "napalmers" arrived on the deck about 1/2 mile from the target. They moved in without slowing down, dropped nape, and continued straight ahead for another 1/2 mile before pulling up in a climbing turn.[121]

The A-1E fitted neatly into night operations, its long loiter time and large ordnance load being excellent for airborne alert. During July-December 1964 the Air Force even tested the aircraft for night fort defense. A Skyraider was outfitted with two 7.62-mm miniguns, each capable of firing 9,000 rounds per-minute. From airborne alert, this fighter responded to calls for help within minutes--hosing down the attackers while orbiting beyond small-arms range. Impressed with the test results, the 34th Tactical Group commander planned to employ the aircraft for permanent night fort defense. Preparations got under way to mount as many as 12 miniguns on every A-1E slated for night alert.†[122] The modification was canceled, however, because the gunship came to South Vietnam.‡ Before examining the AC-47, a look at new weapons that braced the A-1E and other strike aircraft is in order.

The Weapon Arsenal Expands

By 1964 new weapons--some growing out of older ones--began trickling into South Vietnam. One of the deadliest was a refined World War II Daisy Cutter antipersonnel bomb. Ground crews removed the nose fuze from a GP or frag bomb and welded an old gun barrel or piece

---

* The strafing track was 45°-90° off the expected napalm attack heading. The pilot could shallow the dive in open areas.

† It was believed the combined firing rate would be 100,000 rounds-per-minute. Still this rate would last just 15 seconds, since the A-1E carried only 25,000 rounds. Besides, 12 minigun pods on one aircraft would clearly be overkill.

‡ See below.

of pipe to it. The nose plug was then reinserted and a tail fuze (with an instant primer/detonator) was set for no-delay. When the weapon was dropped from a strike aircraft, the pipe hit the ground first and sent shock waves to the tail fuze. This exploded the bomb and threw deadly shrapnel over a wide area, cutting down enemy troops. The lethal Daisy Cutter was a mainstay through the remainder of the war.[123]

Strike crews warmly welcomed two more weapons in 1964--the MK-44 (Lazy Dog) antipersonnel bomb and CBU-14 cluster bomb unit. The clam-shaped, 500-pound Lazy Dog (an area-type weapon) housed 10,000 tiny nonexplosive missiles with razor-sharp fins. The Skyraider dropped the MK-44 out of a steep (45°) dive at 4,000 feet AGL (above small-arms range). The bomb opened soon afterward and scattered its "silent little killers" over a 320,000-square-foot area. The Lazy Dog devastated troops in the open. What's more, the little missiles burrowed into the ground with just the keen-edged fins jutting out--ready to tear at truck tires and the foe's. In addition the MK-44 could be dropped nearly on top of hard-pressed friendlies if they were shielded by good cover. The single drawback was the small reserve of Lazy Dogs that required the Air Force to tap Navy stockpiles in the Philippines. Hence, the weapon was not always on hand when needed.[124]

The CBU-14 contained 114 fragmentation bomblets (BLU-3's), weighing 2 pounds apiece and dispensed from six aluminum tubes (each 6 feet long and 3 inches in diameter). The A-1E could deliver the weapon at the doorstep of dug-in friendlies, the 114 bomblets blanketing an area roughly 70 by 450 feet. Nonetheless, the BLU-3's had to hit the ground to explode, and inflicted scant damage unless the enemy was caught in the open.[125]

Napalm still topped the list of weapons most feared by the enemy, however. But as 1964 opened, napalm's use tapered off due to the danger of low-altitude delivery. Fitting the cannisters with fins let the strike pilot release from a steeper dive and higher altitudes. The bomb's near-vertical path shortened the spread of the nape, but penetrated the trees more easily to the troops hiding beneath. Consequently, use after July rose and in December nearly tripled that of the previous January.*[126]

The FC-47 / --A Friend in Need

In mid-1964 the 2d Air Division could no longer cope with the upsurge in Communist attacks on hamlets and outposts. Strike aircraft on airborne alert and flareships could answer some of the calls for help within 30 minutes--the rest had to wait longer. There are simply too few planes to quench all the brushfires without slighting other air support tasks.

The outlook brightened in November. Word filtered down to 2d Air Division that a C-47 with side-firing miniguns was to be tested in South Vietnam. The Air Staff had already explained the advantages of this aircraft to the Commander in Chief, Pacific Air Forces (CINCPACAF). It would rush to defend hamlets, forts, and troops under attack. Loitering for hours over potential trouble spots, the C-47 could respond without the aid of a flareship. It could adjust firing patterns while pouring a heavy stream of lead into enemy positions. A slant range / of 3,000-8,000 feet from the target would keep the aircraft safe from most small-arms fire. Moreover, it was roomy enough for mechanics to make inflight repairs. Lastly, the suggested gunship could strike targets on steep hillsides or in other hard-to-reach places.[127]

The test team, headed by Capt. Ronald W. Terry, arrived at Bien Hoa on 2 December and quickly set up shop. A week later, 7.62-mm minigun kits, gunsights, and ammunition for modifying two C-47's got there. Three guns were mounted on each aircraft--two firing through open windows on the left side, the third resting in the cargo door. The gunsight, placed in the pilot's side window, was a 16-mm camera reflex viewfinder with a crosshair reticle. On 15 December the two gunships were squared away for testing.[128]

---

* The Air Force tried out other weapons. For example, the 34th Tactical Group mounted a 40-mm grenade launcher on a Skyraider but it fired too slow. Also considered were chemical agents that knocked enemy troops out of action without killing them. The specter of world opinion caused these agents to be used sparingly then not at all.

/ The FC-47 - Subsequently redesignated as the AC-49.

/ The line-of-sight distance between two points not at the same elevation.

The AC-47 carried a 7-man crew plus a VNAF observer. While keeping the aircraft in the correct bank and orbit, the pilot aimed and fired the guns. His copilot monitored the instruments and harmonized crew actions. Besides keeping track of the gunship's position, the navigator helped the VNAF observer verify targets. The two gunners managed the miniguns, and the loadmaster prepared the flares for dispensing out the rear cargo door. The flight mechanic looked after all aircraft systems.[129]

The crews flew day missions the first week to get the feel of their aircraft. They found the miniguns potent against sampans, trails, buildings, and in wooded areas. The first night mission took place on 23 December and left little doubt that the AC-47 could defend friendly outposts. The gunship was on airborne alert when the call for help came in from a South Vietnamese outpost at Thanh Yen just west of Can Tho in the Mekong Delta. Inside of 35 minutes the Dragonship* was dropping flares over the besieged defenders. When this didn't break off the attack, the outpost called for minigun fire on the Communists, located about 300 yards to the south.[130]

The AC-47 therefore took up an orbit † at 3,000 feet AGL around the enemy and stabilized speed at 120 KIAS. The pilot centered the target off the gunship's left wingtip by banking and turning as it passed under the left engine nacelle. Isolating the target in his gunsight, he centered the pipper ‡ on it. He then pressed the trigger on the right side of the control wheel--setting all three guns chattering at a combined 17,000 rounds-per-minute. The withering fire completely demoralized the foe and he fled into the jungle. On the heels of this action, the Dragonship got word of an attack on the outpost at Trung Hung, 20 miles to the west. The FC-47

---

* One of the nicknames for the gunship.

† The orbit looked like the pylon-8 maneuver learned in primary pilot school. The pilot skidded or slipped the plane in the desired direction as he kept the target centered.

‡ The center or bead of a gunsight.

reached the scene in 20 minutes, zeroed in on the enemy's gunflashes, dropped flares, and hosed down the attackers with minigun fire. Again the Communists retreated in confusion.[131]

The 28th of December witnessed a more dramatic display of AC-47 might. The district capital of Ngai Giao (and its fort), some 37 miles from Bien Hoa, came under heavy Communist assault. When the gunship piloted by Captain Terry arrived, the tiny triangular fort had flarepots burning brightly on its three corners and a flaming arrow pointing toward the enemy. The Dragonship dropped MK-6 flares and received tracer fire in return. Captain Terry instantly set up an orbit at 3,500 feet AGL and raked the embattled fort's perimeter, firing one gun at a time to prolong support. After 1 hour and 21 minutes the enemy called it quits and left.[132] The value of the AC-47 now clearly evident, testing and refinement continued at year's end.

Summary

(U) The Gulf of Tonkin Crisis in August 1964 deepened U.S. involvement in the war. Air Force jet fighters streamed in, ready to support ground troops in South Vietnam. Two B-57 squadrons moved to Clark AFB, Philippines, and began rotating in and out of the Republic of Vietnam (RVN).[133] Plans were also taking shape to deploy American ground troops to help defend against the rising Communist menace.

(U) The Farm Gate and early air commando experience had supplied the building blocks for shaping close air support tactics. Trial and error had scrapped questionable techniques. Problems with old ordnance were ironed out and new weapons put to use. The Tactical Air Control System evolved to fit the war's specific needs, and ARVN commanders started to believe in tactical air power. As the forward controller came to be a key link in close air support, his role significantly changed.

(U) At the outset of American involvement, the FAC directed most airstrikes from the ground. Thick jungles, mountains, and fluid battlelines, however, made it hard for him to see the target area clearly. What's more, he couldn't view the battle situation from the same perspective as the strike pilots did. So a few weeks after arrival, the first Barn Door controllers began operating from the 0-1.

(U) Several shortcomings should have kept the O-1 out of even light combat, but it was the most acceptable FAC aircraft available at the time. Built for civilian use, the plane had no armorplating for the engine or cockpit. The single engine wasn't powerful enough to carry all needed equipment and still perform well. Rate of climb averaged just 500-750 feet-per-minute at sea level, and the top airspeed of 80 knots hindered quick reaction and invited ground fire. The plane was often pushed beyond its recommended design limitations. Last of all, it lacked the navigation equipment for good night operations.[134]

(U) Nevertheless, the O-1 had strong points. The FAC found it rather easy to fly, the good view from the cockpit and slow speed being pluses for airstrike control. The aircraft could take off from short dirt strips and stay up for nearly 4 hours, and was simple to maintain under field conditions.[135] For a plane not designed for forward air control, the O-1 gave yeoman service.

(U) As of January 1965, USAF tactical and support aircraft in Southeast Asia totaled 305 (222 in South Vietnam). Plans were firmed up for opening new bases to bed down the influx of F-100's and newer F-4 Phantoms. Additional AC-47's and smaller jet fighters like the A-37 and F-5 would soon appear, swelling the inventory further. The Air Force was settling in for a long stay.

III. CLOSE AIR SUPPORT, 1965-1968

The Military Situation

(U) The Viet Cong, backed by thousands of North Vietnamese infiltrators, held the initiative in South Vietnam at the beginning of 1965. Communist strategy had long sought to drive ARVN forces out of the countryside, isolate the Saigon government from the people, and take control. Concerned about increasing U.S. assistance to Saigon, however, the enemy decided to launch a division-size force against South Vietnamese defenders at the hamlet or Binh Gia, 40 miles southeast of Saigon. The battle, which began on 27 December 1964, raged until 3 January 1965 and proved very costly to South Vietnam--politically and militarily. Its 33d Ranger and 4th Marine Battalions were virtually wiped out. Armor and mechanized relief units, sent into combat without adequate air support, also took heavy casualties. The .30-cal machineguns and small high-explosive (HE) rockets of the helicopter gunships couldn't effectively cut through the jungle cover ringing the hamlet. Strike aircraft were finally called in, belatedly.[1]

(U) The Viet Cong publicized Binh Gia as a great military victory. The enemy announced that it would be followed by bigger field operations that would in time topple the government of South Vietnam. He shortly launched a series of attacks throughout the country, which the ARVN seemed powerless to halt.*[2]

(U) Faced with the possible loss of South Vietnam to the Communists, President Lyndon B. Johnson sought to engage Hanoi in peace negotiations. However, when on 7 February 1965 Viet Cong terrorists hit the U.S. airbase at Pleiku, killing 7 Americans and wounding another 109, the President ordered retaliatory airstrikes against North Vietnam. A few days later USAF crews flew their first combat missions against targets in the southern portion of North Vietnam. On 19 February 24 B-57's also bombed a 9th VC Division base camp deep in the jungles of Phuoc Tuy

---

* Binh Gia was a grim reminder (not lost on Gen. William C. Westmoreland, MACV Commander) that good tactical air power was vital to whipping the enemy.

Province. B-57's and F-100's 2 days later aided a U.S. Special Forces team and a Vietnamese Civilian Irregular Defense Group (CIDG) company, caught in a Communist ambush at Mang Yang Pass on Route 19. The airstrikes forced the enemy to pull back, enabling rescue helicopters to lift out the 220 survivors.[3]

(U) On 2 March President Johnson approved a sustained bombing campaign against North Vietnam. Nicknamed Rolling Thunder, it aimed to strengthen Saigon's sagging defenses and to dampen North Vietnamese support of the Viet Cong. He followed up on 8 March by sending the 9th Marine Expeditionary Brigade to Da Nang as a security force. On 5 May the Army's 173d Airborne Brigade was in place at Bien Hoa. U.S. troop strength that stood at 50,000 as of 30 June swelled to 125,000 inside of a month. The President also allowed American soldiers to fight alongside the South Vietnamese.[4]

(U) The Air Force kept pace with the Army and Marine buildup. Two B-52 squadrons were deployed to Andersen AFB, Guam, prepared to join the air campaign. Four O-1 tactical air support squadrons were formed in SEA to furnish forward air control in strike operations. By December air units had deployed to South Vietnam on permanent change of station (PCS), replacing most of the B-57, F-4, F-100, F-105, and gunship detachments rushed over earlier in the year on temporary duty (TDY).*[5]

(U) General Westmoreland, aware he didn't have sufficient forces to wrest the initiative from the enemy, gave first priority to holding areas already in friendly hands. In Communist-controlled regions he planned a series of sweeps and "spoiling attacks," covered by tactical air and designed to keep the foe off balance. Westmoreland thought this approach would give the United States time to gird for larger offensives.[6]

---

* In December 1965 the Air Force had more than 500 aircraft and 21,000 men in South Vietnam, spread over 8 bases. During October 1965 five F-100 squadrons had moved into Bien Hoa and Da Nang. They were followed in November by F-4C elements of the 12th Tactical Fighter Wing (TFWg) at Cam Ranh Bay and additional FC-47 gunships at Tan Son Nhut. Squadrons in SEA at year's end totaled: 11 fighters, 2 tactical bombardment, 9 air commando, 2 tactical reconnaissance, 3 air rescue, 4 tactical air support, 1 fighter-interceptor, and 8 combat support.

(U) American troops first tasted heavy combat in August 1965, when a 3d Marine Division unit tangled with a VC regiment along the coast just south of Chu Lai. Calling in heavy airstrikes, the Marine commander led his men in a rout of the Viet Cong during the 2-day battle, inflicting more than 700 casualties. Tactical air alone accounted for over half of the 326 enemy killed. Two months later, the Communist attacked the Special Forces camp at Plei Me, southwest of Pleiku near the Ia Drang Valley. Again, liberal use of airstrikes saved the camp and drove the attackers into the valley where a bloody month-long battle ensued. It ended with the invaders retreating back into Cambodian sanctuaries, leaving 600 of their fallen comrades behind.[7]

(U) As American strength in South Vietnam nudged 400,000 in 1966,* General Westmoreland felt the time was ripe to seize the initiative from the Communists. He first wanted to regain control of the central highlands in II Corps and cut off the Viet Cong's sources of food and manpower. To spy out the enemy and pinpoint his weaknesses, SF reconnaissance teams and the Air Force FAC force were shored up and streamlined. Army ground units moved out into the field and USAF fighters stood by, ready to respond at a moment's notice.[8]

(U) Before these operations could really get under way, the enemy dealt a death blow to the Special Forces camp at A Shau. This triangular fort nestled at the base of a narrow valley about 20 miles southwest of Hue and 2 1/2 miles from the Laotian border. As a watchpost it was a stabbing thorn in the flesh of North Vietnamese infiltrators. The attack to dig it out began before dawn on 9 March, sounded by barrages from mortars, 75-mm recoilless rifles, and automatic weapons. Since the enemy had chosen bad weather to mask his movements, the low cloud cover rendered close air support of the camp almost impossible. All day the battle raged, the Viet Cong/North Vietnamese overrunning most of the fort. On the 10th the overcast lifted a bit, enabling strike aircraft to move in and hold off the Communists while survivors were evacuated. Although this setback put a small dent in General Westermoreland's plans, joint American/South Vietnamese offensives launched during the rest of 1966 overshadowed enemy activities.[9]

(U) Among the many operations mounted between April-November 1966 were five notable ones. All five relied a great deal on close air support. Birmingham (April-May) searched out and destroyed Viet Cong stockpiles of

---

* Air Force strength stood at more than 834 aircraft and 49,000 personnel.

food and equipment in War Zone C, north of Saigon. Paul Revere (May 1966) began a series of sweeps to clean the enemy from the vicinity of Pleiku. El Paso (June-July) involved five ground actions near the Cambodian border in III Corps, opening Route 13 from Saigon to the big rubber plantations in Binh Long Province. This allowed 1st Infantry Division and South Vietnam's 5th Division to attack and force the 9th VC Division from the province. Hawthorne (June-July) was a major spoiling operation by the 1st Brigade of the 101st Airborne Division. It defeated a Viet Cong regiment around the city of Toumorong in Kontum Province. Attleboro (September-November) turned out to be the biggest operation of the year. Capping off several campaigns in Tay Ninh Province, northwest of Saigon, it pushed the Communists across the Cambodian border and reduced the pressure on Saigon.[10]

(U) The war became Americanized in 1967 as the number of U.S. troops in SEA topped 480,000. Preparing the South Vietnamese to handle their own conflict took a backseat to punishing the enemy. General Westmoreland gave the screw another turn by touching off Operation Junction City, a full-blown successful attack on the Viet Cong sanctuary in War Zone C. He followed with Sam Houston and Francis Marion that took up the sweeps in Pleiku Province where Paul Revere left off. Other operations soon blossomed country wide. Hit hard and often, the enemy seldom had time to catch his breath or plan attacks of his own.[11]

(U) The enemy bent but didn't break. Gen. Vo Nguyen Giap, North Vietnam's military leader, knew that a spectacular victory was essential to regain momentum. Thus as 1967 waned, the Communist firmed up plans for a key offensive early in 1968, to be heralded by an attack on the U.S. Marine combat base at Khe Sanh. This base in northwest South Vietnam sat on a plateau and commanded the approaches to Dong Ha, Quang Tri City, and to Hue beyond. It straddled an otherwise wide-open invasion route to the two northernmost provinces of South Vietnam. If captured, Khe Sanh might have the psychological clout of a Dien Bien Phu*--stirring waves of anti-American and antiwar feeling that would compel the United States to pack up and leave South Vietnam.[12]

---

* A village in northwest North Vietnam. Led by General Giap, the Vietnamese Communists (Viet Minh) besieged and captured it in 1954, spelling the end of French control in Indochina.

(U) The attack opened on 21 January to the rumbling of a mortar barrage against a hill northwest of the Marine base, the heavy shelling of the base itself. Tactical air, controlled mainly by Air Force and Marine FAC's, reacted swiftly and with devasting force. Strike aircraft pinpointed bombs to within a few yards of dug-in Americans and South Vietnamese. B-52's placed 50,000-pound payloads as close as 500 feet. The vicious fighting swirled for over 2 months before the enemy pulled back--battered and beaten. General Giap had clearly underrated the deadliness of strong air support.[13]

(U) The countrywide Tet Offensive commenced on 30 January, the Communists mounting well-executed attacks on Saigon, 5 other key cities, 34 provincial capitals, and a scattering of military installations, villages, and towns. One of their chief objectives was to destroy or neutralize airfields. They failed to do this, and air power figured prominently in blunting Giap's forces. After the offensive petered out, the Communist threat to South Vietnam receded somewhat. But if the North Vietnamese offensive failed militarily, it succeeded politically. On 31 March 1968 President Johnson announced he would not run for a second term and offered to begin peace negotiations with North Vietnam.[14]

Coordinating Close Air Support

Through 1964 VNAF forward air controllers (often flying as observers with USAF FAC's) were nominally required for all USAF airstrikes in support of South Vietnamese ground forces. However, the flood of U.S. troops into the country during 1965 dictated adjustments. American policy specified that fighter-qualified controllers conduct close air support of U.S. Army troops. Since few VNAF controllers could satisfy the fighter qualification, the rules of engagement were charged to allow USAF FAC's to direct airstrikes. By March 1965 Vietnamese Air Force markings disappeared from American aircraft, and USAF fighter pilots engaged in strike operations without carrying along a VNAF crewmember. Nevertheless, all airstrikes still had to have the Vietnamese Government's stamp of approval.[15]

The first U.S. Army units in South Vietnam brought USAF forward air controllers with them. These controllers had trained with the Army in the United States, directing close air support from the ground.*[16] They soon learned that the rugged and forested Vietnamese terrain hindered control by blocking a ground FAC's view.

Many Army commanders clung to the traditional outlook, that air support would be more responsive if under their direct control. In June 1965 Defense Secretary McNamara tended to back this view by authorizing the move of the 1st Cavalry Division (Airborne) and its armed helicopters to South Vietnam.[17] Confidence of ground commanders in their own "organic air force" was strong, and they took to calling the nearest aviation company for immediate helicopter gunship support./[18] Consequently, the number of air support requests through the tactical air control system leveled off. For small engagements the limited firepower of the helicopters was usually sufficient. In bigger operations, however, the choppers could but harass the enemy until strike aircraft arrived.

To dampen overreliance on helicopters,[19] General Westmoreland COMUSMACV, urged ground commanders to make better use of the TACS for filling air support needs. By the end of 1965, the TACS was being used more frequently, and forward air controllers found themselves directing most strikes from the air. Air liaison officers served as advisers to ground commanders and also controlled airstrikes from the ground when the tactical situation demanded.

---

* In contrast, personnel running the VNAF and Barn Door FAC programs saw at the outset the impact of Vietnamese mountains, jungles, and forests. They decided in 1962 to control strikes from the air whenever possible. Even so, U.S. doctrine had traditionally tied the controller to the ground commander's team. During World War II the forward artillery spotter (forerunner to the FAC) had directed cannon fire and occasional airstrikes. In spite of the success of the Mosquito airborne controller in Korea, the ground controller concept persisted.

/ During experiments conducted by the 173d Airborne Brigade at Bien Hoa, armed helicopters dropped CBU-14 frag cluster bombs as well as nose-fuzed 81-mm rounds. These tests did not show great promise.

Refining the Tactical Air Control System

Geared to a small limited war, the Tactical Air Control System strained to keep pace with the rapidly swirling conflict. In January 1965 the TACS handled an average of 2,000 tactical sorties per month; a year later, more than 15,000.[20] The much-needed expansion and refinement of the system got under way in August 1965. (See Fig. 9). The Air Operations Center became the Tactical Air Control Center, while the Air Support Operations Centers were redesignated Direct Air Support Centers and deployed as shown in Map 1. Additionally, the TACC took over the immediate air request net between Tactical Air Control Parties (TACP's) at battalion level and higher headquarters. It further assumed the task of committing aircraft to preplanned air requests, thus freeing the DASC's to focus on immediate air support needs. To reduce the response time to immediate requests, TACP's (equipped with mobile radios) were attached to each Direct Air Support Center for quick dispatch to trouble spots.[21]

At the same time the Army upgraded its Air-Ground System (AAGS). Ground commanders kept in touch with lower units through this net. They likewise used it to request and tie in close air support with their organic firepower--artillery, helicopter gunships, and small spotter aircraft.[22]

In May 1966 General Westmoreland formed the Joint Air-Ground Operations System (JAGOS) to streamline coordination between the Army Air-Ground System and the Tactical Air Control System.* (See Fig. 10). Under the JAGOS the Army Tactical Air Support Element (TASE)--the top echelon of the AAGS and comparable to the Air Force TACC--moved to the MACV Combat Operations Center (COC), next to the Tactical Air Control Center. This made it easier to funnel air requests through the TASE to the TACC for execution. In addition, the TASE attached Ground Liaison Officers (GLO's) to USAF tactical fighter wings as advisers on ground requirements.[23]

---

* The Joint Air-Ground Operations System also included the tactical air control system of the Marine 1st Air Wing at Da Nang. The JAGOS should not be confused with the Southeast Asia Integrated Tactical Air Control System (SEAITACS), set up in August 1965. The SEAITACS coordinated the activities of all TACS's in Southeast Asia--U.S. Air Force, Vietnamese Air Force, U.S. Marines, U.S. Navy Air Operations, as well as a TACS operated by the Air Force in Thailand.

TACTICAL AIR CONTROL SYSTEM

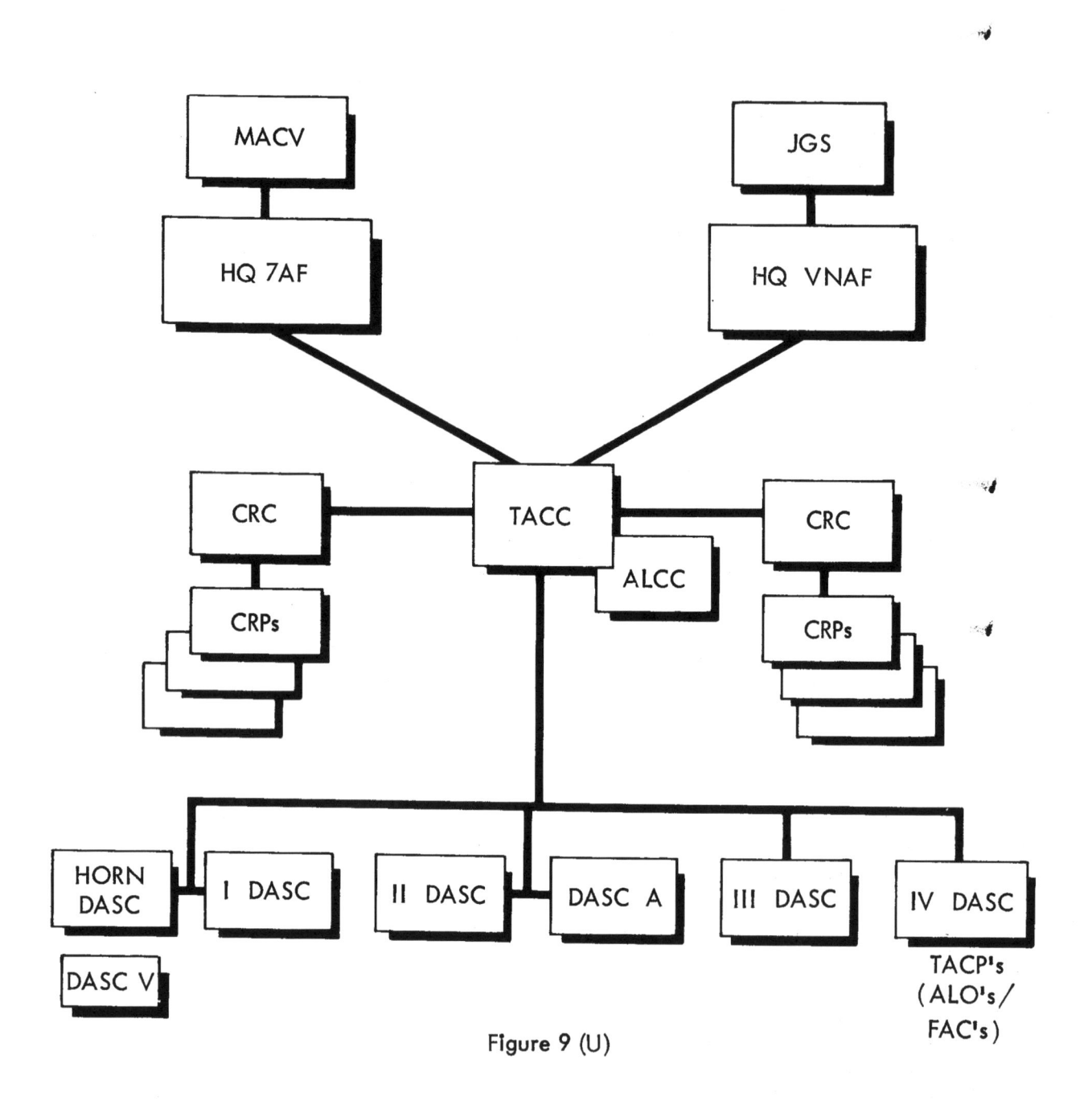

Figure 9 (U)

(This page Unclassified)

Map 1 (C)

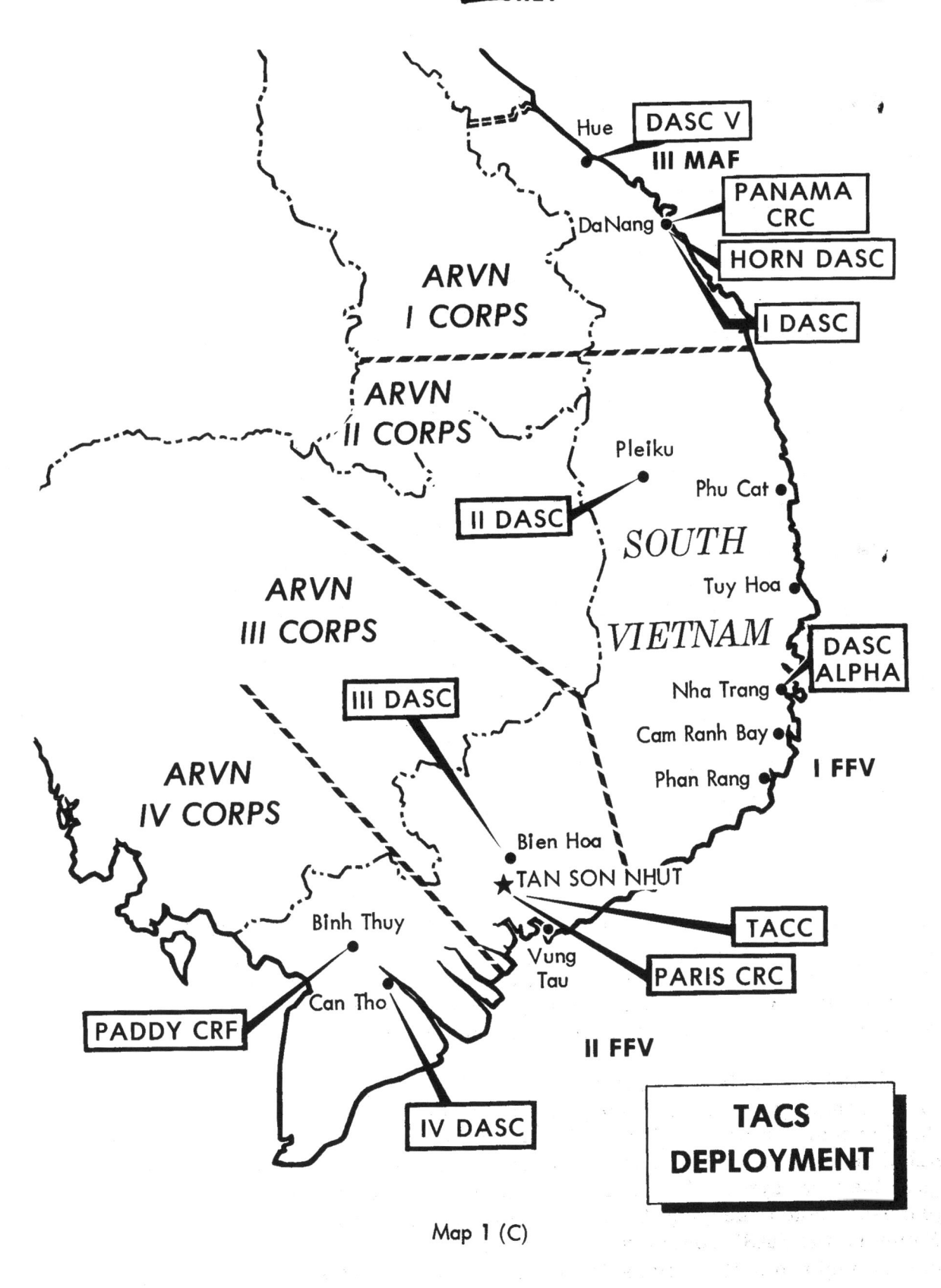

(This page Confidential)

The revamped Tactical Air Control System treated air requests much like before. (See Fig. 10.) Preplanned requests normally began at the unit needing the air support but could originate at any level. For example, a planning conference would commonly be held at a battalion firebase the afternoon before a scheduled ground operation, with the attached Air Force FAC or ALO sitting in. After determining the need for air support, the battalion commander used the Army net to forward a request to the brigade. If the brigade could satisfy the want with artillery or air, the request went no higher. Otherwise, it underwent a similar review at each level while continuing up the line to the Corps Tactical Operations Center. The CTOC sent it on to the Tactical Air Support Element for coordination with the Tactical Air Control Center. The request was then given a priority and a frag order issued.*[24] All strike requests had to have prior approval of a province chief or higher authority. The sole exceptions were strikes in designated free bomb zones and those in support of endangered U.S. ground troops.[25]

An immediate air request, like the preplanned, could start off at any echelon. If at company level, the request went to the battalion command post for validation, after which the TACP or an airborne FAC transmitted it straight to the Direct Air Support Center. Radio silence from intermediate levels signified approval. The DASC passed the request to the Corps Tactical Operations Center located alongside, and commenced action pending final approval by the CTOC. The Direct Air Support Center could divert controller and strike crews from lower priority preplanned missions or from airborne alert. But the TACC alone could authorize the scrambling of ground alert aircraft or the diverting of planes from another corps. †[26]

---

* Key U.S./Vietnamese commanders decided daily how much of the air effort would go to close air support. The Tactical Air Control Center next notified every corps commander how many sorties he could expect. From this pool the commander requested airstrikes--designating priority, target location/description, time-over-target, and desired results. Moreover, he was responsible for the safety of his troops during the strikes.

† Within the Marine system, an immediate request traveled from the FAC to the company or battalion then straight to the Direct Air Support Center over the Tactical Air Request Net (TARN). Silence from intermediate levels signaled assent. The Fire Support Coordination Center, collocated with the DASC, gave the final approval. After that, the DASC could switch any assigned preplanned strikes, keeping the Tactical Air Direction Center (TADC) advised. Further, the DASC could divert or scramble any alert aircraft in its area, but the right to shift fighters from other areas rested with the TADC.

MILITARY ASSISTANCE COMMAND VIETNAM
JOINT AIR-GROUND OPERATIONS SYSTEM (JAGOS)

- MILITARY ASSISTANCE COMMAND VIETNAM
  - Tactical Air Support Element
  - Tactical Air Control Center
- CORPS OR FIELD FORCES VIETNAM
  - Corps Tactical Operations Center
  - Direct Air Support Center
- DIVISION
  - Division Tactical Operations Center
  - Tactical Air Control Party
- PROVINCE BRIGADE/REGIMENT
  - Fire Support Coordination Center
  - Tactical Air Control Party

Control & Reporting Center
Control & Reporting Post

Immediate -------   Preplanned ———

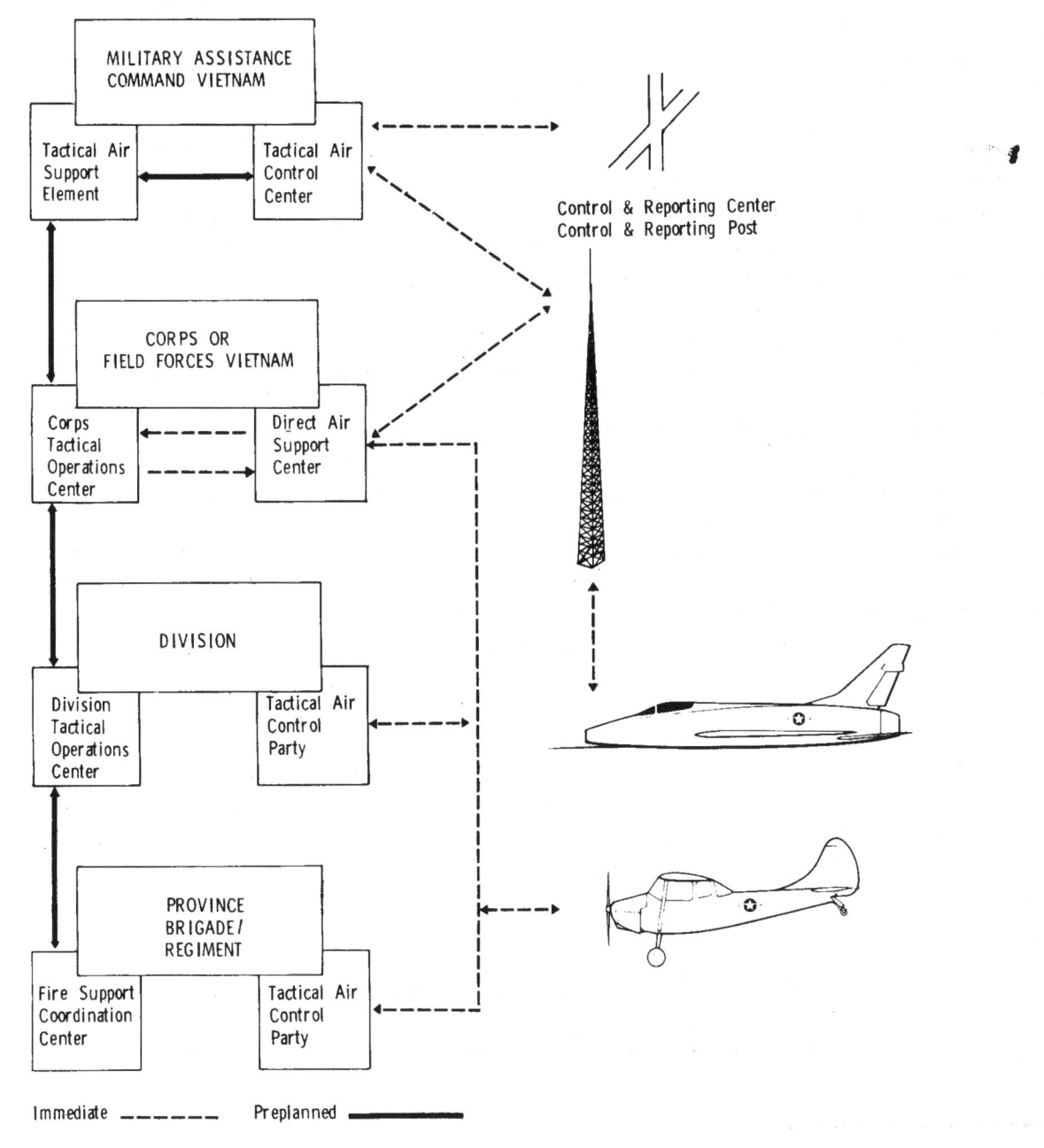

Figure 10 (U)

(This page Unclassified)

When an ARVN commander wanted immediate air support, he and his USAF adviser first had to see eye to eye on the need. Next, they relayed the request to the sector TACP (or division Tactical Operations Center), preferably by way of an airborne controller. From there it went to the Direct Air Support Center through VNAF channels. Approval procedures resembled those for American immediate requests.[27]

Response time to immediate air requests hinged on the circumstances. If strike and controller aircraft happened to be nearby, they could be over the target about as fast as the request could be sent and approved. On the other hand, a jet fighter on ground alert might take an hour or more to get there. The jets were tied to 10,000-foot runways on airfields often distant from the scene of action. Although the propeller-driven A-1's could fly from the nearer and more plentiful 6,000-foot strips, their slower speed canceled out the advantage. There was in addition the time consumed as the requests passed through the system. For example, the Tactical Operations Center needed to sort out various options before turning to the Direct Air Support Center for strike aircraft, and Vietnamese approval had to be secured. Also, strike and FAC crews had to decide on tactics and firm up final details with the ground commander. Tying together these and other loose ends was a must before the first bomb was dropped. Ground alert aircraft could be airborne in 10-15 minutes and in most cases fighters on air alert or diverted responded sooner. Even so, it required 40 minutes to react to immediate requests and put bombs on the target.*[28] Whittling down this response time turned out to be an uphill problem.

Close Air Support Aircraft

(U) During 1965-68 more types of Air Force tactical fighter and FAC aircraft saw combat in Southeast Asia. Some required extensive modification to perform in a close air support role, others only slight changes.

FAC Aircraft

(U) Through 1967 the O-1 Bird Dog was the workhorse for controlling airstrikes and carrying out visual reconnaissance. Its shortcomings and old age, however, had spurred an early search for a replacement. The

---

* Despite lack of heavy firepower, the helicopter gunships could generally be on the scene in minutes and furnish some sort of air support until strike aircraft could take over.

T-28, T-33 and T-6 (the successful Mosquito FAC aircraft in Korea) were examined but dropped as being too old or with deficiencies greater than the O-1's. Finally in 1964, following several years of research and testing, Secretary of Defense McNamara had approved the basic design for the OV-10. It was the first plane actually tailored for airborne forward air control.

Since the OV-10 did not get to SEA until 1968, the Air Force selected the O-2A Super Skymaster as an interim off-the-shelf aircraft and sent it to South Vietnam in May 1967. Although underpowered, the two in-line* engines of this modified Cessna 337 Skymaster gave a cruise speed of 150 knots--50-70 more than 0-1. Besides light armor and smoke-generating equipment, the 0-2A had an aiming device for target marking and under each wing two ordnance stations. Navigation gear consisted of TACAN-distance measuring equipment (DME), automatic direction finder (ADF), very high frequency omnirange (VOR), and identification, friend or foe.† These and a starlight scope ǂ (added later) made it the best FAC aircraft for night operations. There were two major drawbacks however. The plane's side-by-side seating tended to force the pilot into left-hand turns when controlling airstrikes, affording AA gunners an easier target. Furthermore, a clear danger arose when one of the underpowered engines conked out in flight.[29]

) A twin-engine, 2-seat aircraft, the OV-10 boasted a top speed of 250 knots and a combat radius exceeding 300 nautical miles (NM's). The OV-10 carried over 1,500 pounds of ordnance on five external racks plus five 7.62mm machinguns in sponsons @ beneath the fuselage. Armor-plating protected the crew and vital aircraft components. Newer navigation instruments permitted night and all-weather flying. A smoke

---

* Internal-combustion, reciprocating engines in which the cylinders are arranged in one or more straight rows.

† A method for determining the friendly or unfriendly character of aircraft and ships by other aircraft and ships, and by ground forces using electronic equipment and associated IFF units.

ǂ An image intensifier using reflected light from the starts or moon to identify targets.

@ Projections from the side of an aircraft to house guns or other items.

generator aided rendezvous with other planes, and ejection seats bettered the crew's chances for escape in case the Bronco was severly damaged.[30]

Strike Aircraft

Throughout much of the war the prop-driven A-1E proved the most suitable aircraft for close air support. Slow cruise speed let it conduct strikes under 300-foot cloud ceilings and 2-mile visibility. In contrast, jet fighters struggled to work below 1,200-foot ceilings with 4-mile visibility. All the same, the A-1E could muster barely one-third the speed of most jets.* [31]

The North American F-100 Super Sabre had originally been built in 1952 as an air-superiority fighter. In Southeast Asia, however, it easily adapted to close air support operations and flew more than 92 percent of all its combat missions in that role. The aircraft's six external stations carried a bomb/rocket load in excess of 3,000 pounds. In addition the F-100 had four internally mounted M-39 20-mm cannon and room for 800 rounds of ammunition. When flying close air support, the Super Sabre usually hauled bombs on the two inboard and two outboard stations and a 335-gallon fuel tank on each of the two intermediate ones. The extra fuel extended the combat radius to 275 nautical miles with 15 minutes in the target area. The Super Sabre was second only to the A-1E in bombing accuracy, its visual gun/bomb/rocket sight having a circular error average (CEA)/ of 130 feet. / [32]

---

* The A-1E's characteristics are discussed more fully in Chapter II.

/ The bombing error in a given bombing attack, expressed as the average radial distance of the bomb impacts (or mean points of impact) from the center of the target.

/ The pilot favored an alternate aiming method for dive-bombing. He centered the bombsight reticle on the tip of the F-100's nose antenna. As the target passed under the nose, he pickled the bombs.

There were a few flaws in the F-100's fine close air support performance. A heavy bombload on the outboard stations would shift the center of gravity rearward, making the Super Sabre unstable and hard to control. Consequently, 1,000-pound bombs could not be hung there. When the outboards were used, their bombs had to be dispensed first and in pairs (wiring for separate release didn't come until 1968). Hence half the payload was gone after the first pass. Then too, the aircraft demanded runways of 8,000-10,000 feet, confining dispersal to 8 or 10 airbases in South Vietnam. (The A-1E could be deployed to almost 50 different strips.) Lastly, the heavy wing-loading* restricted the Super Sabre's maneuvering and resulted in a very large turn radius.[33] Despite these weaknesses, the F-100 remained the most heavily used jet for close air support up to the time it was removed from the war.

(U) The Martin B-57B Canberra was a 1953 modification of the English Electra Canberra--Great Britain's first jet bomber. The B-57 became the first USAF jet aircraft to be based in South Vietnam and the first jet to drop bombs in combat there. A twin-engine, 2-man bomber, it had been beefed up to withstand 4 G's, thus allowing the full sweep of maneuvers during tactical delivery. The combined capacity of its eight external wing stations and rotary bomb bay was over 10,000 pounds of bombs. The Canberra also mounted either eight .50-cal machineguns (with 24,000 rounds) or four 20-mm cannon (1,160 rounds). Inside of 20-35 minutes (cruising at 400-450 KIAS) it could give close air support to a ground unit 100-200 miles away. Second only to the A-1 in loiter time, the B-57 could travel 200 miles and stay in the target area for at least an hour-and-a-half before heading back to base.[34]

(U) Its broad wing area enabled the B-57 to maneuver extremely well at every altitude. This and a bombing speed as slow as 350 KIAS let it acquire targets easier and deliver ordnance at closer slant ranges. Unlike most other jets, the Canberra didn't mush† when pulling out of a dive.[35]

The first B-57 crews to reach South Vietnam in the fall of 1964 were unqualified for night combat operations. During January 1965 intensive training began in the Philippines, and by June half the 28 authorized crews

---

* In stress analysis, the gross weight of an airplane divided by the wing area.

† To fly partly stalled with controls sluggish or ineffective.

were checked out.[36] The 2-man Canberra crew paid dividends, particularly at night. The pilot focused on flying the plane as the navigator monitored the radio, coordinated with the FAC, kept the course, and armed the guns for each firing pass. On each bombing run he called off airspeed, altitude, and angle of attack.[37]

(U) The B-57 had several drawbacks. Perhaps the major one was a lack of replacement aircraft and parts. Moreover, the size of the Canberra made it more vulnerable to ground fire and confined its use to low- and medium-threat areas. The plane could not be refueled in flight, and the big wing blocked the crew's view to the rear, making it difficult to keep other aircraft in sight. By late 1968, attrition was hampering B-57 operations. In October 1969 the Air Force pulled the Canberra out of Southeast Asia.[38]

(U) The McDonnell-Douglas F-4 Phantom II turned out to be the most versatile strike aircraft of the war.* This 2-seat multipurpose plane began life as a Navy shipboard interceptor and wound up as the Air Force's primary land-based tactical fighter in SEA. The first Phantoms arrived at Ubon, Thailand, on 7 April 1965. ╫ Within 2 years they had fanned out from there to many bases in Thailand and South Vietnam.[39]

The payload of the Phantom exceeded that of any other USAF tactical fighter. As a rule, the aircraft hauled 6,000-9,000 pounds of ordnance on nine external stations, but could carry as much as 16,000 pounds if need be. In addition, a low-altitude airspeed up to 700 knots let the F-4 slip swiftly in and out of high-threat areas--almost before enemy gunners could manually track it. A fairly short takeoff roll (3,000 feet under ideal conditions but considerably more under combat loading) allowed the plane to use airfields judged too small for other jet fighters.[40]

---

* The Phantom for the most part performed out-country where its full potential could be exploited. Even so, it conducted quite a lot of close air support in South Vietnam.

╫ These were planes of the 45th Tactical Fighter Squadron (TFSq), 5th TFWg, deployed from MacDill AFB, Fla.

Besides using a manually depressed reticle bombsight (reminiscent of World War II), the F-4 D/E crew could bomb automatically with a weapon release computer set (WRCS) and radar. All F-4's, except the E model, had been built without internally mounted guns. However, when strafing became necessary, an M-61 20-mm cannon could be strapped to the Phantom's centerline station.[41]

The superior speed of the F-4 proved a handicap in some ways. It forced the pilot to bomb from higher altitudes which diluted accuracy. Requiring a greater area than slower aircraft to turn and maneuver in, the Phantom was not so flexible in low-level operations. Additionally, a shorter loiter time without refueling (20 minutes at 200 miles range) diminished its airborne alert value. Also the location of the two engine intakes, just below and behind the crew compartment, cut off part of the rear view.[42] These limitations were nevertheless lived with to capitalize on the F-4's strengths in close air support.

On 23 October 1965 the F-5 Freedom Fighter commenced its combat test and evaluation (Skoshi Tiger) in South Vietnam. This single-seat, lightweight tactical fighter was modified from the Northrup T-38 trainer (Talon) and meant for foreign sales. After passing the evaluation, the F-5 was used in training Vietnamese Air Force pilots. Turned over to the VNAF in April 1967, the Freedom Fighter flew almost entirely close air support missions.[43]

The F-5 had two internally mounted M-39 20-mm cannon and five external stations that could carry up to 6,000 pounds of bombs. To secure best flight performance, however, the bombload seldom surpassed 2,000 pounds. The Freedom Fighter featured a manually depressed reticle gunsight for both bombing and strafing. In addition to presenting enemy gunners a small target, its extra protection stemmed from armorplating beneath the cockpit and a light honeycombed structure under the skin.* Other pluses were simply designed systems for better maintenance, a good view from the cockpit, smooth response to the slightest touch of the controls, and ease of maneuver.[44]

---

* The plane's survivability was a key advantage. Between April 1967 and December 1969, the VNAF flew more than 14,800 F-5 sorties--losing just two aircraft.

On the other hand, the F-5 did not live up to its designed short takeoff roll and combat radius of about 230 miles. A more practical range seemed to be 120-150 miles, while it ate up 7,000-9,000 feet of runway when taking off with a full bombload and external fuel tanks. The two engines were powerful enough for training flights, but faltered under the added weight for combat operations. Hence the weapon load was trimmed to step up acceleration, climb rate, and range.[45]

(U) The A-37 Dragonfly was delivered to Tactical Air Command in May 1967 for combat testing. Plans called for this modified version of Cessna's twin-engine T-37 pilot trainer to supplement and then replace the A-1 and F-100. The Dragonfly boasted souped-up engines (doubling thrust), armor-plating, wing ordnance racks, a 7.62-mm minigun in the nose, manually depressed reticle gunsight, self-sealing fuel tanks, and 90-gallon tip tanks. Commonly conveying 2,500 pounds of bombs at a top airspeed of 416 knots, the aircraft could throttle back to bomb more accurately. Requiring as little as 2,800 feet of runway for takeoff, the A-37 could operate from nearby all hard-surfaced airfields in South Vietnam.[46]

The A-37 evaluation (Combat Dragon) ran from July to December 1967 and in general showed good results. The flights met with light to moderate ground fire, but the small silhouette and quick maneuver of the Dragonfly held its losses to less than half the F-100's. Then too, the plane's simple design lent itself well to maintenance in the field. During a scramble,* its quick starting allowed the A-37 to be rolling down the runway inside of 10 minutes.[47]

Combat Dragon did reveal a few deficiencies in the A-37. Its loiter time was only about two-thirds that of the F-100, and it strained to reach targets more than 170 miles distant from home base. The Dragonfly's best attack speed of 250-350 KIAS enhanced accuracy but extended exposure to AA fire. Moreover, the plane's side-by-side seating hindered the crew's view and encouraged predictable left-hand patterns during strike operations. The A-37 nevertheless stacked up favorably against the F-100 in overall performance, and stayed in South Vietnam after the evaluation ended.[48]

Tactics

The swift upsurge of the war in 1965 threw hundreds of young USAF pilots into combat for the first time. The majority of these had never flown tactical fighters or used strike tactics prior to retraining for service in

---

* The whole action for getting planes into the air in the shortest time possible, sometimes without adequate warmup.

SEA. The newcomers therefore relied heavily on the combat experience of Farm Gate and 1st Air Commando Squadron crews. However, a lot of early tactics developed in low-threat areas had to be adjusted when enemy ground fire heated up. Straight-in attack headings gave way to new approaches-- many constantly changing which degraded accuracy. Fighters began hiding in the sun or clouds from the enemy until the last possible moment. Then as jets assumed a greater share of the sorties, approach patterns such as the "floating wheel" and the "curvilinear" became common.* Crews also turned to terrain more often to shield them from AA fire.[49]

Forward Air Controller

(U) The rules of engagement called for a forward air controller to direct all close air support, and in nearly every instance he was vital to success. Spending up to 60 percent of his time in visual reconnaissance, the airborne FAC could quickly detect the telltale signs of an enemy lurking in ambush--new dust on bushes by roads and trails, muddy tracks leading out of mudholes, tiny wisps of smoke trailing up through the undergrowth, or small knots of people in spots unoccupied the day before.[50] If at all possible, a controller steeped in the area of operation would be picked to control the strike. He could more surely pinpoint trouble since he knew the locale, the people, and their habits. Nonetheless at times--chiefly in immediate air request situations--this was not possible. So while en route to the target area, the FAC selected would have to receive a radio briefing from the Direct Air Support Center and the ground commander.[51]

After takeoff on a preplanned mission, ╡ the controller called his own TACP for final coordination. He next gave his estimated arrival time to the ground commander's TACP and got any changes in the combat

---

* In the "floating wheel" the strike aircraft flew a circular base leg around the target before picking the attack heading. In the "curvilinear" the fighter continuously turned while descending to the bomb run heading. These and other tactics are treated in detail below.

╡ If responding to an immediate request, the FAC got in touch with his TACP. The steps from then on were similar to those of the preplanned mission, except that the controller was given a more detailed briefing by the DASC and ground commander.

situation. Following a check on artillery clearances with the Army fire support control center, the FAC confirmed target information with the ground commander and discussed the type of ordnance to be used. He also noted those landmarks he could easily identify such as seacoast, railroads, rivers, roads, and prominent hills Afterwards, he alerted the commander to stand by for marking his position at a predetermined time, and to have his men under suitable cover.[52]

Meantime, the DASC dispatched strike aircraft and relayed their call signs and ordnance loads to the FAC and the TACP in the target area. The fighters then contacted the control and reporting center for flight following, and the DASC moved out of the picture. To rendezvous with the forward air controller, the strike crews generally relied on TACAN fixes. As an added help, the FAC could talk the fighters in by referring to landmarks, or by generating smoke.[53]

On the way from the rendezvous point to the target area (usually 10-25 miles), the FAC and fighter crews reviewed the target situation and tactics. The method of attack pivoted largely on the ground battle's progress and the type of ordnance to be employed. If troops were not in contact, CBU, Iron bombs, or napalm could be dropped. Iron bombs were ruled out when the opposing forces were close-in on each other, but napalm or CBU could be used if the friendlies had good cover. Whenever possible, the controller and strike orbits were set up with attack headings moving parallel to friendly positions and away from the sun.*[54]

As FAC and fighter aircraft penetrated the target area, the forward air controller called the ground commander for the prearranged marker. This could be a colored smoke grenade, signal panels, tracer crossfire, signal mirrors, or artillery/mortar rounds. To confuse the strike team, the enemy at times sent up colored smoke matching that of the friendlies. Whereupon, the controller had the option of asking for a new mark and identifying the color himself.[55]

---

* Sometimes the controller had strike crews orbit out of the target area, if he was directing other fighters or waiting for the friendly ground situation to clear up.

Target Marking *

▮ The forward air controller first made doubly sure he had identified the target. Then keeping an eye on the fighters, he marked it from the same heading (or its reciprocal) they would use for their bomb runs. If the strike pilots found it hard to pick out the target, the marking was done over.56

(U) O-1 forward air controllers favored two basic target marking deliveries in close air support--the "steep and close-in" against lightly defended targets and the "turning" where small-arms fire heated up. In the first delivery, the

STEEP AND CLOSE-IN DELIVERY

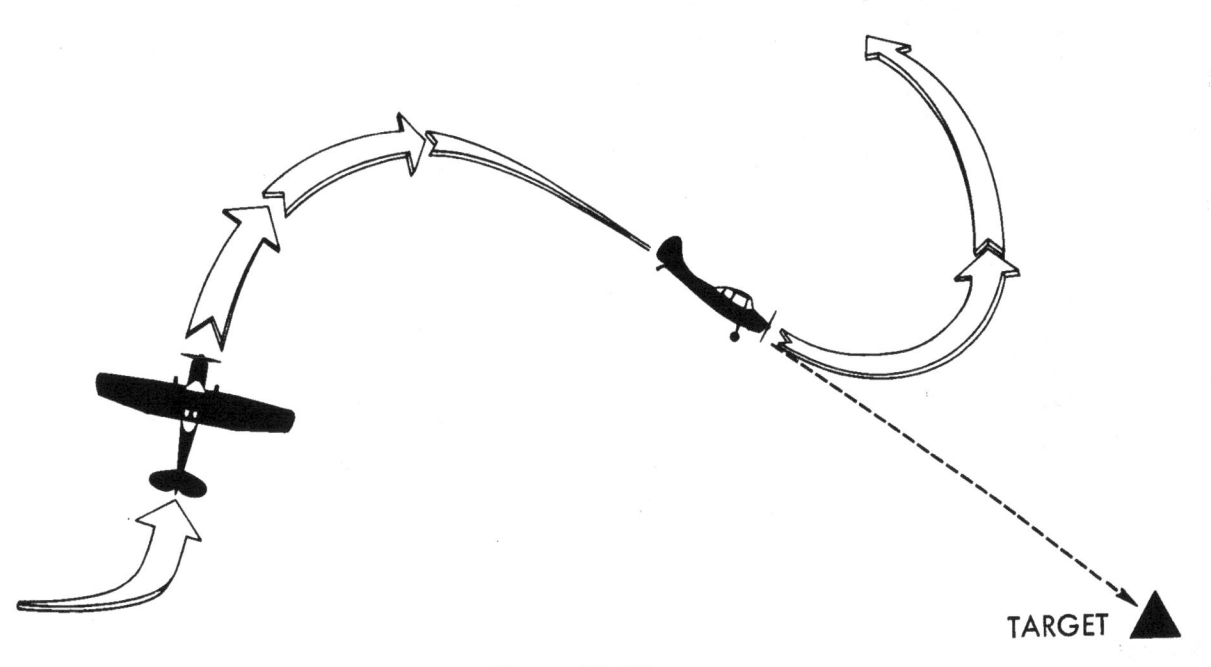

Figure 11 (U)

* White phosphorous 2.75-inch rockets were the most common target markers, but wind quickly blew their smoke off-target. Also, in swampy areas they often buried themselves harmlessly in the mud. Airborne controllers accordingly decreased the penetration by shallowing their diving approaches.

controller held close-in and parallel to the target at 2,000-2,000 feet AGL, set to mark. When ready he closed the throttle and pulled the plane's nose up. As the speed dropped off to 50 KIAS, he kicked the rudder hard right or left. The nose fell down and through the horizon, while at the same time pivoting rapidly toward the target. After leveling the wings and lining up to mark, the FAC fired a rocket. He immediately pulled out at about 1,500 feet, using his airspeed to complete a steep banking turn 60°-80° off the attack heading. He climbed back to altitude in an arcing maneuver that let him keep the rocket's impact and the target in view.[57] A variation of this delivery involved a simple wingover, with the 0-1's nose sinking down and past the horizon as the bank angle steepened. Recovery was made the same way as before.[58]

(U) In the turning delivery, the controller did not roll wings and line up on the target. He marked instead from a turn that gave the rocket a curved path. He therefore fired slightly high and before the aircraft passed through the target picture.[59]

TURNING DELIVERY

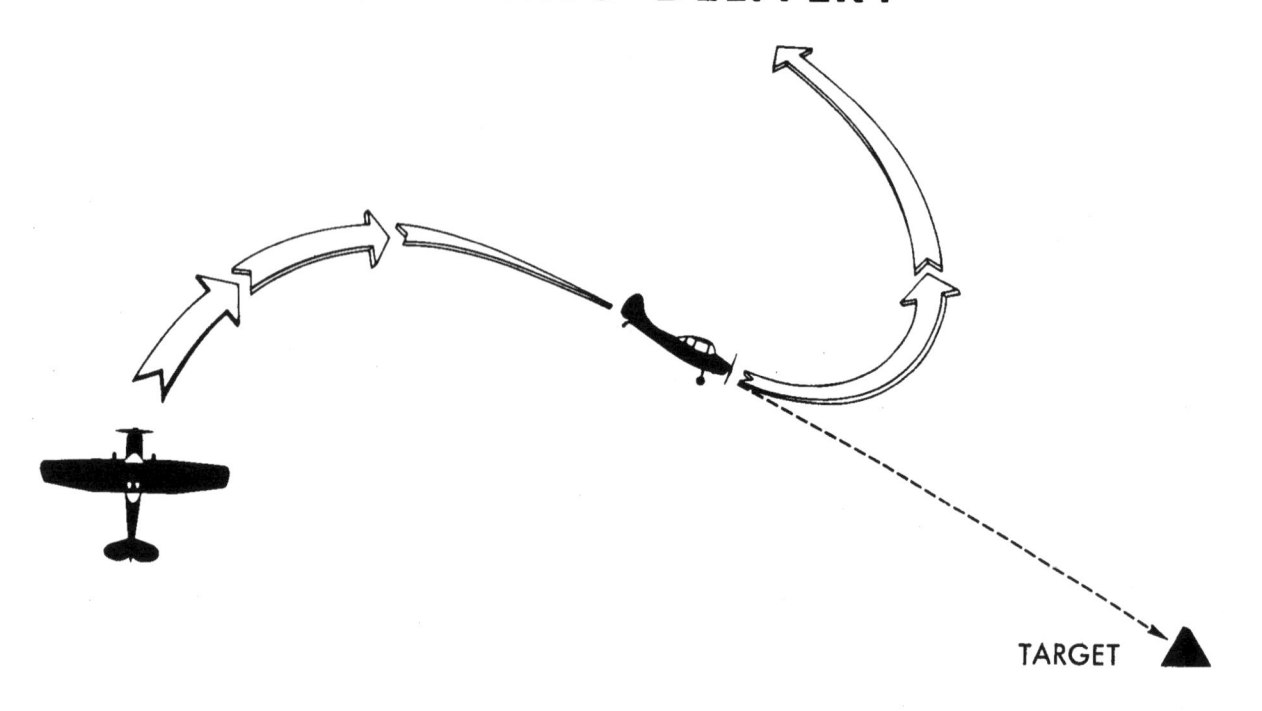

TARGET

Figure 12 (U)

(This page Unclassified)

(U) Besides being more stable than the O-1 for marking targets, the O-2A boasted a noncomputing gunsight that refined marking accuracy. This oval, mirror-type, glass device sat on the instrument panel in front of the pilot, tilted 45° away from him. A rheostat-controlled dot of light (pipper) adjustable for delivery altitude, could be reflected on the glass. The pilot flew straight and level at 140 KIAS to mark, setting the dot on one of the calibrated lines of elevation/depression inscribed on the gunsight's surface. [60]

(U) O-2A marking methods in general followed those of the O-1, with but minor exceptions. The O-2A propeller speed setting, for example, stayed at 2,600 revolutions per minute (rpm), and delivery approaches started 800-1,000 feet above desired release altitudes. The power-off approach, commonly used, was a lot like the O-1's steep and close-in technique. With the target at 3 or 9 o'clock, the controller retarded throttles, lifted the nose a little to drain off airspeed to 100 knots, and rolled into his final approach. As the aircraft came around, the FAC dipped the nose so he could bring the gunsight pipper up to center on the target at release point. [61] The power-on approach was adopted when ground fire intensified. A higher altitude and airspeed were its chief differences from the power-off. [62]

(U) The OV-10 featured a target marking system that computed winds, dive angles, and release altitudes. In theory the system could score a shack* every time, but in practice the forward air controller often had to make corrections during the pass. Even so, the Bronco proved to be the best aircraft for target marking. Its greater airspeed also let it fly off the wing of the A-1 and the A-37. The controller could thereby direct the strike pilot, mark the target, and make last-minute adjustments in the bomb run. Then a quick loop out and back over afforded the FAC time to meet and give final corrections to the second fighter coming in. [63] This tactic was sparingly used, however, due to its element of danger. Other OV-10 marking procedures were similar to those of the O-2.

(U) After marking the target, the FAC took up a holding pattern fitted to the type of ordnance, terrain, and friendly and enemy positions. If the strike aircraft dispensed slicks (free-fall bombs) from higher altitudes, the controller held high to avoid the blast. He flew a lower holding orbit

---

* A direct or perfect hit.

OUTSIDE HOLDING PATTERN

- HIGH ANGLE – HIGH RELEASE
- 1,500 – 2,500 FEET ALTITUDE
- WORK STRIKE AIRCRAFT PARALLEL TO FRIENDLY POSITIONS

TARGET

FRIENDLY POSITIONS

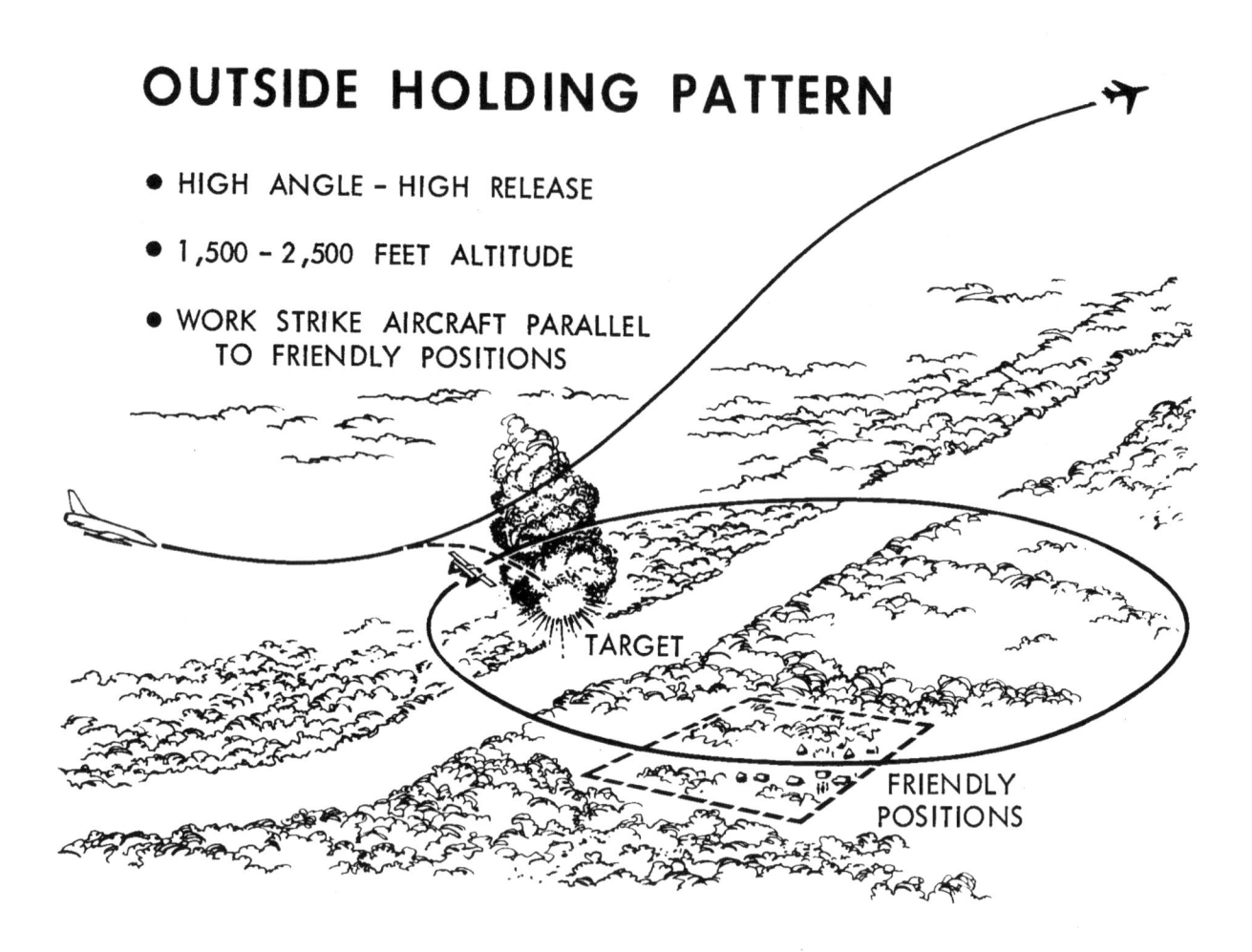

Figure 13 (U)

when high drags (finned or parachute-retarded bombs), napalm, or blueys (BLU's)*were released at low altitude. Thus two basic patterns emerged-- the outside and the overhead.[64]

(U) The outside orbit suited high angle and steep delivery bomb runs. The forward air controller would set up a racetrack pattern over friendly positions at 1,500-2,500 feet AGL, opposite the strike orbit and short of the weapon release point. (See Fig. 13). He could see the incoming fighters clearly as they expended ordnance, and they were able to climb out without pulling through his orbit. An offshoot of this pattern, the figure eight, allowed the FAC to view both strike aircraft and target at all times. (See Fig. 14.) When neither one of these filled the bill, the controller could try the inside orbit. Here, he again traced his racetrack route over the friendlies but inside the strike pattern. (See Fig. 15).[65]

(U) The overhead orbit had the FAC circle at 2,000-3,000 feet directly above the target as the fighters zoomed in beneath. (See Fig. 16). This pattern worked well when strikes needed to be made down a valley, or with friendly positions pressing close to either side of the target. Looking straight down on the impact points, the controller could furnish the fighter pilots corrections without having to consider slant ranges.[66]

Directing the Strike

If tactical conditions permitted and the element of surprise was unnecessary, fighter pilots could make dry passes ⁄at the target. They also had the option of going over "dry" when unsure of the target's exact location. Moreover, if the forward air controller spotted a change in the ground situation that meant undue danger to friendly troops, he told the strike polots to withhold their ordnance.[67]

---

*BLU's (bomb, live unit) applies to various ordnance, for example, the bomblets dropped from dispensers or from special purpose bombs.

⁄ Orientation passes with no ordnance drops.

FIGURE EIGHT PATTERN

STRIKE AIRCRAFT AND TARGET CAN BE KEPT IN SIGHT AT ALL TIMES

- 1,500 - 2,500 FEET ALTITUDE AGL
- 120 - 150 KNOTS
- WORK STRIKE AIRCRAFT PARALLEL TO LONG AXIS

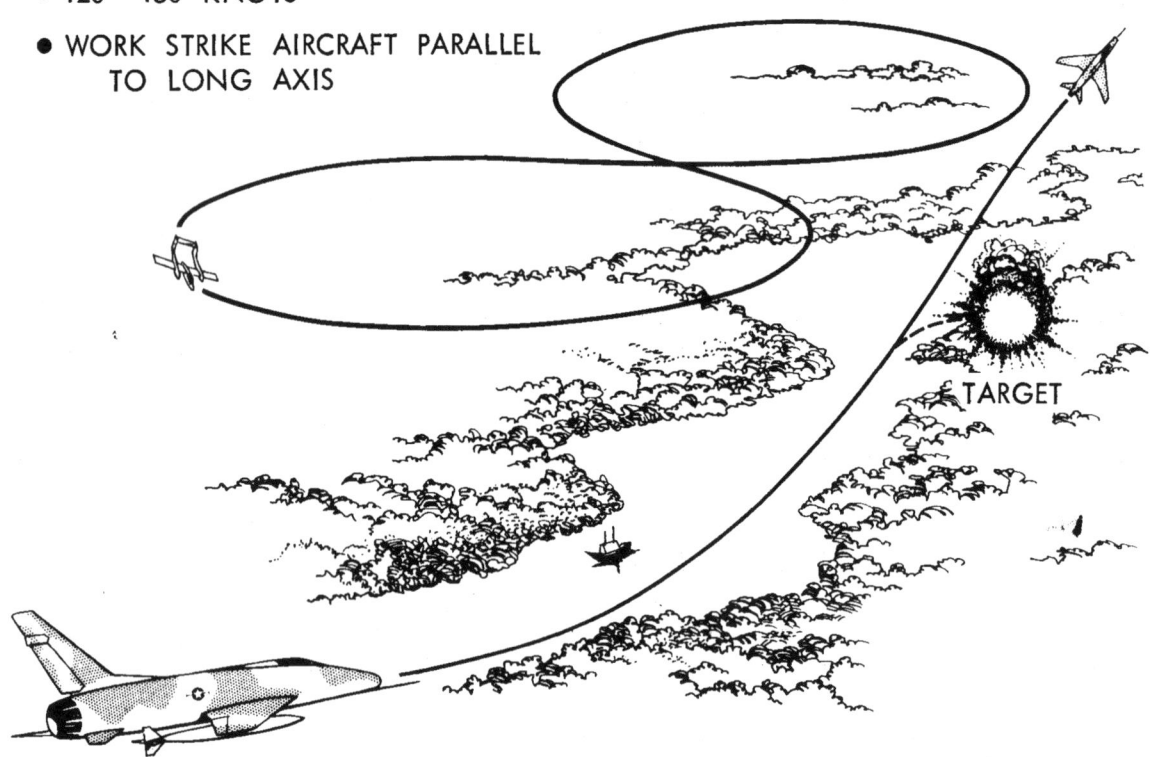

Figure 14 (U)

(This page Unclassified)

INSIDE HOLDING PATTERN

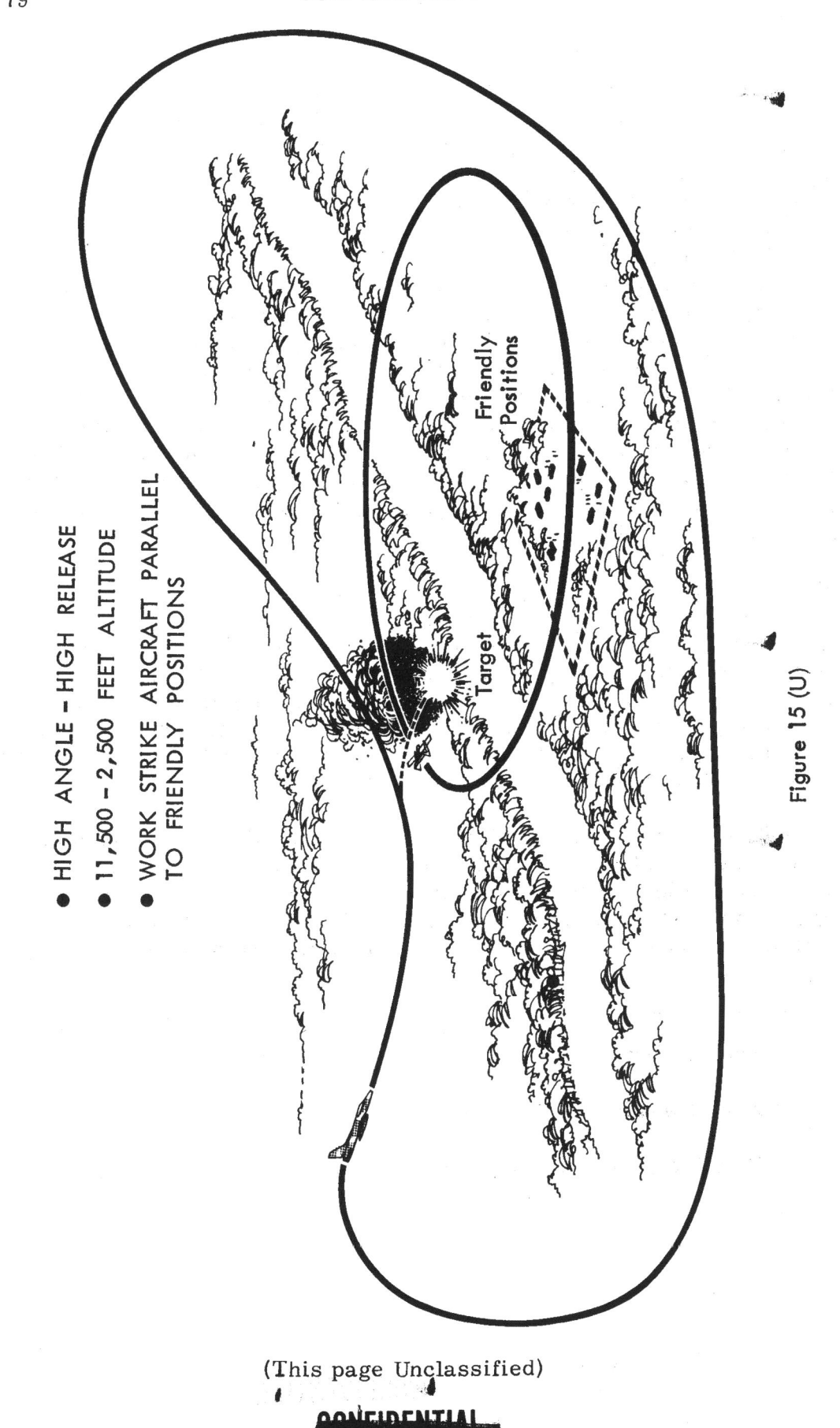

- HIGH ANGLE – HIGH RELEASE
- 11,500 – 2,500 FEET ALTITUDE
- WORK STRIKE AIRCRAFT PARALLEL TO FRIENDLY POSITIONS

Figure 15 (U)

(This page Unclassified)

(C) The explosion of the first bomb commonly served as a reference point for the controller to adjust follow-on strikes. He gave corrections crisply and in the clear,* citing cardinal headings† and prominent landmarks. In addition, he kept in constant contact with the ground commander to secure a running account of strike results.[68]

(U) Frequently the FAC coordinated airstrikes, artillery fire, and helicopter gunship support on the same target. This required reliable radio contact between him and the fire support coordination center, the ground commander, and the helicopter gunship commander. His decisions had to be made quickly and were based first on the needs of the ground troops, then on the loiter time of the fighters. Whenever the Communists were deeply dug-in or were attacking in force, the strike aircraft dropped heavy bombs, with artillery and gunship fire mopping up. But if lighter firepower would do, the fighters held "high and dry." The controller never directed tactical airstrikes and helicopter gunship fire on a target at the same time.[69]

Slow Movers ‡

(C) After 1965 the A-1E continued to be the chief slow mover strike aircraft in close air support operations. Because of its side-by-side seating, pilots tended to fly left-hand orbits, rolling in on and turning off the target in the same direction. Since this let enemy gunners predict their flight path, Skyraider crews had to steel themselves to fly a mix of right- and left- hand turns and orbits.[70]

(C) A-1E tactics changed only slightly from 1964 on, the Skyraiders preferring 2- and 4-ship flights. However, they did use a wider variety of attack headings to escape the stepped-up ground fire. Usually the flight leader set up a circular or racetrack orbit, the other aircraft in trail and so spaced that at least one could attack on the strike heading.

---

* That is, not in cipher or code.

† North, south, east, and west.

‡ Relatively slow-moving aircraft.

OVERHEAD HOLDING PATTERN

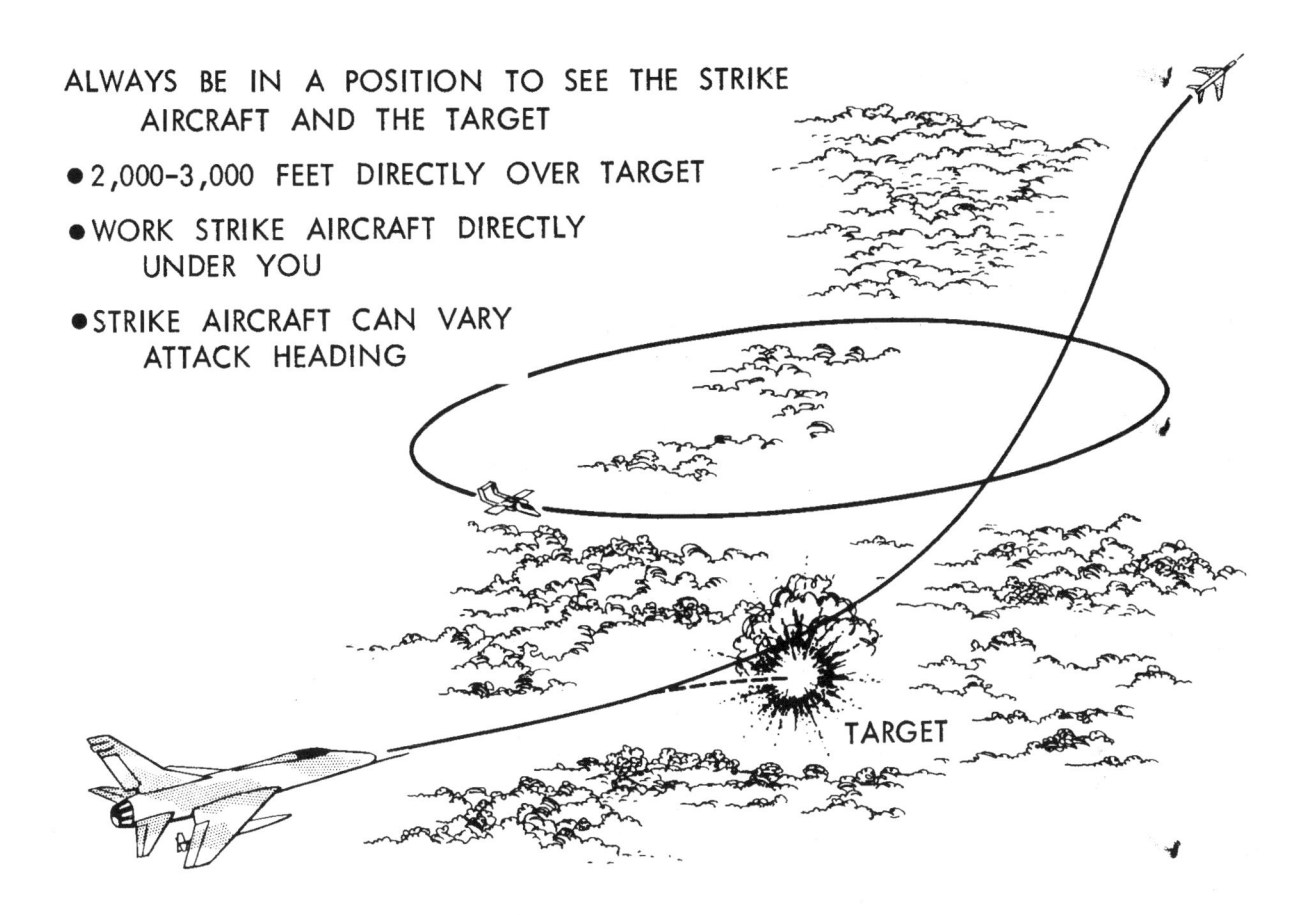

ALWAYS BE IN A POSITION TO SEE THE STRIKE AIRCRAFT AND THE TARGET

- 2,000-3,000 FEET DIRECTLY OVER TARGET
- WORK STRIKE AIRCRAFT DIRECTLY UNDER YOU
- STRIKE AIRCRAFT CAN VARY ATTACK HEADING

Figure 16 (U)

(This page Unclassified)

An alternate method was the moving figure eight. (See Fig. 17). The leader dove toward the target as number two positioned to come in from nearly a reciprocal track. After the lead dropped bombs and pulled away, two started his run. Meantime, three and four got ready to sweep in from still slightly different headings.[71]

Previous to delivering mixed loads, Skyraider crews made sure of safe aircraft and altitude separation. High-explosive bombs were usually dropped from above 1,000 feet AGL, but napalm and other incendiaries could be released from as low as 50 feet. It therefore behooved an A-1E pilot not to begin his nape run too close behind a Skyraider dispensing general purpose bombs. Doing so risked heavy damage from shrapnel or even being blown from the sky by the concussion of the bomb blast. Hence a general rule required that GP bombs go first, followed after a safe interval by napalm and cluster bomb units.[72]

While A-1E crews polished their strike tactics, Communist gunners devised two basic ways to counter them. The first method strung out hundreds of troops along an anticipated attack heading, sending up barrages of small arms fire as the aircraft passed overhead. The second and better tactic placed seasoned gunners at strategic points of an expected strike path. From these positions, they expertly "lead-aimed" and fired on the fighters, severly damaging those who ventured too low. Barrage fire grew hotter by 1966, stoked by an influx of machineguns, the .30-cal and the rapid firing .50 cal (540-600 rounds-per-minute). Then in 1967, 23- and 37-mm guns (having ranges of more than 6,600 and 8,200 feet, respectively) swung into action.* They took their toll of the slow-flying Skyraiders.[73]

) The enemy added still another ground-fire wrinkle in November 1967. During the battle for Bo Duc in III Corps, he bolted together four .50-cal machineguns to make "quad-50's." He put them several kilometers/ from the expected target at the point he believed the fighters would make their final roll-in on the attack heading. Once the strike aircraft had

---

* 57-mm guns, with a lethal range of 19,700 feet, began appearing in South Vietnam a short time later.

/ A kilometer is 3,280.8 feet, about two-thirds (.62) of a mile.

completed their turn and leveled off, the Communists unleashed the quad-50's then threw up a heavy smokescreen to obscure the target area. Disrupted by the gunfire and smoke, the A-1E pilots were forced to go over dry on nearly one-third of their passes.[74] After Bo Duc, quad-50's with smoke were widely used.

A-1E crews explored quite a few ways to foil the hot ground fire. They tried descending into the target area earlier for a low-altitude attack, but barrage fire remained a serious threat. High-speed, turning/diving approaches worked better but met with fire over the target. A further tactic had number one roar in low to bomb, trailed by number two with guns blazing. This kept enemy heads down long enough for the third fighter to sneak in from a different direction with bombs.[75]

High and medium dive angles (30°-60°) cut down the danger from ground fire in the course of Skyraider strafing attacks. Though the steeper angles diminished firing accuracy, it was precise enough to permit recovery above 1,500 feet AGL. Each pilot took care not to follow other strafing aircraft too close, lest he fly through spent cartridge casings and links.* He also steered clear of friendly positions, because the links and casings could be well-nigh as deadly as bullets to the troops below.[76]

The sharp Communist fire curbed low-level delivery of napalm. Then too, the nape tended to hang up in the trees and ignite before striking the ground.[77] These problems were solved by attaching fins to the rear of the cannisters. Now, the Skyraider pilot started a high-speed, 40°-45° dive from 3,000-4,000 feet AGL and released the weapon at about 2,000 feet and 240-280 KIAS. He quickly climbed back to orbit without ever having been within lethal small-arms range. Meantime, the fins steadied the path of the napalm and let it punch down through the trees to the ground before erupting. The nape's burn pattern was circular instead of long and narrow as in low-altitude drops.[78]

Dispensing napalm by glide bombing secured the best features of the low- and high- level methods. The attack began with a medium angle (15°-20°) dive from 2,000-30,000 feet AGL. When airspeed edged up to

---

* A link is the metal part that links one cartridge to another to form an ammunition belt.

220 KIAS and altitude nudged 500-800 feet, the A-1E pilot triggered off an unfinned cannister and started his recovery. Like in other nape deliveries he aimed short, and the fireball rolled into the target. This attack angle as a rule allowed the bomb to pierce the trees with finer accuracy and lengthened the spread of the mixture.[79]

Fast Movers*

In 1965 the F-100 and B-57 crews pioneered in forging close air support procedures for jets in Southeast Asia. Since a few of them had flown combat, they relied on Korean War tactics learned in school. F-100 pilots, for example, set up the old rectangular box orbit and stuck to the same dive angle and attack heading during follow-on passes. These simple patterns had to be changed, however, once the enemy gunners mastered tracking and barrage firing.[80]

The jet pilots had also picked up the habit of dropping explosives before strafing. Consequently, the Communists stayed hidden until all bombs were expended, then emerged to pour withering fire into the fighters streaking in low (often under 500 feet AGL). Hence by the close of 1965, the strike crews had started to vary their bombing and strafing runs. After dropping one or two bombs the flight leader usually climbed back to orbit altitude, while numbers two and three strafed. As the enemy troops came out shooting, the lead pilot swooped back in and hit them with the rest of his bombs.[81] Experience further taught the crews to use steeper (25°-30°) dive angles for strafe and to pull out at 1,000-1,500 feet. / They likewise limited these runs to two at a time, thus making it harder for the Viet Cong to get ready for firing.[82]

---

* High-performance aircraft (jets).

/ At first jet fighter pilots were cool to any change in strafing tactics. Since 1951 the standard training pattern had been a 5°-15° dive angle with firing to begin at about 1,900 feet. Pilots believed this method was the only way to "rip" the target. In any case, the continuing battle damage slowly convinced them that varied attacks with steeper strafe angles would do the job more safely.

As the ground-fire threat grew, strike crews sharpened dive angles to 45° or more for hard bombs. Angles for high-drag bombs, rockets, napalm, and cluster bomb units crept up to over 30°. Delivery altitudes rose to 2,000 feet AGL and above, forcing pilots to begin attacks from as high as 9,000 feet, and often pushing airspeed to 500 knots at release point. The number of strike passes were also scaled down, and the same attack headings were rarely repeated.* When low clouds or the need for extreme accuracy called for low-level runs, the jet fighters zipped in and out at high speed. They constantly made small heading and altitude changes during the attack and recovery, leveling out just long enough to line up on the target.[83]

Deemed the least desirable attack maneuver, the old box pattern commonly proved best for working close in to ground troops, during night strikes, or under low cloud ceilings. Jet crews further found that the box simplified the job of keeping track of one another. The pattern induced single-heading attacks, however, and so was used only when other tactics were out of the question.[84]

The circular pattern came to be one of the most popular and flexible maneuvers for close air support. It gave the jet pilots a wide choice of attack headings, differing as much as 90°. The tactic consisted of two circles with the edge of one crossing over the other. Four fighters were best, two in each circle and all keeping up a clockwise or counter-clockwise flow. From orbit altitude of 7,500-9,000 feet AGL, the lead pilot in the first circle began a dive as he turned onto his strike heading (calling out his position and direction to the other fighters and the controller). At release altitude (500-2,000 feet, depending on the type of ordnance), he dropped his bombs and at once commenced a wings-level climb. He turned sharply off-heading at 2,500 feet ǂ (again alerting the others). This signaled the lead pilot in the second circle to take up his attack heading,

---

* A few situations dictated a single strike heading of its reciprocal-- for example, the support of troops in a long and narrow valley, within a box canyon, or on a hillside.

ǂ Turning any earlier would extend his exposure to ground fire in the target area.

90° from that of the first pass. Since the circular pattern held dangers, the crews had to keep the other aircraft constantly in view, and strictly adhere to altitude separations. Attack intervals were usually spaced at least a minute apart. They could be made longer or shorter by altering the sizes of the two circles.[85]

CIRCULAR ATTACK PATTERN

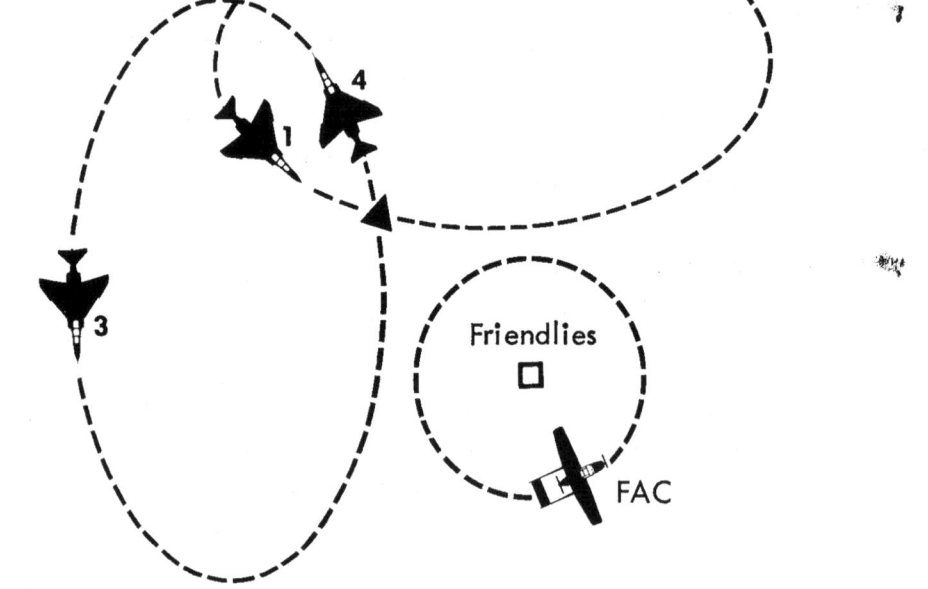

CIRCULAR PATTERN LEFT OR RIGHT WITH ONE ELEMENT IN EACH CIRCLE. THE FLOW OF TRAFFIC CONTINUES ROTATING IN A COUNTERCLOCKWISE DIRECTION, OR VICE VERSA.

Figure 17 (U)

When strikes had to be held to a single run-in heading, the attack-by-element pattern worked well. The tactic in addition suited the delivery of mixed ordnance loads. A 2-fighter element orbited in each of two circles on opposite sides of the target. Keeping inside one of these orbits, the FAC circled over the friendly troops. As a rule, strike aircraft of the lead element dove steeply and dropped GP bombs, pulled up in a turn away from the other element, and streaked back to altitude. After the bombs exploded, the second element launched a low-level napalm run. The pilots set up a medium dive (20°-30°), gunned to 450-500 KIAS, and released the nape at 1,000 feet or lower.* They recovered in a turn, swinging into position to suppress ground fire during the first element's follow-on pass.[86]

ATTACK BY ELEMENTS

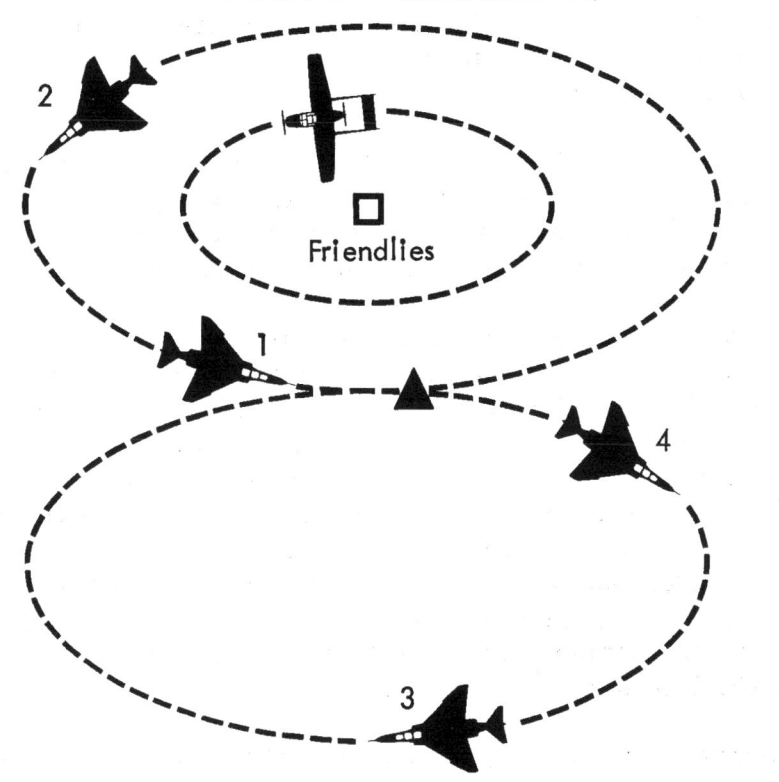

ATTACK BY ELEMENTS FROM RESTRICTED HEADING.
1 AND 2 MANEUVER ON THE LEFT, 3 AND 4 MANEUVER ON THE RIGHT.

Figure 18 (U)

---

* Release was 300-500 feet higher for cluster bomb units.

By 1967 random attack patterns had pushed to the fore, but were used with caution in close air support due to heading restrictions. Considered the most flexible random tactic, the floating wheel was employed solely when friendly troops stayed outside the fighter flight path. (See Fig. 19). The wheel was nothing more than a circular base leg flown around the target generally at 6,000-7,000 feet AGL. Each strike pilot picked an attack heading at random, based on that of the fighter directly in front of him. After departing the wheel, he kept turning and descending to the final heading in a curvilinear approach. (See Fig. 20). Between 2-3 seconds prior to release, the pilot straightened out and brought wings level, holding steady until the bombs were triggered. He started a straight-ahead pullup and at 2-4 G's stabbed to above 2,500 feet. Once clear of other aircraft, he continued on a climbing arc back to orbit.[87] Inasmuch as the fighters were commonly in different phases of the attack, the floating wheel upped the chances of collision. Every pilot therefore kept tabs on the other fighters. He called out the direction of his approach and the kind of ordnance being dropped. During pullout he gave his position and direction of turn.[88]

The floating wheel in addition let the controller or ground commander set the delivery sequence. The FAC, for example, could ask for the GP bombs. The fighter packing them would turn in on the proper heading and dive angle, while the others remained in orbit.[89]

The B-57 unlike the F-100 could not take the physical pounding or G-stresses during strike and evasive maneuvers. Hence the Canberra pilots flew rectangular and circular orbits but avoided the punishing curvilinear approaches. The basic B-57 tactic for both weapons delivery and strafing was a straight-ahead, 30°-45° dive from an orbit altitude of 9,000 feet AGL. Airspeed often topped 400 knots as the aircraft neared 5,000 feet. The pilot then sighten in by offsetting the gunsight ring the estimated distance from an aiming point to the target. When the crosshairs lined up with the pipper, he pickled the bombs and began a pullout on the same heading. After passing above small-arms range, he climbed back to altitude in a shallow turn.[90]

(U) F-4 pilots for the most part adopted F-100 close air support tactics. Being heavier than the Super Sabre, the Phantom did not maneuver as well at similar airspeeds. In consequence it required wider turns and larger strike patterns. When the support of ground troops pared the number of attack headings, F-4 pilots as a rule chose reciprocal tracks for follow-on runs. During the strike, the backseater helped the pilot line up on the target by locking on with the air-to-air radar and giving heading/dive-angle corrections. At 1,500-3,000 feet AGL (depending on the type of ordnance and

FLOATING WHEEL ATTACK PATTERN

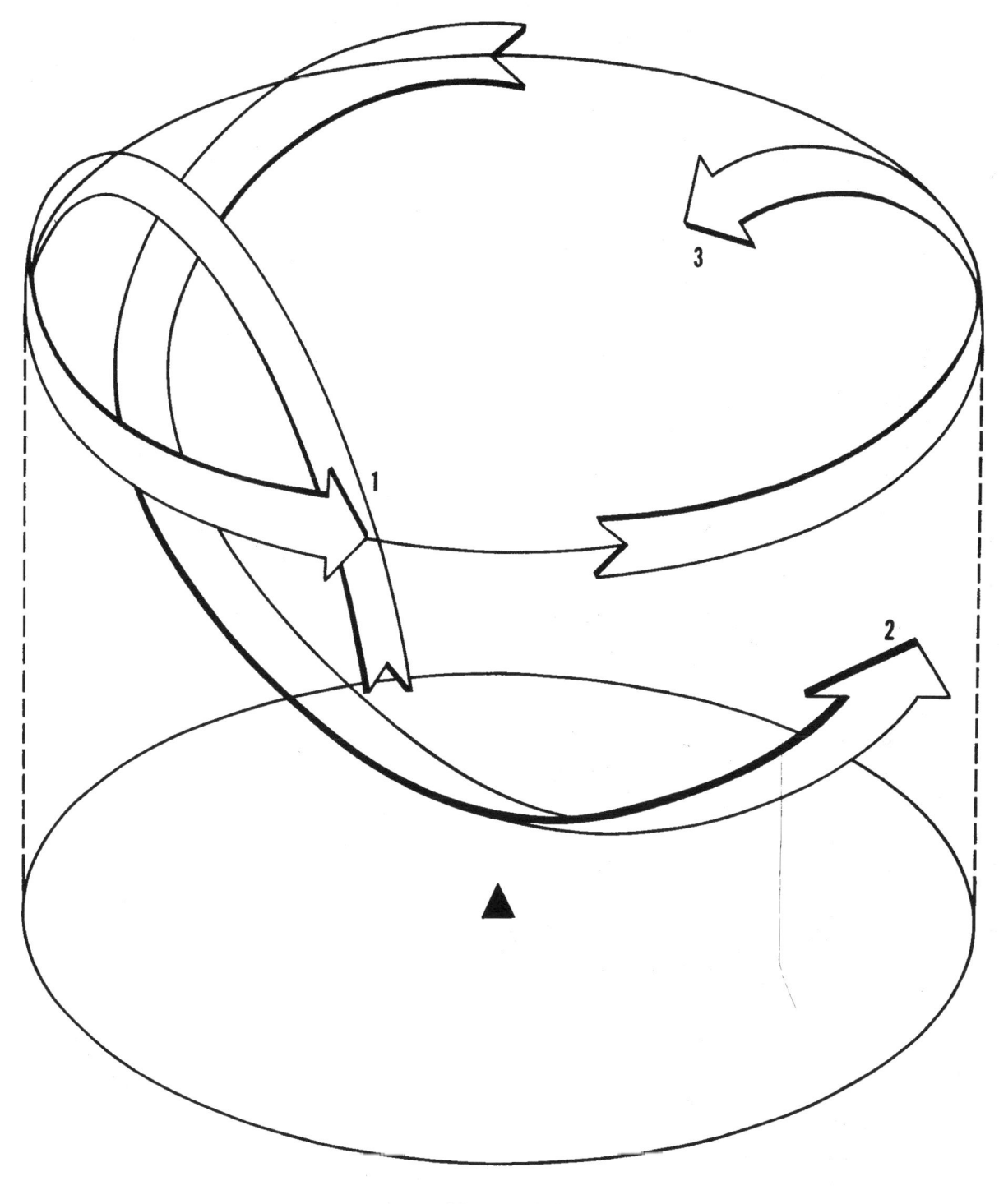

Figure 19 (C)

CURVILINEAR APPROACH AND ATTACK

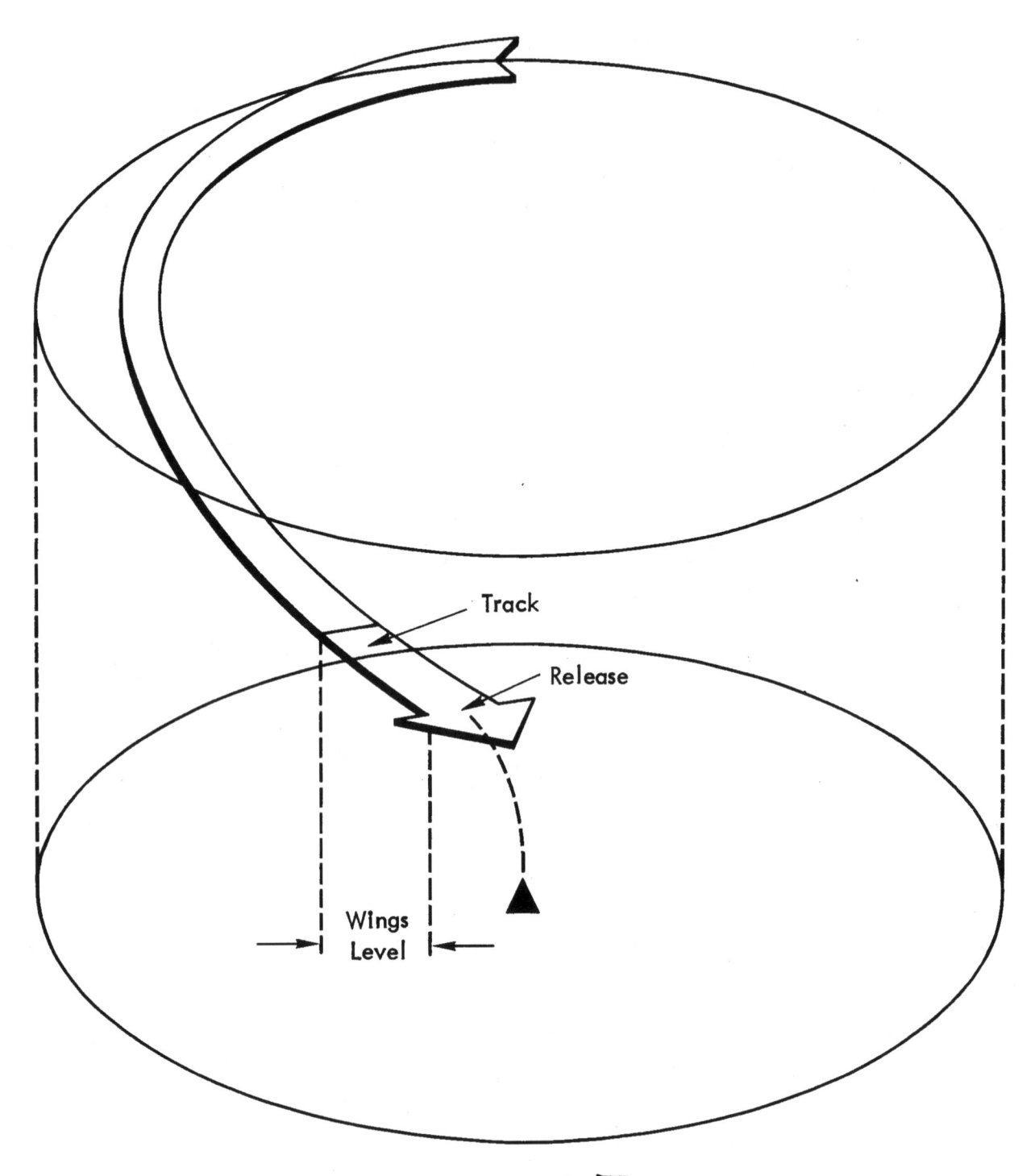

Figure 20

tactics), the pilot placed the gunsight pipper on the target. He flew on until the pipper matched the crosshairs, released the bombs, and commenced a straight-ahead pullup at 2-4 G's to get free of small-arms fire. He later made a 180° climbing turn that formed a narrow figure eight and aligned him for an attack from the opposite direction.[91]

(U) When offered a wider choice of strike headings, F-4 pilots opted for the floating wheel pattern and curvilinear approach. The wheel was regularly set up at 6,000-8,000 feet AGL, with the fighters dropping off into a medium-to high-angle attack. Turning toward the target, the Phantom pilot leveled out just long enough to put the gunsight pipper on it and trigger the bombs. Without switching heading he climbed out past small-arms range, and gunned to altitude in a turn. To drop napalm the F-4 attacked at 600-800 feet, holding a straight-and-level approach to heighten accuracy.*[92]

(U) The F-5 and A-37 employed F-100 close air support tactics. If not loaded down with ordnance, both aircraft maneuvered better than the F-100 or F-4. They could therefore support ground troops in tight places that bigger aircraft couldn't get into.

Ground Controlled Radar Bombing

The Air Force's support of ground troops fell off sharply in bad weather and at night, the controllers finding it very hard to direct airstrikes. The Viet Cong and their North Vietnamese allies exploited this weakness by launching most of their attacks during these periods. The fall of the Special Forces camp at A Shau in March 1966 served as a grim reminder of how darkness and weather could choke off close air support.[93]

Seeking a way to conduct tactical bombing around the clock and in all sorts of weather, the Air Force tested the MSQ-35 bomb scoring computer. Since the early 1950's, SAC and TAC had used the system to score simulated bomb runs. The van-mounted MSQ-35 could be programmed with the ballistics

---

* If friendlies were in deep trouble, the pilot kicked off the nape attack below 6,000 feet. He descended to the deck in a low-angle dive at 450 KIAS or more. Considering that the slightest error in judgment could spell disaster, this tactic was used sparingly.

of the weapons to be dropped and the grid coordinates of the impact point. After receiving the bombing crew's true airspeed (TAS), altitude, and true heading at release, the computer could precisely gauge the accuracy of the attack.[94]

(U) This scoring procedure had been successfully reversed in the Korean War. The radar controller directed the strike pilots to fly a specific altitude, heading, and airspeed to the target. At a given point the countdown commenced, and the bombs were released when the controller got to zero.[95] To find out if the reverse MSQ method could be of use in SEA, the Air Force ran tests at Matagorda Island, Tex., during late 1965 and early 1966. Mostly F-100 aircraft took part and dropped live bombs. Picking up their skin-paint blips* at 50 nautical miles on the MSQ scope, the controller recorded a circular error average of less than 500 feet. With range stretched to 95 NM, the CEA still registered only 607 feet. In light of these results, the Air Force modified the MSQ-35 into the MSQ-77 Combat Skyspot. The new system had a range of 200 nautical miles for aircraft equipped with beacon transponders.†[96]

In March 1966 the first MSQ-77 arrived at Bien Hoa. Others followed to Pleiku, Dong Ha, and Dalat in South Vietnam, as well as to Nakhon Phanom in Thailand. Once tied into the tactical air control system, Combat Skypot gave a sizable boost to 24-hour air support of ground troops. The MSQ sites within a year controlled more than 15,000 strike sorties, chiefly flown by F-100's. Skyspot's accuracy let heavy bombs be dropped on occasion within 250 meters of friendly positions. Moreover, the fighters could release their ordnance from above the range of ground fire.[98]

Until the bomb run began, preplanned and immediate sorties under Skyspot control went much like other close air support missions. The DASC and CRC in most cases bypassed the FAC, handing off the fighters direct to the proper MSQ-77 site. The radar controller kept contact with the strike pilots and ground commander to coordinate target information and ordnance requirements. He fed into the computer the type of aircraft and weapons,

---

*A skin-paint blip is a radar indication caused by the reflected radar signal from an object.

† A transponder's blip appeared much larger on the radarscope than did a skin-paint blip.

TAS, release altitude, run-in headings, and target grid coordinates. Since many maps of South Vietnam contained distance errors of up to 300 meters, the controller rarely brought ordnance in that close unless the ground commander insisted. Even then, the attack heading paralleled the line of friendly positions as a safeguard. [99]

When working with Combat Skyspot, the F-100's flew a bombing altitude of 25,000 feet AGL and 400-knot true airspeed.* After departing the initial point (IP), ✝ 70-100 miles from the target, the strike crew followed to the letter each small correction in heading, altitude, and airspeed furnished by the radar controller. The last 2 minutes of the run were crucial. Final computations had already been set into the MSQ-77 computer and further changes would seriously impair bombing accuracy. At 1 minute and again at 30 seconds before bombs away, the controller called for the crew to steady the aircraft and prepare for countdown. As zero sounded, the pilot pickled the bombs and turned off-target. [100]

Escort Tactics

(U) The A-1E Skyraiders handled most of the air cover for helicopter operations and convoy or troop movements. Their tactics resembled those of Farm Gate T-28's. To escort helicopters flying low-altitude contour patterns, the Skyraider element split up. One fighter flew low and in front of the copters, sweeping back and forth in slow S-turns to draw enemy fire. The others (one to three) held above and behind, similarly weaving. When the Communists opened fire, the high formation began at once to bomb and strafe the guns into silence. [101]

(U) When the helicopters flew at medium altitude (2,500-3,000 feet AGL), three A-1E's commonly covered them. One strike aircraft flanked each side of the formation, executing the same S-maneuver. The third flew back of and higher than the copters. All Skyriders stayed in position to suppress ground

---

*This altitude afforded the MSQ-77 good line-of-sight transmission. Some time later, the altitude was lowered and the airspeed increased.

✝ A well-defined point, easily distinguishable visually and/or electronically, used as a starting point for the bomb run to the target.

LOW-ALTITUDE HELICOPTER ESCORT (A-1E)

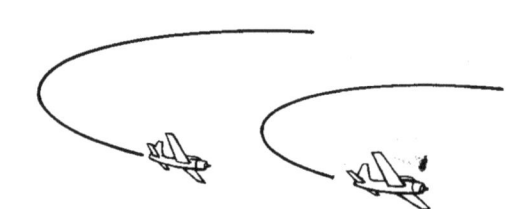

HIGH ELEMENT S - TURNS BEHIND AND ABOVE FORMATION

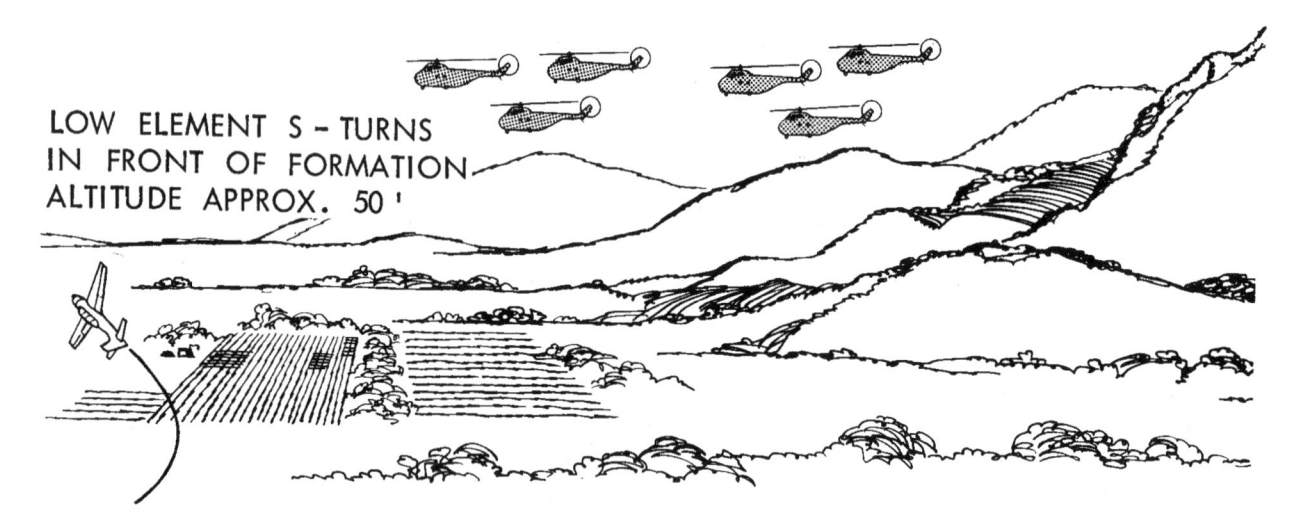

LOW ELEMENT S - TURNS IN FRONT OF FORMATION ALTITUDE APPROX. 50'

Figure 21 (U)

(This page Unclassified)

fire the instant it erupted. The choppers also stood ready to mark gun positions with smoke grenades or machinegun fire.[102]

A-1 ESCORT--HELICOPTERS MEDIUM TO HIGH ALTITUDE

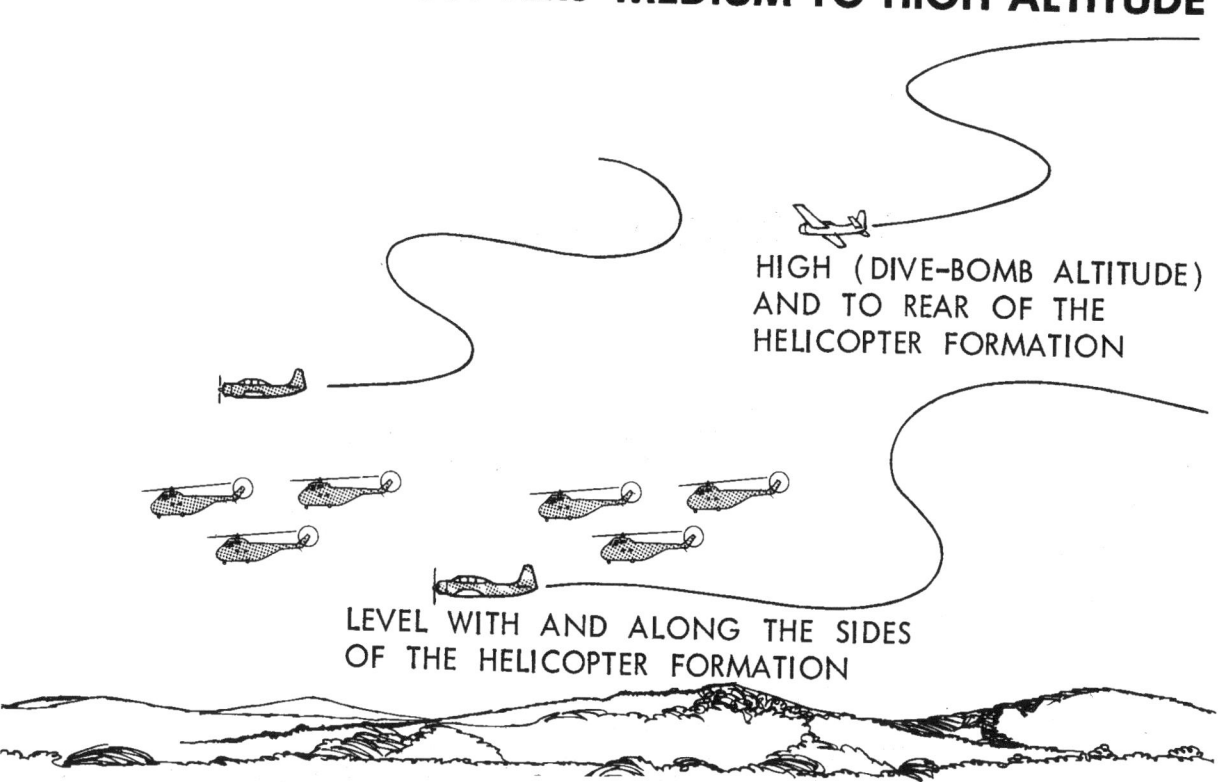

HIGH (DIVE-BOMB ALTITUDE) AND TO REAR OF THE HELICOPTER FORMATION

LEVEL WITH AND ALONG THE SIDES OF THE HELICOPTER FORMATION

Figure 22 (U)

(U) The forward air controller entered the picture whenever the A-1E's escorted troop convoys. In the course of the preflight briefing, the crews went over departure and destination arrival times, travel route and terrain, and defensive tactics. As the vehicles rolled out, the controller flew several hundred yards to the fore in lazy back-and-forth swings across the road. The Skyraiders tarried a bit behind the convoy, barely high enough to clear most small-arms fire. The moment the FAC spotted hostile fire or enemy troops, he marked and called in the fighters. One pilot kept high to cover the attack, then traded positions and made his run. [103]

A-1E CONVOY ESCORT

FAC FLIES SLOW S-TURNS IN FRONT OF CONVOY

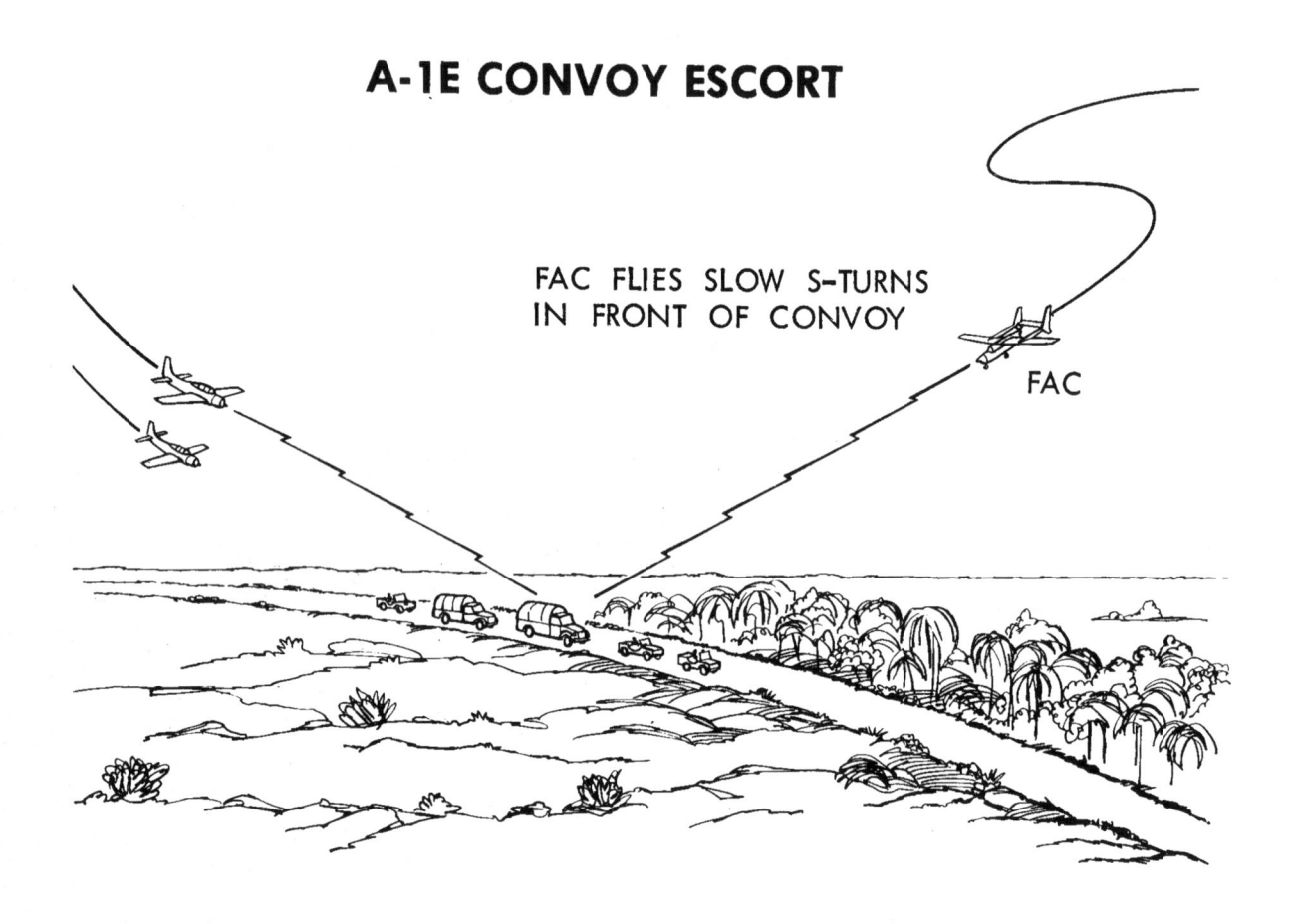

FAC

Figure 23 (U)

(This page Unclassified)

(U) If a FAC was not to be had, one of the Skyraider pilots reconnoitered out ahead of the convoy. In case enemy gunners opened up, he halted the trucks and counterattacked. He used the ordnance impact point as a marker in directing the strikes of the other crews.[104]

(U) At night a flareship joined the escort team. It flew at 2,500 feet AGL, while the fighters moved up to a 4,500-foot perch* altitude. Since the trucks often traveled with lights out, a slightly different tactic was used. Based on the planned departure and arrival times of the convoy, the escorts followed a flightpath that kept them over it for most of the trip. A prearranged signal (flares or tracer fire) warned of an attack. The flareship then dropped parachute flares, and airstrikes began as soon as the enemy was pinpointed.[105]

Once in a while jet strike aircraft escorted convoys. A controller accompanied them in every instance, covering the road ahead in slow S-turns. If flying a high escort pattern, the fighters stayed in a shallow-banked racetrack orbit above and a little back of the convoy. This allowed them to peel off from any point in the orbit for a bombing or strafing run, right after the FAC marked the target.[106]

To do low-level strikes during convoy escort, the jets formed a racetrack or a floating wheel pattern. For the racetrack, one fighter orbited on either side of the trucks, at 3,000-4,000 feel AGL and 400 KIAS. The two aircraft timed their orbits so at least one of them was set for instant attack. The floating wheel employed the same altitude and airspeed as the racetrack. It had the advantage, however, of placing both planes directly over the convoy at all times. In either pattern the strike pilot could descend from orbit in a curvilinear approach to the attack, jinking as necessary.[107]

Supporting Special Forces

Irregular forces loyal to the South Vietnamese Government grew from modest beginnings in 1961 to a potent countrywide influence 4 years later. U.S. Army Special Forces provided advisers and logistic support,

---

* An airborne position assumed by a fighter/bomber aircraft in preparation for or anticipation of an air-to-ground strike maneuver.

stationing small but highly trained teams of Americans at scores of border and remote camps. Often straddling infiltration routes, the camps helped keep tabs on Communist movements and offered the rural people protection. Civilian Irregular Defense Group (CIDG) troop units were created for camp and hamlet defense. Specially skilled CIDG guerrillas penetrated Viet Cong strongholds, probed for weaknesses, and tried to draw Charlie out in the open where ground troops and air power could hit him. Small AF reconnaissance teams were formed outside the CIDG. They slipped behind enemy lines, ferreted out intelligence, and directed airstrikes.[108]

Most strategic hamlets and SF camps were in isolated areas, frequently quite far from the nearest friendly base. Seldom having adequate fortification or artillery support to fend off large attacks, they relied heavily on tactical air. Moreover, special reconnaissance patrols and teams usually operated deep within enemy-held territory. Their very survival often hinged on timely close air support.[109]

Forward air controllers were central to the defense of SF camps. Still none worked full-time with Special Forces except for certain operations.* Requests for FAC assistance funneled instead through routine TACS channels, generally to USAF controllers attached to ARVN units.† If a FAC was airborne (and available), he could commonly respond to a call for help within 5 minutes.[110] On numerous occasions, however, the forward air controllers were tied up with other operations when the SF units radioed in for airstrikes. Precious time was then lost in finding a way to respond. In February 1967 Seventh Air Force made inroads on this problem. Beginning with I Corps, an air liaison officer (assisted by two controllers) was attached to every corps headquarters. He worked under the Corps ALO, coordinating all SF forward air control with his counterpart at 5th Special Forces Group.‡ [111]

---

* For example, USAF controllers had been permanently assigned to Project Delta since December 1965. Delta handled the bulk of the recon patrols and clandestine infiltrations into enemy strongholds.

† These FAC's did make periodic visits to SF camps in their sectors, keeping current intelligence folders on each outpost.

‡ This group had been set up in October 1964 to harmonize Special Forces support for South Vietnam. Its commander reported direct to COMUSMACV.

More progress came with the carrying out of Seventh Air Force Operations Plan 443-68, dated September 1967. Tactical fighter squadrons took responsibility for specific camps. On each one they prepared a folder containing photos, maps, intelligence summaries, radio frequencies, and camp layout. Strike crews received periodic briefings on the characteristics and defense/evacuation plans of "their" camps. In addition, they visited them regularly to talk over tactics and get acquainted with the troops. Whenever a fighter pilot overflew one of his assigned outposts, he radioed it to find out how things were going. Also under the plan, Air Force AC-47 gunships* and Army fire support elements were tied into a single firepower net that gave around-the-clock coverage to the camps.[112]

Tactics

Tactics for defending Special Forces differed a little from those of other close air support operations. Every CIDG camp, for example, had compartments that were sealed off for individual defense when the enemy breached the perimeter. Then too, the special reconnaissance patrols posed singular problems. These teams often operated clandestinely behind enemy lines, at times even dressed in Communist uniforms. Since they could not afford to be mistaken for Viet Cong by "unknowing" support aircraft, seasoned forward air controllers watched over them. Serving as eyes and ears, the FAC scanned the surrounding jungle for any sign of the enemy and alerted the patrol of impending danger.[113]

Once attached to a long-range reconnaissance team, the controller with other support people moved into a forward operating base (FOB)--commonly a nearby SF camp. Next, the corps commander sealed off the area of operations from all other ground troops and aircraft. The forward air controller had blanket clearance from the DASC to request the air support needed--no questions asked.[114]

Ground and air personnel at the FOB work in close harmony. The Special Forces FAC flew over the area to be infiltrated, sizing up possible helicopter landing zones (LZ's). He gave his choices to the ground commander who went out in a helicopter (or with the FAC) to look them over. Final site selection reflected the size of the force. A team of 6-8 men could get by with an LZ just big enough for 1 helicopter, but a patrol of 40-50 men would

---

* The AC-47 saved many SF camps along the South Vietnam border. At night Spooky's flares were often enough to drive off attackers. Since the gunships flew virtually a 24-hour airborne alert, they could move in at any time to aid an outpost.

need a zone capable of handling from 6 to 8 choppers. If a suitable site couldn't be found, airstrikes blasted one out with 500-pound or heavier GP bombs.[115]

Action to insert the team now commenced. The infiltration force included 1 forward air controller, 1 helicopter to carry the team and 1 for command and control, plus from 4 to 10 helicopter gunships. If the commander expected ground fire, he requested air cover (normally A-1E's) ahead of time. To keep from tipping its hand, the formation set a flight pattern that carried it directly over the landing site. At that point, the other helicopters tuned the pitch of their rotor blades to blend with the noise of the team ship. The latter copter dropped like a stone, unloaded in seconds, then shot skyward to rejoin the others and move a little way off.[116]

The controller meantime stayed 1,000 feet above the formation, keeping in constant touch with it and the higher orbiting fighters (offset some distance away). After leaving the helicopter on the run, the recon team members dug in not far from the landing zone. If not detected by the enemy, They moved off on their mission. The formation and fighters then returned to base, but the FAC lingered a while longer to watch over the patrol's progress.[117]

The forward air controller flew to daily prearranged contacts with the patrol--at dawn and at dusk. He spent the rest of his time at the FOB, set to react at once to the team's call for help. The only surveillance he performed took place on the way to and from the contact area. If he spotted something he checked it out.[118]

When the team ran into trouble,* its commander radioed the base camp command post. If the FAC was not already airborne, it took him and the accompanying helicopter gunships about 15 minutes to get there. En route he called the DASC, using a special call sign. His request held the highest priority so strike aircraft were diverted from other missions. The fighters were over the present rendezvous point by the time the controller was ready to link up and bring them in to attack.[119]

---

*"Trouble" meant (1) the team had come upon the enemy without being detected, or (2) the enemy had spotted the team and was searching for it, or (3) the enemy knew the team's location and was closing in.

Coordination became crucial at this point. The team commander could ill afford to give away his position if it had not yet been discovered by the enemy. When the Communists stole so near as to rule out even whispered radio conversations, the patrol used quiet ways to catch the controller's attention. A cloth panel was spread on the ground, waved in the air, or opened and closed like an accordian. In lieu of this, a signal mirror could be flashed or a balloon inflated and let rise through the trees. At night the team turned to a shielded strobe light (visible only from the air) or to a hand-held flaregun (pengun).[120]

If the team had to be extracted, the fighters needed to pin down the enemy or force him to break off so the helicopters could pop in and whisk out the survivors. This demanded utmost FAC skill because in most every case the patrol and Communists were nose-to-nose and the airstrikes would be almost on top of the friendlies. Furthermore, the controller could not always count on the strike aircraft having the "right kind" of ordnance. Heavy GP bombs or napalm placed too close in to the exposed troops would be nearly as disastrous as being overrun. The final decision was up to the ground commander. If his patrol stood in danger of being wiped out, he gave the go-ahead and had his men dig in behind or beneath any shelter they could find.[121] The airstrikes went on until the last man was heli-lifted out.

Resupply Operations

Special Forces recon teams in the field for 2 or 3 days took along their own supplies but relied on aerial resupply if out longer. Since paradrops from cargo aircraft told the Communists where a patrol was, two enterprising officers* hit upon an alternate scheme that was used through 1968. Food and supplies were put in 500-pound napalm cannisters and dropped bomb-run fashion. The fairly slow speed of the A-1E let the cannisters fall accurately and with least danger of rupture on impact.[122]

After packing supplies into a cannister, the ground crew tied the two sections together at the seams with parachute cord rather than bolts, so the team could open it easier. The cannisters were rigged either for paradrop or for free-fall into trees. A forward air controller aided in

---

* Lt. Col. Eugene P. Deatrick, 1st Air Commando Squadron Commander at Pleiku, and Lt. Col. Eleazer Parmley, USA, I Corps Special Forces Detachment Commander.

locating the patrol and coordinating the drop. The A-1E normally swept in low and used strike support procedures for identification. The patrol marked its location by day with three panels in the shape of an "L", the Skyraider lining up its "bomb run" on the two panels forming the stem. At night a fire arrow was substituted, the head pointing toward the team. When visual signals could not be used, the ground commander spoke softly over the radio, vectoring the fighter in by the sound of its engines.[123]

Once the A-1E pilot had definitely identified the team, he began a descending circular turn. The ground commander or the FAC (flying some distance away) guided him onto the "attack" heading. The pilot skimmed over the patrol at 250 feet AGL and 120 KIAS, releasing, the cannister at the command "drop" from the ground. He flew straight ahead for 2-3 miles before climbing back to altitude. Afterwards, to add a spark of realism, A-1E's set up a formation and came back around on a low-level strafing adjacent to the team's position. By 1968 the Communists had figured out what was going on, and the tactic lost much of its value. Resupply was gradually turned over to tactical airlift aircraft.[124]

Out-Country Operations

In 1965 special operations teams* of the combined USA/ARVN Special Forces began crossing the border into Laos. As part of Operation Shining Brass (Prairie Fire after 1 March 1967), they harassed North Vietnamese infiltrators along the Ho Chi Minh Trail. These operations depended heavily on Air Force support, with forward air controllers and A-1E strike crews having a key role.[125]

When an area was slated for infiltration, a FAC "reconned" for suitable landing zones and assisted the team commander in choosing one. Insertion of the team was generally done at night and in the same way as in South Vietnam. If bad weather canceled out tactical fighter cover,

---

*Each team commonly consisted of 12 men--3 Americans and 9 natives of the area of operation (often mercenaries).

the helicopter gunships filled in. Arriving at the area, the controller flew in low and marked the LZ. But the operation did not continue until the helicopters had dropped down to check out the site for "bad guys." On the ground, the patrol dug in and cleared the support aircraft to leave. The command and control detachment at Da Nang remained in continuous radio contact with the team.[126]

If radio communication was lost, the airborne battlefield command and control center (ABCCC)* or the forward air controller tried to regain it. When this failed, immediate air support was requested. Before any strikes were made, however, contact with the team had to be restored and its position pinpointed. Silencing of enemy ground fire and rescue of the patrol followed.[127]

Operation Daniel Boone got under way in May 1967, sending special operations reconnaissance patrols into the border areas of Cambodia. During insertion and extraction of these 6- to 12-man teams, the presence of a controller was a must. At other times the FAC stayed close by to lend a hand. Nevertheless, the patrols were warned that if detected by the enemy their only tactical air support would be for pickup. Hence they went all out to avoid discovery.[128]

If discovered, however, the Air Force's 20th Helicopter Squadron rushed close air support to the scene. The force commonly consisted of three helicopters (two gunships and one lightly armed). The two gunships each carried fourteen 2.75-inch rockets and two side-firing, 7.62-mm miniguns./ They flew a figure eight pattern ǂ at treetop level, passing over the patrol's position at the "crossing of the 8." The copters poured minigun and rocket fire into the Communists (the rockets usually being triggered before rollout from the end loops of the "8"). With the enemy pinned down by withering fire, the third chopper whipped in and lifted out the team.[129]

---

* As an extension of the Seventh Air Force Command Center, the ABCCC was usually a C-130 deployed in support of out-country air operations.

/ The minigun on either side of the gunship was independent, manually controlled and electrically fired.

ǂ This and an alternate "dogbone shape" maneuver were the two basic fire-suppression methods used by USAF helicopter gunships. Both patterns were flown no higher than 10 feet above the terrain.

IV. NIGHT CLOSE AIR SUPPORT, 1965-1968

(U) During 1965 the enemy's mastery of night operations raised new problems for the expanding U.S. ground forces in South Vietnam. The Communists often took advantage of the rugged terrain and heavy jungles to shield their movements. They mounted frequent mortar, rocket, and infantry attacks, melting back into the darkness before counterattacks could be made. Moreover, the Viet Cong launched many night assaults in bad weather when FAC and strike aircraft had to remain on the ground.

(U) Nighttime likewise magnified the drawbacks for aircrews engaged in close air support. They had trouble detecting ground reference points and could not see the horizon at all--making them easy prey for spatial disorientation. Since judging closure rates accurately became more difficult, pilots hesitated to use steep dive angles with the greater danger of plowing into the ground. The chances of midair collision also climbed, underlining the need for crews to hew to altitude reservations and aircraft separation requirements.[1] Lastly, aircrews found it harder to tell friend from foe at night. The Communists realized this and often avoided airstrikes by crowding in close to American or ARVN positions.

(U) This latter problem was solved in late 1965 by a forward air controller with the Army's 1st Cavalry Division. He suggested 105-mm howitzer shell casings be filled with sand-soaked fuel. When the enemy attacked at night, these "torches" could be placed around friendly positions and lit. One of the ground commanders said, "Gee, then they'll know where we are." The FAC replied, "When they hit you they [already] know where you are. Give us the chance to find out too." The glowing torches proved an excellent reference for directing airstrikes.[2] Another method devised by the division had 50-gallon oil drums cut in half, filled with jellied gasoline mixed with sand, and spaced on a position's perimeter. The wire of the tripflare attached to each drum snaked out on the ground. When an infiltrator broke the wire, it triggered the flare and ignited the drum torch.*[3]

---

* Ground troops further used ground flares, strobe lights, and fire arrows--when support aircrews could be sure the illumination stemmed from friendly sources. Such care was a must because the Viet Cong could easily steal and employ these items.

Flareships were a boon to night strike operations, lighting up the sky and ground of the target area. Still flare operations produced problems of their own. Many times the initial flash blinded aircrews during final run-in. Swinging beneath its parachute, the flare heightened ground glare and created the effect of moving shadows. This in turn led to crew disorientation * and visual loss of target. Furthermore, flares igniting below an overcast helped enemy gunners track the fighters. If flares were dropped too high, they burned out before reaching the ground. Those dispensed too low gave off little light. Finally, inaccurate flaredrops failed to illuminate the target area well enough for good ordnance delivery.[4] Despite these shortcomings, flare operations in support of ground troops were clearly an asset.

Marking targets under flarelight was at best a tricky business. The 2.75-inch WP marker rocket (a mainstay for day operations) worked poorly at night. Its smoke lasted only 2-3 minutes, quickly drifted off-target, and on dark nights couldn't be seen at all. If aircrews diverted their attention even for a moment, they could easily miss the rocket's short impact flash. The ideal marker would be a long-burning, high-intensity, ground-type flare that could be fired as a rocket and illuminate a target in any kind of weather.[5] No such marker was developed during 1965-68.

Nevertheless, adoption of ground marker logs did make inroads on night target-marking problems. These logs--often converted flares--ignited after reaching the ground. Although a good reference for controlling airstrikes, the markers at times couldn't be seen in mountainous or forested areas. Then too, the enemy began kindling fires of his own to confuse the controller and strike pilots. This tactic was countered by dropping brighter, longer-burning red/green logs.[6] Furthermore, the accurate delivery of the ground markers was difficult, what with no aiming device and the need to consider wind, airspeed, altitude, and angle/direction of approach. Forward air controllers usually released the markers from either the cockpit or wing pylons. Flareship crews ejected them from the cargo doors in much the same way as regular flares.[7]

---

* Crewmembers additionally experienced the milkbowl effect. Particles in the air picked up rays of flarelight and reflected them back, giving one the feeling of being in an inverted milkbowl.

(U) The best overall marker log turned out to be the MK-6 (Mod-3). It had a 90-second delay fuze, triggered upon leaving the aircraft by an attached lanyard. Burning brightly for 40-60 minutes, the MK-6 could be used alone or with air flares. As an alternate marker, controllers commonly favored the LUU-1B (a modified MK-24 flare). This log emitted a fierce red flame that stood out starkly from other ground fires. Its chief drawback was a timer that could not be reset during flight to fit changes in the tactical situation.[8]

Starlight Scope

(U) Flarelight alerted the enemy, curbed his movements, and canceled out the element of surprise. Seeking a better way to pick up targets in the darkness, the Air Force noticed the Army's success with a rifle-mounted starlight scope and selected it for testing in 1965.[9] The starlight scope consisted of an objective lens, a 3-stage, image-intensifier assembly, and an eyepiece. Powered by a 6.5-volt battery, the scope collected available starlight/moonlight and amplified it up to 40,000 times. The operator could see objects invisible to the naked eye--people moving about, canal/tree lines, buildings, roads, trucks, and sampans plying waterways. But all this vanished if clouds obsured the moon and stars.[10]

The 1965 testing of the starlight scope started off in the 0-1 Bird Dog. However, the small rear cockpit cramped the scope operator and hampered good coverage. Having no suitable mount, he held the scope in his hands as the aircraft vibration defied steadiness. Just the same, forward air controllers found the scope helpful in visual reconnaissance and continued to use it whenever they could.[11]

In March 1966 the starlight scope was used with spectacular success in an AC-47 Spooky, during a close air support mission over the strategic town of Attopeu in the Laotian panhandle. Straddling a major junction of the Ho Chi Minh Trail, Attopeu was a thorn in the side of North Vietnamese infiltrators. As March began, the Communists overrun two neighboring villages to the east, Muong Cau and Fangdeng. They then moved toward Attopeu and its tiny airfield, completely confident of meeting with only token resistance. The AC-47, stripped of all U.S. markings, responded to the request of Gen. Thao Mao, Royal Laotian Air Force (RLAF) Commander. The gunship commenced covering the area early in the evening of 4 March. A starlight scope had been jury-rigged in the open main cargo door in the rear. The navigator operator sat in the doorway, a rope around his waist to keep him from falling out. After some preliminary reconnaissance, he spotted 150-200 Communists wedged between two known friendly positions in rice paddies just east of town. The Laotian officer on board confirmed the sightings with his counterpart on the ground, and the Spooky opened fire without the customary flaredrop. Results were sensational. The enemy fled the field in panic, leaving more than 100 dead comrades behind.[12]

Heartened by the Attopeu success, the Air Force pushed its own starlight scope development. The AN/AVG-3 was ready by mid-1967 and put in the 0-2A and the C-123/C-130 flareships. Solidly mounted, this 6-pound scope proved more stable, easier to handle, and better for picking out ground targets.[13]

Strike Tactics

During a night close air support mission, the FAC as a rule reached the target area ahead of the fighters or flareship. He contacted the ground commander to find out the location of the friendly and enemy troops. He talked over with him the type of ordnance and strike tactics planned, and settled on the best attack headings. If the element of surprise did not matter, the controller at times would ask for artillery-or mortar-fired flares to enhance the operation of his starlight scope.* After spotting and identifying the target, he moved away from it to await the other aircraft.[14]

Meanwhile, the strike crews took off and were turned over to the control and reporting center for flight following. They navigated to the rendezvous point for TACAN. If that proved unreliable, the fighters could home in on the controller's UHF transmissions and fly down the "frequency beam." Rendezvous could also be done by radar when the FAC had a MSQ-77 transponder.[15]

Once in the rendezvous area, the fighters held above the forward air controller's altitude. Join-up usually entailed a showing of wing lights or rotating beacons ("Go Christmas Tree!"). Should this fail, the FAC could drop a flare or have the flareship--if present--do so. Upon seeing the

---

*Flarelight shining or reflecting into the scope caused a "whiteout" or (in the newer instruments) an automatic shutdown. Too much light ruined the scope or crippled it by burning spots on the lens. Flaring to one side of an area staved off this scope damage.

strike aircraft, the controller completed the join-up by clock code, for example, "I'm in your 3 o'clock position, low."[16]

On the way to the target area the FAC and fighter crews reviewed strike and orbit tactics, weather and terrain conditions, and expected enemy defenses. After arrival the forward air controller cleared the fighters for descent to orbit altitude (6,000-1000 feet AGL). He dropped down to around 3,500 feet and began dispensing flares. Ideally, they were released far enough upwind to drift by or across the target at half-burn point. Whenever possible the controller bracketed the target with marker logs. This gave him two more reference points from which to control airstrikes, and also aided the strike pilots in judging distances.[17]

(U) Target marking at night paralleled daytime procedures, except that the FAC stayed several hundred feet higher and flew his patterns with more caution. In most cases the fighters used steeper dive angles and delivered ordnance from higher altitudes. Hence the controller flew an outside holding pattern (2,000 feet AGL), over the friendly troops but opposite the strike orbit. (See Fig. 24). He had a good overall view of the attack and still was clear of the fighters.[18]

(U) IF a flareship linked up with the strike team, spacing took on special significance. Offset patterns were flown and a 1,000-foot altitude separation maintained. (See Fig. 25). The forward air controller held to one side of the target but inside the strike orbit. On the other side the flareship flew a tight pattern, above and opposite the FAC. It dropped flares every 2 1/2 - 3 minutes, which kept three burning most of the time. From yet a higher perch, the fighters circled on a heading reciprocal to the flareship's. During run-in the strike pilots dove between the controller and flareship, pickled their bombs, executed a straight-ahead pullup, and streaked back to altitude.[19]

(U) Sometimes a gunship replaced the flareship on the strike team to suppress ground fire. It commonly circled the enemy position while hammering gun emplacements and dropping flares. The FAC set his holding pattern opposite the fighter orbit. (see Fig. 26). This tactic required the strike aircraft to pass 500-1,000 feet below the gunship during roll-in, and climb back through its altitude after pulloff. Consequently, the gunship stopped shooting and dispensing flares throughout the bomb run. The offset pattern (Fig. 26) reduced the collision risk and let flaring continue for the entire

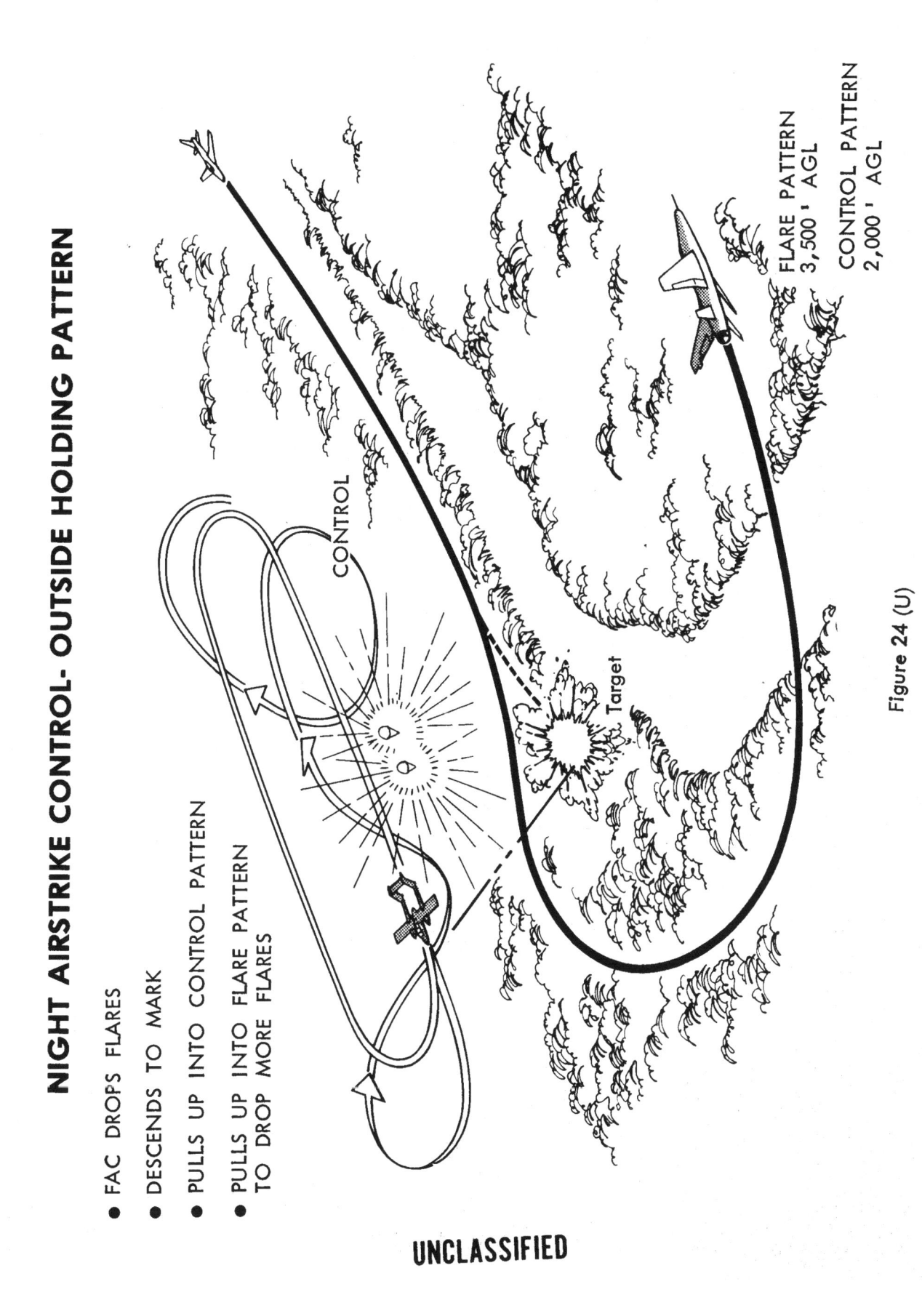

NIGHT AIRSTRIKE CONTROL- OUTSIDE HOLDING PATTERN

- FAC DROPS FLARES
- DESCENDS TO MARK
- PULLS UP INTO CONTROL PATTERN
- PULLS UP INTO FLARE PATTERN TO DROP MORE FLARES

FLARE PATTERN 3,500' AGL
CONTROL PATTERN 2,000' AGL

Figure 24 (U)

NIGHT AIRSTRIKE CONTROL WITH FLARESHIP

- FLARESHIP SELECTS INBOUND HEADING
- STACK TO PROVIDE 1,000 FEET SEPARATION BETWEEN FAC, FLARESHIP AND STRIKE AIRCRAFT
- AVOID BEING SILHOUETTED BY FLARE
- DUD FLARES AND EMPTY FLARE CANISTERS CAN BE HAZARD
- FAC HOLDS INSIDE STRIKE AIRCRAFT PATTERN

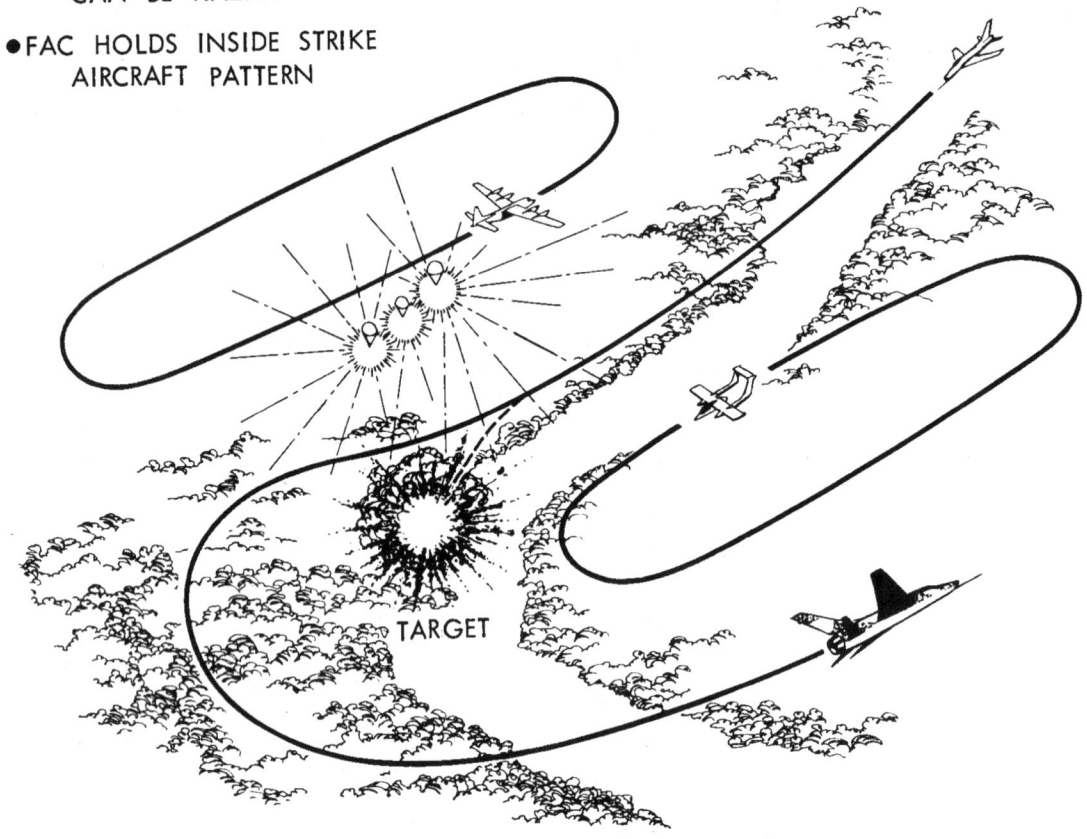

Figure 25 (U)

FAC/GUNSHIP STRIKE PROCEDURE PATTERN
NIGHT TACTICS

- GUNSHIP CIRCULAR PATTERN AND DROPPING FLARES

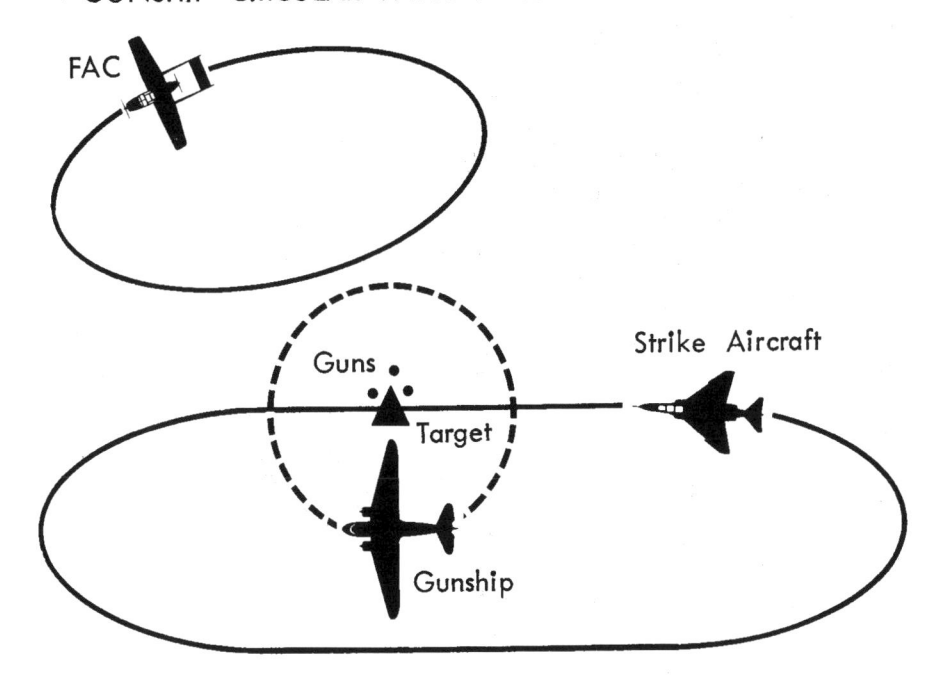

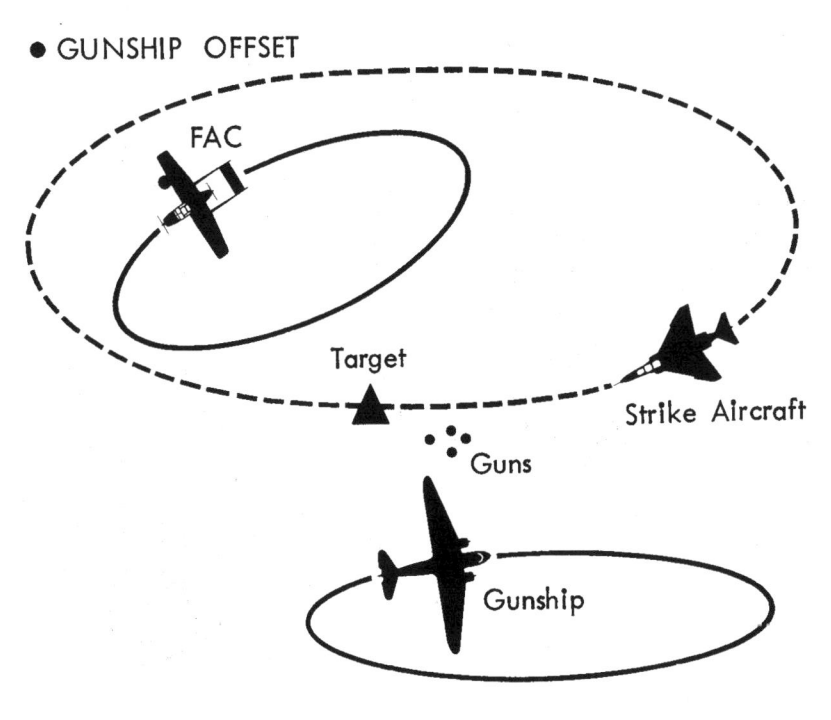

- GUNSHIP OFFSET

Figure 26 (U)

155MM HOWITZER ILLUMINATION FOR AIR STRIKES

155MM HOWITZER BATTERY LOCATED PARALLEL TO STRIKE RUN-IN HEADING

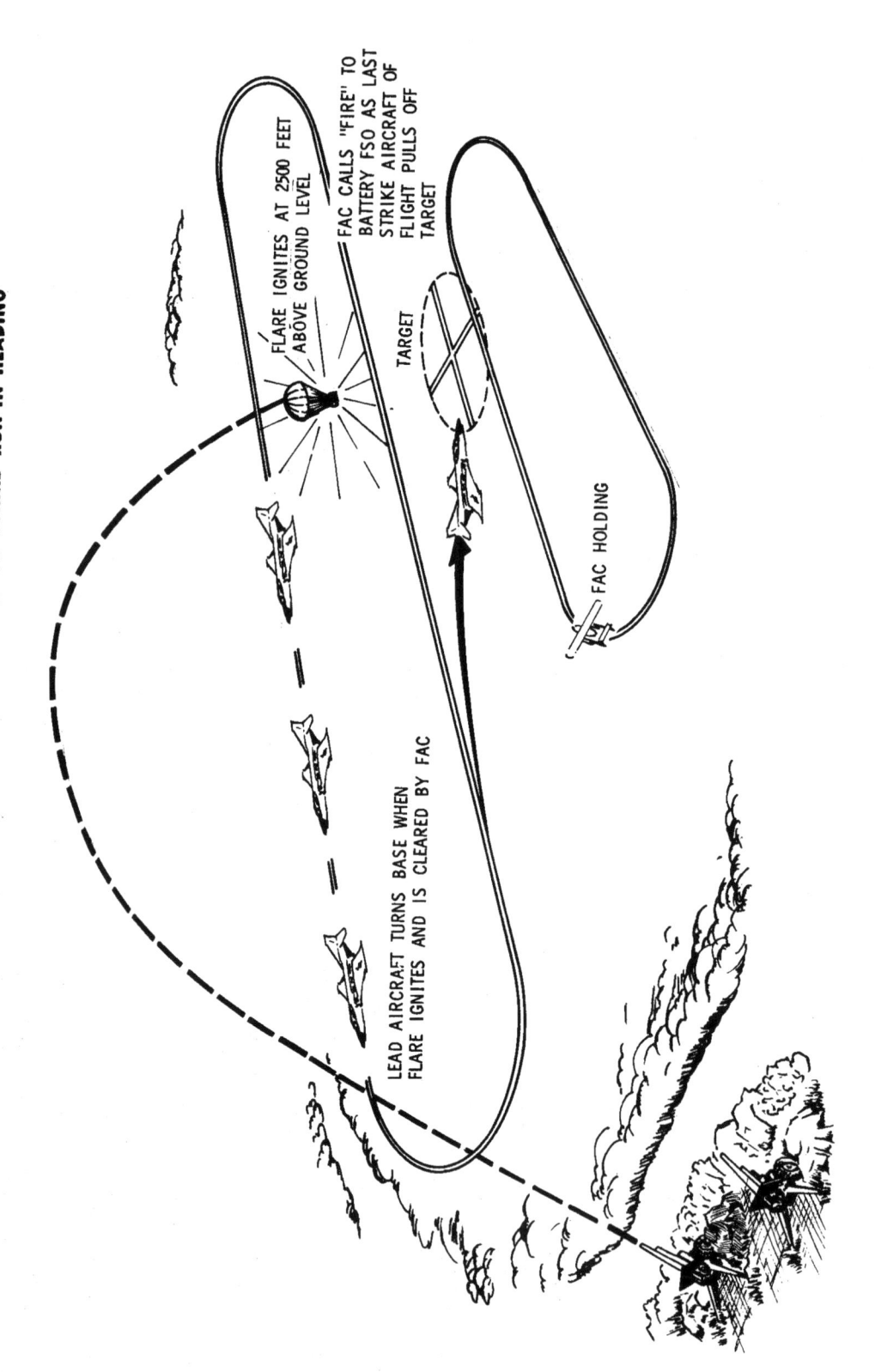

FLARE IGNITES AT 2500 FEET ABOVE GROUND LEVEL

FAC CALLS "FIRE" TO BATTERY FSO AS LAST STRIKE AIRCRAFT OF FLIGHT PULLS OFF TARGET

TARGET

FAC HOLDING

LEAD AIRCRAFT TURNS BASE WHEN FLARE IGNITES AND IS CLEARED BY FAC

Figure 27 (U)

period of the attack. The gunship circled on the opposite side of the target from the controller, who held outside the strike orbit.[20]

If the need arose, the forward air controller requested flare support from the fighters. The leader brought his flight down the bomb-run heading in loose trail,* at 350 KIAS and 4,500 feet AGL. Arriving over the target he triggered four flares at 5- to 10-second intervals.✝ As the flight broke downwind, he called for the FAC to mark the target. The airstrike then progressed like other night close air support missions, except that lead re-flared as necessary.[21]

The controller also had the option of requesting artillery-fired flares from nearby firebase. (See Fig. 27.) The battery--commonly using 155-mm howitzers--fired a flare round toward the enemy on a trajectory parallel to the strike heading. Timed to coincide with the first fighter's turn on base leg, the flare ignited at about 2,500 feet AGL. When the last aircraft of the flight pulled off-target, the TAC radioed for another flare. A variation had the battery fire three rounds at 1-minute intervals, lighting the area for the forward air controller to acquire and mark the target.[22]

Night strike tactics differed hardly at all from day techniques. Maneuvers became less abrupt (no banking turns over 60°), dive angles shallower, and bomb-release altitudes at least 500 feet higher. Strike crews stayed chiefly with standard box and rectangular patterns, calling off position when turning: "off-target," "downwind," "base leg," and "final." If possible each fighter pilot made a dry run across the target to fix it in his mind. Run-in headings differed up to 15° between aircraft, pilots jinking during most of the run if ground fire heated up. Dive angles rarely exceeded 30° for general purpose bombs, or 10°-20° for soft ordnance such as napalm and cluster bomb units.[23]

---

* Aircraft directly behind one another and spaced fairly far apart.

✝ Fighter pilots believed flares worked best when ignited just behind the target, thereby keeping the approach and recovery areas in shadow.

The AC-47 Gunship

The striking success of the experimental FC-47 in late 1964 and early 1965 led Secretary of Defense McNamara to direct the modification of more Gooney Birds into gunships. The initial request for PACAF was for 50 FC-47's. By June 1965, however, it had been trimmed to the 20 aircraft* of the 4th Air Commando Squadron (ACSq), Forbes AFB, Kans. This unit deployed to South Vietnam after further testing and training, the last gunship arriving on 14 November.[24]

The mission of the AC-47‡ was "to respond with flares and firepower in support of hamlets under night attack, supplement strike aircraft in the defense of friendly forces, and provide long endurance escort for convoys."[25] Inasmuch as the defense of hamlets, towns, and outposts held priority, this soon became the gunship's key task.[26]

AC-47 tactics had been worked out before the 4th ACSq arrived. Moreover, the rules of engagement had been modified to permit gunships to support hamlets or outposts under night attack--without a VNAF observer aboard. The gunship crews nevertheless preferred to pick up a bilingual observer whenever they could, to ease the job of talking to the Vietnamese ground commanders.[27]

A call for help from a friendly unit in the field touched off the typical gunship mission. The request went through ARVN or U.S. Army channels to the TACS. The proper DASC then dispatched an AC-47 Spooky from airborne patrol or airstrip alert to the target area. Enroute the crew reviewed whatever information they had on the combat situation--location of friendlies and enemy, type of terrain, weather conditions, and emergency procedures. The gunners went through their checklist and the loadmaster readied his flares.[28]

---

* 16 plus 4 for command support and attrition.

† The gunship could carry 48 MK-24 flares. Its pneumatically operated flare launcher was placed in the fifth window on the left, forward of the main door. In the early days the launcher often malfunctioned, and the loadmaster usually chose to kick most of the flares out the rear cargo door.

‡ Redesignated "AC-47" from "FC-47" in September 1965. Its call sign was Spooky.

(👁) The crew navigated mainly by dead reckoning or map reading, aided by TACAN or radar vectors from ground sites. Once over the friendly position, the copilot radioed the ground commander to find his location and defense status, where the enemy was, and the type of support desired (flares or firepower).* The enemy then expended a flare so the enemy position could be positively identified.[29]

(👁) The ground commander marked his position with a fire arrow, flare, or strobe lights. When such showing of light was undesirable, he (or the FAC) helped the Spooky identify the location by reference to visible landmarks. After marking the target, the controller climbed 500-1,000 feet above the gunship, orbited outside its pattern, and watched for enemy ground fire. (See Fig. 28).

(👁) Upon getting the go-ahead to fire from the ground commander and DASC, the gunship pilot descended to 2,500-3,500 feet AGL† and flew a constant 120 KIAS. As he approached a crosswind heading (upwind from the enemy position), he tried to keep the target a shade outside and ahead of the left propeller dome. Turning crosswind he cleared the loadmaster to drop a flare, and flew straight and level for 15 seconds to give it a chance to ignite. When the target passed under the engine cowling, the pilot rolled into a 30° bank.‡ This steepened the declination angle of the guns to 42°, since they had been installed at a 12° tilt. Centering the gunsight popper on the target, the pilot fired a short burst from one gun to confirm the target. Thereafter all guns were fired in 3- to 7-second volleys. To stay on target, the pilot corrected the bank angle by

---

* Frequently the Spooky's first contact on the scene was with a forward air controller who supplied this information.

† Altitude could be altered for weather, anemy ground fire, and target acquisition/identification troubles.

‡ A dive-bank-and-climb maneuver tried in 1964 was discarded as too complex and a potential danger.

GUNSHIP CONTROL PATTERN

- FAC MARKS TARGET
- THEN CLIMBS 500 – 1,000 FEET ABOVE THE GUNSHIP AND MOVES REARWARD TO WATCH FOR ENEMY GROUND FIRE ... MARKS GROUND FIRE FOR GUNSHIP

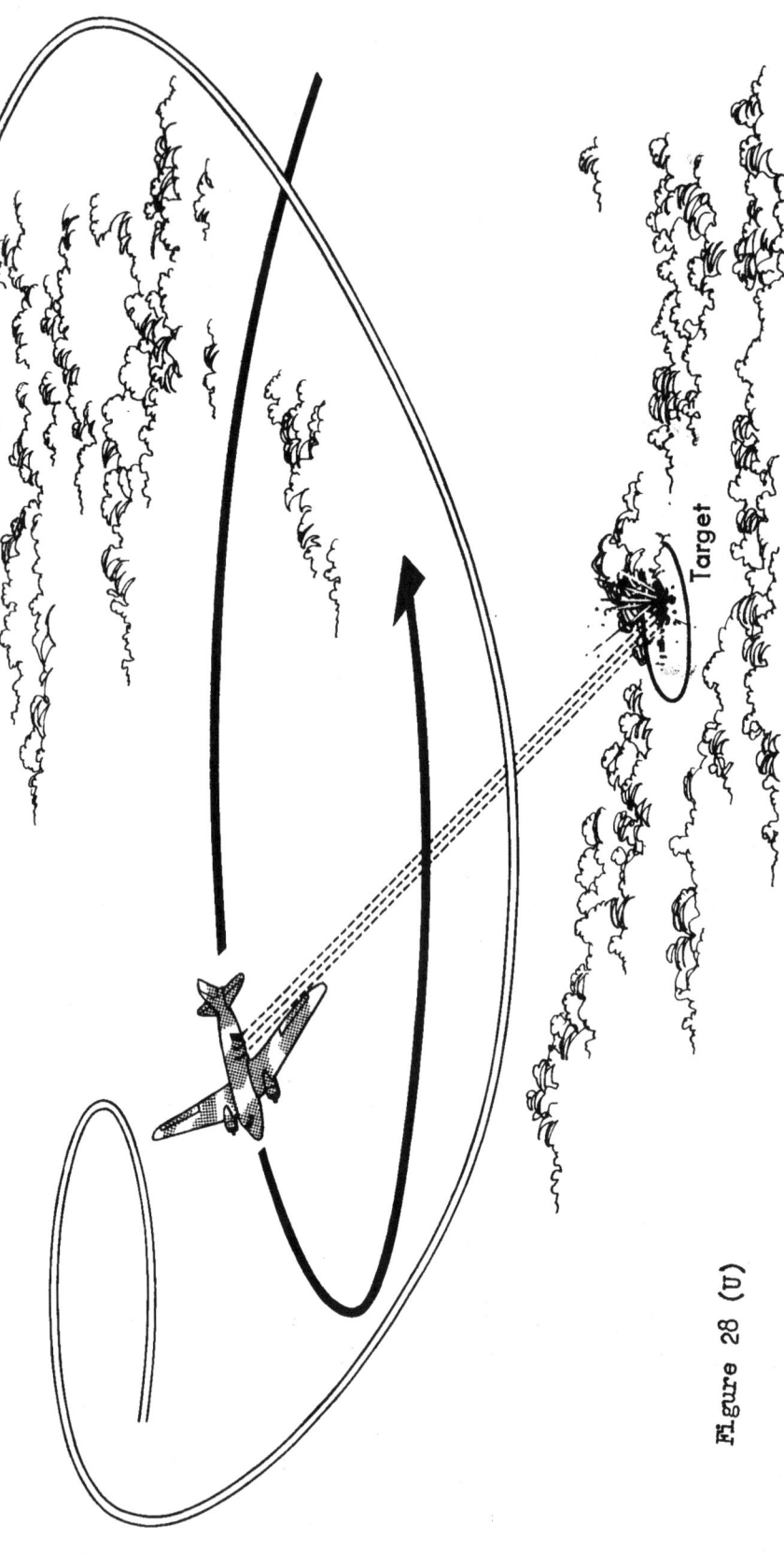

Figure 28 (U)

(This page Unclassified)

adjusting the feed-in of top rudder pressure. If the pipper drifted off-target to the rear, he ceased firing and recentered it by shallowing the bank. When the pipper strayed to the front, he had to sharpen the bank angle. The copilot meanwhile checked the Spooky's altitude and airspeed while keeping an eye out for other aircraft. If danger threatened, he called at once for a breakoff of the attack.[31]

At a slant range of 8,000 feet, a 3-second burst from one of Spooky's guns covered an elliptical area of about 52 yards in diameter, placing a bullet every 2.4 yards. The gunship could therefore orbit and sweep enemy positions with nearly continuous fire, bringing it accurately to well within 50 meters of friendly troops. Finally, a loiter time of 5 1/2 hours let the AC-47 remain on station long enough to outlast most attacks on hamlets and outposts.[32]

Through June 1966 the AC-47's of the 14th Air Commando Wing (ACWg) had saved an average of one fort or hamlet per night. A gunship coming on the scene in time could almost without exception drive off the Communists.[33] Not so during the defense of the A Shau Special Forces camp (9-10 March 1966). A 400-foot cloud ceiling stifled airstrikes on the first day. The Spooky slipping in under the cover was soon downed by the withering ground fire.*

(U) Of the many successful gunship missions, the defense of the fort of Thanh Anh affords a resounding example. Thanh Anh was among the fortresses in the Mekong Delta that ringed Binh Thuy AB and the provincial capital of Can Tho. Situated 7-8 miles southeast of the airbase, it defended a point where the Bassac River and a canal joined, denying the Viet Cong use of an excellent waterway to the interior. One morning in July 1966, Than Anh's 26 men heard Communist bullhorns: "Leave the fort. Leave now and you will live. Stay until the next dark of the moon and you will be killed. No one will be spared."[35]

(U) The no-moon period neared, heralded by stepped-up shelling of Thank Anh by the Viet Cong. Narrow zigzag enemy trenches inched closer to the fort's perimeter. A single AC-47 routinely kept the Communists from attacking at night. On 13 July, however, four gunships were brought in shortly after dark to repulse a mass assault. The Spookies fired more than 50,000 rounds and dispensed

---

* The consensus was that the camp could have been saved, had the weather lifted a little or the gunship been able to fly 1,000-2,000 feet higher.

over 50 flares to break the back of the siege. A few days later, the enemy melted back into the jungle. The fort, like numerous others, had been saved by its "own private air force" of gunships.[36]

By 1966 the role of the gunships had expanded. They became key to most major ground offensives and search and destroy missions, flew interdiction along the Ho Chi Minh Trail in Laos and supported friendly Lao troops, backed up American Marine operations, and furnished much of the firepower for airbase defense.[37]

In spite of combat successes, the AC-47 had several shortcomings that eventually caused its replacement. The small cockpit windows and low wing prevented a full view of the target and ground action. High winds hindered handling, the pilot finding it well-nigh impossible to maintain the pylon turn while firing the guns. The gunsight could not compensate for the wind and the use of "Kentucky windage" diminished accuracy. Vulnerability to ground fire posed a severe problem. Having a top airspeed of under 200 knots, the Spooky could not safely venture below 2,500 feet AGL, and above 3,500 feet the guns became practically useless. Hence operating altitude was restricted to between 2,500-3,500 feet. *[38]

The landing of the last Spooky at Phang Rang AB on 1 December 1969 signaled the close of USAF AC-47 operations. A glance back over the year revealed that the gunship had averaged over 20 sorties each night in South Vietnam. During 4 years the 4th Special Operations Squadron alone had successfully defended 3,926 outposts and hamlets. The crews fired more than 97 million rounds, dropped 270,000 flares, and were credited with killing 5,300 enemy troops. The phaseout of Spooky did not mean it was being retired. After all, the aging aircraft was still simple to operate, versatile, very dependable, and easy to maintain. Consequently, the remaining AC-47's were transferred to the VNAF and RLAF where they saw further combat. As for the Air Force, it selected the AC-130 (GunshipII) to spearhead the gunship mission in SEA.[39]

---

* Weight limitations added to the AC-47's woes. Its old underpowered engines lacked the thrust to carry sizable payloads and still climb and maneuver well.

The AC-130 (Gunship II)

The search for a follow-on aircraft to the AC-47 had begun in 1966 when Project Little Brother looked at several smaller planes. This project died, however, when the Air Force decided to reconfigure the C-130 Hercules (Project Gunboat). The Lockheed-built C-130 had entered USAF service in 1956, becoming the backbone in air transportation. Having four turboprop engines and a 15-ton payload, it cruised at 290 KIAS and had a top airspeed in excess of 330 knots. In the spacious C-130 the planners foresaw a gunship housing bigger, more accurate guns, a huge supply of ammunition and flares, plus sensors and all-weather gear for around-the-clock operations.[40]

The AC-130 (Gunship II) carried four 7.62-mm miniguns and four 20-mm Vulcan cannon,* all located on the left side. A night observation device (NOD)--a large starlight scope--was mounted on a yoke at the left crew entrance door. A forward-looking infrared (FLIR) was situated in the wheel-well fairing,/ its operator being stationed in the cargo compartment. While the NOD lost a truck or other hot target disappearing under the trees, the heat-seeking FLIR could continue to track it. Other Gunship II features were a side-looking radar (SLR), a Bell optical gunsight, and a pneumatic flare dispenser. A 40-kilowatt xenon≠ lamp illuminator was attached to the cargo-ramp door. By flipping a switch, its operator could select visible light or invisible infrared/ultraviolet radiation. Further refinements consisted of a 40-kilowatt searchlight, doppler radar for navigation, radar homing and warning (RHAW) equipment, an FW radio transceiver, @ inert fuel tanks, # and armor-plating.[41]

---

* The miniguns could fire 3,000 or 6,000 rounds-per-minute; the 20-mm cannon, 2,500 rounds-per-minute.

/ An auxiliary member or structure on an aircraft that reduces drag.

≠ A heavy, colorless, inert, gaseous element used in specialized electric lamps.

@ A radio transmitter-receiver that uses many of the same components for both transmission and reception.

\# A cellular foam lining prevented fire should incendiary shells pierce the tanks.

The AC-130's computerized fire-control system linked the sensors and guns. The computer established a line-of-sight reading to a designated point by taking sensor inputs and correcting them for wind, airspeed, and altitude. All the pilot had to do was line up his gunsight pipper on the target reticle and begin firing.[42]

From September to December 1967, the AC-130 (call sign Spectre) underwent combat testing in Southeast Asia. The Spectre surpassed the Spooky in almost every aspect of close air support and interdiction. However, its mission duration was shorter--5 hours opposed to Spooky's 5 1/2. The second evaluation (February-May 1968) went equally well, so the Air Force gave the go-ahead to produce and deploy Gunship II. In October the first AC-130 unit, the 16th Special Operations Squadron (SOSq),* began operating out of Ubon, Thailand. Its gunships took part in the Lao interdiction campaign,[43] and flew close air support to South Vietnam upon request.

For close air support missions the AC-130 carried an 11-man crew--aircraft commander, copilot, fire direction officer, navigator, NOD operator, IR/radar operator, flight engineer, master armorer, two gun armorers, and loadmaster./ The TACC exerted operational control of the AC-130's through the DASC in the area of operations. Each DASC held both scramble and divert authority, with the TACC retaining veto power. The Special Operations Branch of the TACC drew up the gunship alert schedule. It could be readily adjusted to changing combat situations, but this required close coordination beforehand with the 14th Special Operations Wing (SOWg).[44]

Requests for air support followed the same routine as used for the AC-47. After approval the DASC scrambled or diverted an AC-130 to the target area. En route the copilot secured a rundown on the situation from the ground commander (or FAC), and determined the kind of help needed--flares or gunfire. If friendly artillery fire would be employed, the FSCC was brought into the picture. The ground

---

*On 1 August 1968 the "Air Commando" designation was changed to "Special Operations."

/ The loadmaster handled the flares, illuminator, and searchlight.

commander then marked his position with a fire arrow, flare, or strobe light. However, when he wanted to keep his location hidden, he resorted instead to IR strobes or retroreflective panels. These markers were visible to the Spectre's infrared gear or night observation device.[45]

As the gunship's sensors fed information into the fire-control computer,* the pilot got ready to attack. Sizing up the ground-fire threat, he selected an altitude between 2,500-5,000 AGL and set up a left-hand orbit. He circled the target at a slant range (6,000-12,000 feet) that would yield the best results. The established orbit seldom needed adjustment. When it did, the computer furnished the corrections, and the pilot changed bank/altitude as necessary to keep the pipper aligned on the target.[46]

The AC-119 (Gunship III)

Although the AC-130 emerged the best gunship in the war, it had several drawbacks. Installation of the sensors and fire-control equipment proved expensive. The sensors malfunctioned frequently but less so as the bugs were worked out. Perhaps more important, the C-130 remained the spine of the tactical airlift. Few Hercules could be spared without hurting the airlift mission.[47]

Consequently, the Air Force in May 1967 looked to other aircraft to augment the AC-130. Among those studied were the C-123, C-54, C-119G/K. All excelled the AC-47 in airspeed, loiter time, and payload, but the C-123 and C-119 alone possessed the high wing desired in a side-firing gunship. Such design gave a clear line-of-sight the length of the fuselage for observation, firing, and use of sensors. Being more readily available than the C-123 for deployment to South Vietnam, the C-119 was the choice for gunship conversion.[48]

---

*In poor weather the ground could be seen every now and then or not at all. Nonetheless, the target range and bearing from a continuous wave (CW) ground beacon could be set into the fire-control computer. This and an assist from the side-looking radar permitted blind firing through the undercast.

(�) Modification of airframes into the AC-119G got under way quickly but work on the AC-119K moved more slowly. When evaluation and testing ended in December 1968, two 16-ship squadrons were slated for SEA. The AC-119G's (call sign Shadow) of the 17th SOSq began operations at Nha Trang AB on 5 January 1969. Extra modification and testing delayed until October the deployment to Phan Rang AB of the 18th SOSq and its AC-119K's (call sign Stinger).[49]

(�) The planned one-for-one replacement of AC-47's with AC-119's bogged down because Communist attacks surged throughout the countryside. Since the enemy struck widely separated hamlets and outposts simultaneously, even a joint gunship fleet was hard-pressed to cover them all. Hence at first the Shadows served as a much-needed supplement. The phaseout of the AC-47's started just before the Stingers arrived at Phan Rang.[50]

(�) The AC-119G featured four 7.62-mm miniguns, a 4-tube pneumatic flare launcher (at the right-rear cargo door), a night observation device locked into the fire-control system, a lead-computer optical gunsight (in the pilot's left window), and an airborne illuminator. The crew numbered eight--pilot, copilot, navigator, NOD operation, two gunners, illuminator operator, and flight engineer.[51] In responding to immediate requests for help, the Shadow could muster 180 KIAS (compared to the AC-47's 130 KIAS) and stay aloft more than 6 1/2 hours.[52]

(U) The fire control system of the AC-119G contained an analog computer linked to the NOD and the pilot's optical gunsight. The system could be operated in manual, semiautomatic, or automatic mode. During manual mode the pilot needed to see and orbit the target so as to align it with a fixed reticle in the gunsight. While firing the guns he had to mainain his altitude and a 30° left bank. In semiautomatic mode the pilot fed heading (or turn rate), bank, and altitude into the computer. The target was then represented by a moving reticle in the gunsight. After visually selecting an offset aiming point, he entered its coordinates into the computer. Finally, he centered the reticle in the sight and fired without ever seeing the target.* Automatic mode

---

*The computer automatically corrected for wind, target offset, altitude, heading, and aircraft roll.

AC-130A GUNSHIP II SPECIAL EQUIPMENT ARRANGEMENT

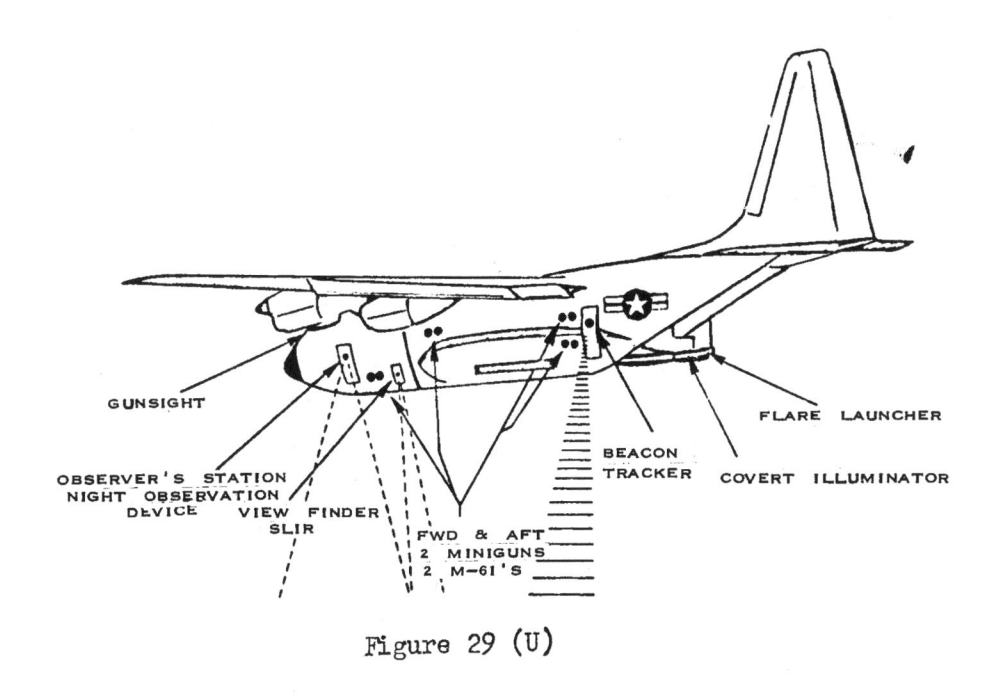

Figure 29 (U)

AC-119K FUSELAGE - GENERAL ARRANGEMENT

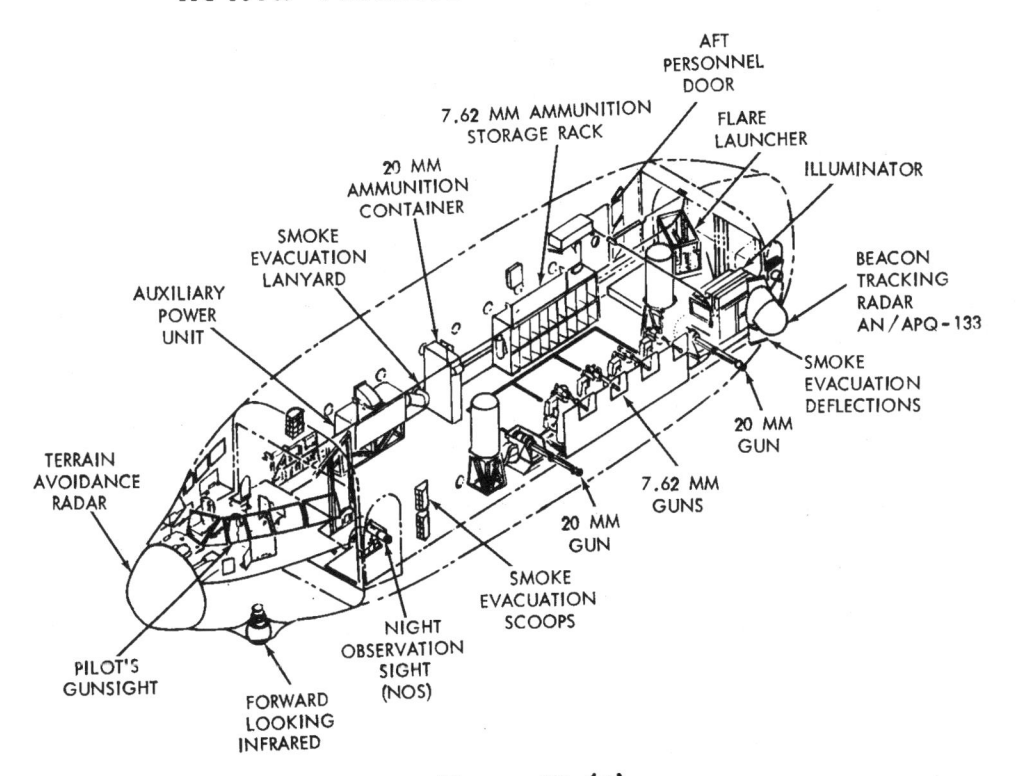

Figure 30 (U)

differed from semiautomatic solely in the need to center the moving reticle before firing could begin.[53]

Extra features enabled the AC-119K Stinger to surpass the Shadow in performance. Two autiliary jet engines, mounted farther out on the wings, boosted airspeed by over 20 knots but pared endurance time to 5 hours. Beacon-tracking radar and FLIR* afforded an all-weather capability. Two additional 20-mm cannon allowed an attack orbit of 6,500 feet AGL (Shadow's was 3,500 feet). Terrain-avoidance radar, RHAW equipment, and a doppler computer were other extras. All this new gear pointed the AC-119K more toward an interdiction than a close air support role. The Stinger's primary mission accordingly became armed reconnaissance in the panhandle of Laos.[54]

AC-119G GUNSHIP

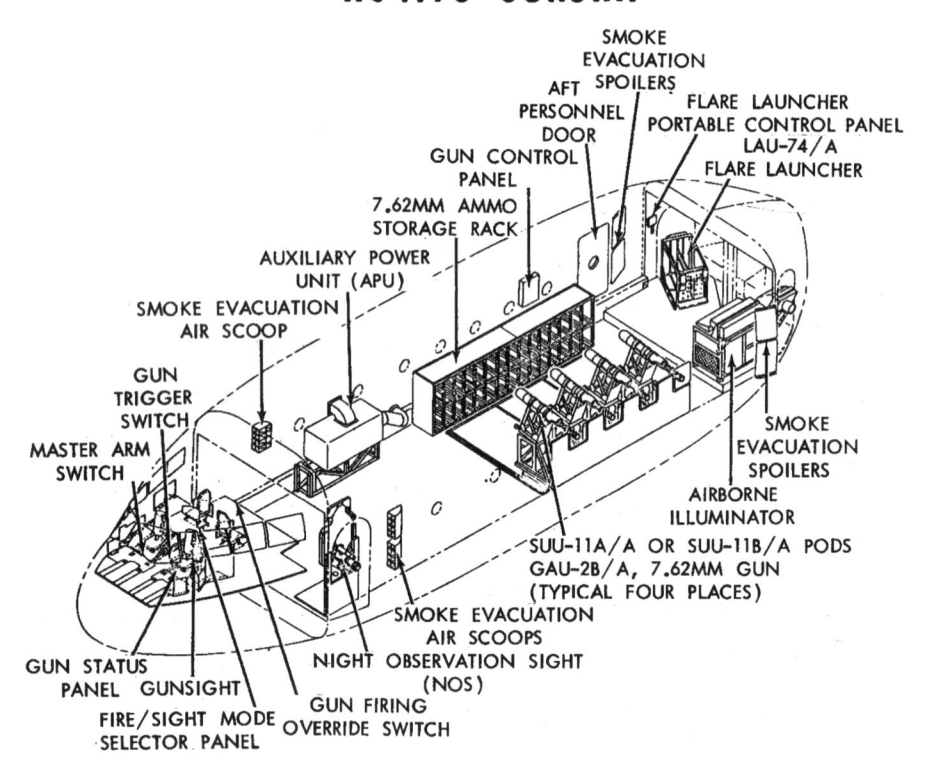

Figure 31 (U)

---

* Like the NOD, these systems were tied into the fire-control computer.

(U) The Shadows and Stingers shaped AC-47 tactics to their needs. One of two gunships flew airborne alert each night, ready for dispatch by the DASC to an outpost in trouble. Once in the target area, the crew coordinated with the ground commander and FAC, identified the target, and swung into action. The pilot took up his left-hand orbit at an altitude dictated by the ground-fire threat and weather. He fired the miniguns in the manual, semiautomatic, or automatic mode.[55]

By December 1970 the AC-47's of the VNAF were shouldering a great deal of the gunship load in South Vietnam. This freed the AC-119G's to join the AC-119K's in the support of Lao ground troops-- although the Stinger still flew mostly interdiction. Meantime, the growth of the Vietnamization program prompted the Air Force in September 1971 to turn over the AC-119G's to the VNAF.[56] The AC-119K's and AC-130's went on flying some support missions until hostilities ceased in January 1973, and in 1974 remained as a part of the USAF close air support concept.

Rocket Watch

In 1965 the Communists commenced standoff hit-and-run attacks on outposts, airbases, and urban centers throughout South Vietnam. The attackers favored mortars and rocket launchers because they could be easily assembled and dismantled. Unless caught in the act of firing, they were packed up and gone before their launch sites could be pinpointed. Such strikes proved most devastating to large base complexes like Da Nang and Tan Son Nhut, having perimeters difficult to defend.[57] On 15 July 1967 a small band of Viet Cong and North Vietnamese soldiers struck Da Nang. From as far away as 6-7 miles, they rained rockets onto the runway and parking apron for 20-minutes-- killing eight Air Force personnel and doing $1.5 million damage/destruction to 43 USAF and Marine aircraft. These surprise attacks stepped up, peaking just before the 1968 Tet Offensive.[58]

To curb the numerous rocket attacks around Da Nang, MACV in February 1968 formed a night watch of forward air controllers. The results were swift and gratifying as the FAC's zeroed in on areas used repeatedly for previous night barrages. During the first week they discovered and directed airstrikes/ground sweeps against 32 rocket and mortar sites, driving off the enemy before he could do much damage.[59]

Extension of rocket watch in March to the Saigon area briefly curtailed the upturn in attacks there. Normal FAC visual reconnaissance was flown over the area in the daytime. Two O-1 controllers continued the coverage during the hours of darkness, supported by two A-1E's on ground alert and two AC-47's on airborne alert.[60]

A spate of successful rocket attacks on Saigon between 5-May-21 June underlined the need to bolster the watch. MACV therefore set up the Capital Military Advisory (Assistance) Command (CMAC) to coordinate the area's overall defense. The CMAC director divided the region into four corridors corresponding to the cardinal points of the compass. Army helicopters covered the east, south, and west corridors. O-1 forward air controllers monitored the north corridor, aided (and soon replaced) by O-2A FAC's. Daily general direction of the rocket watch fell to the helicopter gunship duty officer.[61]

Two O-1's worked the north corridor nightly from 1900 to 2300, then two O-2A's took over until 0700. An AC-47 flew airborne alert during 1900-0630. To keep clear of artillery fire and each other, the controllers flew above 3,000 feet AGL, while the gunships stayed at 3,700 feet or higher. In August the Air Force added the east corridor to its surveillance.[62]

The linking of rocket watch and ground sweeps begun to pay off. More and more the ground troops netted large caches of mortars and unfired rockets, left behind by the fleeing Communists. Switching tactics, the attackers imbedded two sticks in the ground at the desired launch angle, leaned a rocket against them, and adjusted its aim. A timer touched off the rocket after the enemy escaped into the darkness. In most cases only one volley was fired.[63]

Staving off at least one volley of rockets was virtually impossible. As a rule, however, keener detection and quick-reacting sweeps stopped followup firings. The rocket watch also reduced the element of surprise by centering on routes the attackers could be expected to travel to their launch sites.[64]

To pinpoint these sites during an attack was far from easy. Since the initial rocket flash lasted but a moment, the forward air controller could miss it if he so much as blinked his eyes. What's more, he had to fix his position swiftly and still keep an eye on the flash's source for pinpointing in turn. Hence the FAC had to know his area well--prominent landmarks, villages, streams, and friendly troop locations.[65]

To afford controllers more experience in pinpointing launch sites, Army artillery units fired no-notice "flash tests" nightly. They further put up white phosphorous airburst rounds on present coordinates. The rocket watchers (airborne and on watchtowers) recorded and tried to fix each flash, translate it to a ground position, and call in the coordinates. Early erratic results vanished as practice progressed. The watchers pinpointed bursts to within 300 meters of actual positions and trimmed to 45 seconds the time required to sight, plot, and call in a flash. [66]

) Rocket watchers generally reported an attack and requested immediate air support through Army channels. The FAC (or ground observer) spotting a launch site advised the Saigon Artillery Center at once, then notified the tactical operations center at CMAC. He next passed the coordinates (a 6-digit figure) to the controlling helicopter gunship, and asked for a strike clearance. The gunship commander obtained a blanket clearance covering a 1,000-meter radius around the site, and the attack began. Best results, usually came from an AC-47 gunship, but light fire teams* or artillery could also be used. Sometimes all three took part. [67]

(U) Toward the end of 1968, the rocket watch was trimmed down as enemy rocket/mortar attacks sharply declined. It stood ready, however, to build up again should the attacks once more intensify.

---

* These were ground elements that attacked rocket/mortar sites. The controller watched their movements carefully while keeping an eye on incoming artillery rounds and AC-47 fire.

V. THE FINAL YEARS, 1969-1973

(U) After President Johnson halted the bombing of North Vietnam in November 1968, the full weight of Allied tactical air power shifted to interdiction and close air support. Air interdiction quickened in the Laotian panhandle and northern Cambodia, seeking to stem the flow of enemy troops and supplies into South Vietnam. In-country close air support also expanded, pounding the Communists and warning them that future forays would prove costly. The enemy, weakened by losses in the 1968 Tet Offensive and possibly influenced by the Paris negotiations, presented a lower profile of operations in South Vietnam.[1]

President Richard M. Nixon took office in January 1969 and in June announced his intent to withdraw U.S. troops from the war. His plan called for a buildup of South Vietnam's armed forces to replace the departing Americans. The Vietnamese Air Force, for example, would swell to 45 operational squadrons by 1973--17 helicopter, 7 liaison, 4 cargo, 4 gunship, 9 tactical fighter, 1 reconnaissance, 1 training, and 2 F-5.* This in turn required a rise in the number of VNAF personnel from 16,000 to 35,000.[2] At the outset, MACV believed it would take 5 years to round out the President's program. In April, however, Secretary of Defense Melvin R. Laird advanced the deadline to December 1971. To speed the major training effort, MACV recommended that many of the Vietnamese personnel be attached to U.S. units in Vietnam. Seventh Air Force adopted MACV's suggestion and shaped it to Vietnamese Air Force needs.[3]

In March 1969 Seventh Air Force and the Vietnamese Air Force set in motion a plan to upgrade and Vietnamize the Tactical Air Control System by early 1971. Specifically, VNAF personnel would be collocated with their USAF counterparts for side-by-side training at the TACC and in the DASC and TACP's of each corps area. Dual manning of positions would continue until the VNAF could take over parts of and eventually the entire TACS.

---

*By the time the Air Force left South Vietnam in early 1973, the number of squadrons had been upped to 54--18 helicopters, 8 liaison, 9 cargo, 3 gunship, 12 tactical fighter, 2 reconnaissance, 1 training, and 1 special air mission.

New VNAF controllers, ALO's, and liaison aircraft pilots were to be brought under the program and similarly trained.[4]

(S) As Vietnamization made headway, American troops were gradually disengaged. The first withdrawal came in mid-1969, and by 15 December U.S. force levels in South Vietnam were slimmer by 60,000 men.[5]

The Armed FAC in Close Air Support

During the disengagement, USAF aircraft supported American and South Vietnamese ground troops until the VNAF could take complete charge. The Air Force therefore tried to sharpen responsiveness to air support requests, but physical limitations left little room to shrink reaction times without coming up with a new technique. For example, airspeed and distance from the target area affected a strike aircraft's response. The fighter could get to the target in 40 minutes from strip alert; 18 minutes, if dispatched when airborne. However, it seldom arrived under 10 minutes even if close by, due to the time consumed by the TACS in handling the request, and by the FAC in briefing and marking the target. The AC-119's and the AC-130's remained one of the best sources for close air support, featuring long loiter time and fast-firing miniguns of deadly accuracy. Still, there were too few gunships because of the need for transport airframes in tactical airlift. Moreover, those on hand operated widely in out-country interdiction campaigns, confining their in-country support for the most part to hamlets and outposts.[6]

(S) Statistics showed that just 23 percent of all troops-in-contact engagements were large ones. A full 53 percent ended within 20 minutes and involved fewer than ten enemy soldiers. Even from airborne alert, fighters arrive too late to affect the outcome of these brief actions. The final 24 percent of the TIC's entailed small contingents but lasted beyond 20 minutes. Although strike aircraft generally reacted in time to support many of these, they often wasted firepower in overkill.[7]

Mounting light armament on FAC aircraft seemed one way to hurry air support to troops in small engagements. Further, armed forward air controllers could serve as a stopgap in the larger actions until heavier firepower arrived. Since controllers were in the air almost constantly, they could respond to calls for help at a moment's notice. During visual reconnaissance the FAC's commonly came upon tiny knots of Communist troops, and if armed could neutralize or destroy them. As it was, the enemy frequently vanished before the fighters got there.[8]

Suggestions to arm the forward air controller had been made as early as 1965. Supporters pointed out the above advantages. They stressed that an armed FAC could strike small fleeting targets, saving the fighters and gunships for the higher-priority ones. Admitting that the controller would be more exposed to danger, backers believed he wouldn't be shot down if he stayed clear when ground fire heated up. Opponents of the concept argued that an armed FAC would be tempted to forget his main job of VR and strike control and "play fighter pilot" instead. This could be fatal to him and the troops supported as well. After sifting these and related arguments, Seventh Air Force came out against arming forward air controllers.*[9]

(U) Despite this decision, controllers found it hard to stand idly by while the enemy chewed up a friendly unit. Many of them accordingly jury-rigged grenade launchers and machineguns to aircraft wing struts and carried extra rounds for their M-16 rifles. Capt. Donald R. Hawley, a dedicated FAC, devised his own brand of Molotov cocktail. Nicknamed "Hawley's cocktail," it consisted of a grenade (with pin pulled) stuffed inside a peanut butter jar. The sides of the jar held the release handle down. He dropped his cocktails out the 0-1's side window onto Communist troops.[10]

(U) Another controller, Capt. Hilliard A. Wilbanks, won the Medal of Honor for ingenuity and bravery while supporting friendly troops. On the afternoon of 24 February 1967, he was flying air cover out in front of two companies of the 23d Ranger Battalion. The rangers were sweeping a plantation just west of Di Linh (100 miles

---

*Seventh's position rested in part on World War II experiences of tactical reconnaissance crews. Flying armed P-51's/P-38's, these crews often fought air battles in lieu of taking pictures. Once the aircraft armament was removed, however, reconnaissance activity picked up.

northeast of Saigon). They threaded through the waist-high tea bushes and grass, unaware of a larger Viet Cong force dug in nearby and waiting in ambush. Captain Wilbanks spotted the enemy trap and flashed a radio warning to the ground commander. The Communists (listening in) instantly opened fire with machine-guns, mortars, and automatic rifles--pinning down the rangers.[11]

(U) Two Army helicopter gunships soon whirled to the scene and Wilbanks directed their fire against the enemy emplacements. Return fire quickly crippled one of the ships and it limped from the field escorted by the other. As the Viet Cong sprang from their foxholes and moved to the attack, Wilbanks knew the friendlies would be overrun before air support could come. He put his O-1 into a steep dive and launched a rocket marker at the advancing foe who replied with withering fire. After using up his rockets, he grabbed an M-16 rifle and renewed the assault--weaving, turning, climbing, and diving again and again at the Communists. Finally hit and brought down, Captain Wilbanks perished in the crash. His life had bought precious time--tac air arrived and saved the two companies.[12]

The demand for speedier more flexible air response did not diminish, so arming the forward air controller was again considered. Air Force Headquarters in May 1968 gave the green light for a combat test of the concept.* The O-1 was declared unfit for the testing role, lacking armament and being too vulnerable to ground fire. The O-2A looked better for it had passed preliminary tests earlier at Hurlburt Field Fla., using miniguns, bomb racks, rockets, and flares. A full combat load, however, overtaxed and made the Super Skymaster dangerous to fly. Consequently, Tactical Air Command and Seventh Air Force turned it down in favor of the OV-10 Bronco.[13]

---

* A possible factor in the USAF decision were the reports filtering in from Southeast Asia. They recounted the many occasions when forward air controllers employed whatever means were at hand to relieve hard-pressed troops. With the O-1 as their principal aircraft, the chances of successful support were slim.

The OV-10 seemed an ideal armed FAC aircraft.* Besides four forward-firing M-60 (7.62-mm) machineguns hung in sponsons from the bottom of the fuselage, its five armament stations could carry 3,600 pounds of ordnance. Before testing began, TAC cautioned that the OV-10 should not be considered a "fighter or attack aircraft" and thus its ordnance loads should be solely for light action.[14]

The test (code name Misty Bronco) took place in III Corps from 4 April to 13 June 1969, following a stateside evaluation ǂ at Eglin AFB, Fla. Seventh Air Force assigned six OV-10's and nine forward air controllers to the TACP of the 25th Infantry Division's 2d Brigade at Cu Chi. Besides testing the armed FAC concept, these controllers carried out VR, strike control, and emergency support of ground troops. They flew a total of 508 sorties (an average of 7 per day). Only a handful were night ones, and then mostly emergency scrambles. Each Bronco was limited to 2,000 rounds of ammunition (500 per gun), 14 marker rockets, and 14 high-explosive rockets.[15]

During Misty Bronco the armed FAC's responded to 98 requests for immediate air support, handling 78 by themselves. Their reaction times outstripped those of strike aircraft. Jet fighters, for example, took just under 40 minutes to respond when scrambled from ground alert. Even if diverted while airborne, they couldn't cut the time below 10 minutes (5 of the 10 could be consumed by the FAC's briefing and target marking). On the other hand, the armed controller (generally flying in the immediate area) responded and fired within 5.1 minutes of the initial air support request. For fleeting targets he needed 8.7 minutes, the extra time being taken up with identifying the enemy. Even so, his response time for all strike requests averaged 7.3 minutes.[16] The armed FAC's strafing

---

* The Navy and Marine version of the OV-10 had been conceived as a light armed reconnaissance aircraft.

ǂ This test (code name Combat Cover) had three phases, the final one being merged into the Misty Bronco evaluation. See Rowley, FAC Operations, 1965-1970, p. 121.

tactics resembled those of the A-1E, but rocket delivery copied his own target-marking methods.

The 25th Infantry Division Commander praised and endorsed the efforts of the Misty Bronco armed FAC's. Similarly pleased, Gen. George S. Brown, Seventh Air Force Commander, directed that all USAF OV-10's in South Vietnam be armed. Work started on 14 June 1969 with the fitting of HE rocket pods on the first Broncos. The next and last step called for adding M-60 machineguns by 15 September. However, a shortage of armament specialists, guns, and parts delayed completion until 1970.[17]

1970-1971 Operations

The Allied incursions into Cambodia during the spring of 1970 scuttled Communist plans to step up the war in South Vietnam.*[18] In December, however, intelligence reports alerted MACV to a fresh North Vietnamese buildup having three apparent aims. Phnom Penh was to be cut off and force the fall of the Lon Nol Government. To support bigger operations in South Vietnam, logistic bases would be built along the Cambodian border adjacent to III Corps, and in the southern Laotian panhandle. Lastly, the troop expansion and stockpiling around Tchepone pointed to an invasion of Quang Tri and Thua Thien, South Vietnam's two northernmost provinces. As the threat grew more menacing, MACV and South Vietnamese military leaders agreed to a preemptive thrust into Laos. The operation (designated Lam Son 719) would try to strike across the Ho Chi Minh Trail toward Tchepone, wipe out the enemy, and interdict supply lines./ Only ARVN troops would take part, supported by American Air power.[19]

For a week prior to the invasion, troops of the U.S. XXIV Corps attacked enemy positions between Khe Sanh and the Laotian border, clearing a pathway for ARVN troops to their jump-off point.

---

* The incursions afforded the GVN more time to bolster its own buildup. By December the VNAF burgeoned to 9 tactical wings, 40,000 personnel, and nearly 700 aircraft (A-1H's, A-37's, F-5's, AC-47's, O-1's, and C-119's). Vietnamese pilots were also flying almost 40 percent of all tactical strike sorties in-country.

/ Earlier, MACV and South Vietnam had considered and encouraged a Laotian invasion as a sure way to impede the enemy's trail activity. Lam Son 719 could now do this.

On 8 February 1971, a 3-division force crossed over the border on the way to Tchepone, the major objective. To coordinate air support for the ARVN, Seventh Air Force set up a separate direct air support center (DASC Victor) at XXIV Corps Headquarters in Quang Tri. The DASC served the TACP's at each of the division headquarters.[20]

The invasion got under way smoothly but problems soon surfaced. The battle plan called for extensive use of tactical air power in supporting ground troops. However the invasion force commander, Lt. Gen. Hoang Zuan Lam, relied too heavily on helicopter gunships and artillery for close-in support.* In addition, he shifted his troops about without notifying the VNAF, Seventh Air Force, and XXIV Corps far enough in advance. The roundabout method for requesting immediate air support also hindered the operation. A request from the field had to work its way through the ARVN command post (CP) at Khe Sanh to the I Corps CP at Dong Ha, then to the XXIV Corps CP at Quang Tri. At this point, DASC Victor (which commonly kept tabs on a request from its inception) was tasked to furnish the air support. Finally, USAF forward air controllers covering Lam Son 719 often had trouble understanding the ground commanders due to the language barrier.[21]

By the end of the operation's second week, these problems were well on the way to solution. MACV and Seventh Air Force convinced General Lam to use tac air more often for close-in support. He also gave more lead time to coordinating his troop movements with the other military services. To help remove the language barrier between USAF controllers and ARVN ground commanders, the VNAF let bilingual observers fly in the backseat of the OV-10's.† On 1 March a joint coordinating group began operation at Khe Sanh, made up of members from ARVN I Corps, XXIV, and an air liaison officer from DASC Victor. The result was faster and better air support for ARVN troops.[22]

---

* During the operation's first 10 days, helicopter gunships averaged 465 sorties daily as opposed to 96.4 for tactical air and 6.1 for B-52's. In its final 10 days, however, these averages stood at 321.8, 157.4, and 12.4 respectively.

† Accustomed to the O-1, these observers tended to get airsick during their first few flights in the faster, abrupt-turning Bronco.

As the ARVN forces pushed close to Tchepone, they came upon sizable stockpiles of enemy supplies and equipment. Many of the caches had been uncovered by the massive B-52 strikes. The C-130's aided the advance by dropping 15,000-pound BLU-82 bombs that carved instant helicopter landing pads out of the jungle. Seventh Air Force assigned an airborne battlefield command and control center chiefly to support night operations.[23]

Near-disaster loomed however. Possibly forewarned of the invasion, the North Vietnamese had buttressed the defenses of their logistic bases in Laos. Predicting the operation's travel route, they placed large numbers of tanks, artillery, and AA weapons at strategic points. The heaviest firepower they massed near Tchepone. Even though the ARVN units had met with stubborn resistance from the moment they crossed into Laos, their airpower umbrella had largely neutralized it. But as the force crept closer to Tchepone, the opposition sharply stiffened. Then on 25 February, an estimated 24,000 Communist soldiers, supported by about 120 tanks, slammed into the flank of the stalled ARVN troops. The intensive ground fire took a heavy toll of the low-flying Army helicopters, and tactical air power replaced them in the hotter areas. Wave after wave of USAF fighters and B-52's were thrown into the battle, the fighters often attacking the foe inside the perimeters of friendly defenses.[24]

The Director of DASC Victor described one of that day's actions. The strike aircraft battered the Communists without letup, yet some reached the wire of the defensive perimeter. While the attackers were still about 800 meters away, the fighters riddled them with CBU-24 fragmentation cluster bombs and 2,000-pound HE Daisy Cutters. When darkness fell, the gunships took over from the strike aircraft--circling and pouring minigun fire into the enemy all night long. Then

> in between gunships, three to four minutes, the enemy would be up and into the wire. The gunships would then shoot them back off and do this until the next gunship came up. There is no doubt in my mind that [the friendlies] would have been overrun if it had not been for tac air and gunships.[25]

Massive airstrikes prevented the North Vietnamese from grouping for an all-out attack. On 3 March the back of the counter-offensive was finally broken, and South Vietnamese forces were in Tchepone by the 7th. After destroying as many stockpiles and roads as possible, they began their withdrawal from Laos on 18 March. The enemy waited along the way and exacted a stiff price in men and materiel--many trucks, tanks, and armored vehicles had to be abandoned. By the 24th the withdrawal was virtually complete, the operation officially ending on 6 April. The cost to both sides had been high. For example, an estimated 13,000 of the enemy were killed and 20,000 tons of food and ammunition destroyed. The ARVN suffered 1,519 killed, 5,423 wounded, and 651 missing in action. The overriding lesson learned in Lam Son 719 was that helicopter gunships alone could not support such an operation.* Neither the invasion nor the withdrawal could have been achieved without the extensive use of tactical air power.[26]

(U) Lam Son 719 highlighted military operations in 1971, and frustrated North Vietnamese plans to attack the northern provinces. Of necessity the Communists spent several months in replacing and reequipping many of their crack units, and rebuilding supply bases. This gave the South Vietnamese breathing space for pursuing their buildup as the American presence declined. By December 1971 the VNAF operated its own TACC and handled around 70 percent of all combat air operations in South Vietnam. The DASC's had come under VNAF control and were located alongside the ARVN tactical operations centers in the military regions (formerly corps areas).[27]

1972 Operations

The first weeks of 1972 witnessed sporadic fighting in South Vietnam. By March the VNAF Tactical Air Control System was virtually self-sufficient, directing over 90 percent of the total tactical air operations in-country. Merely a handful of USAF TACP's remained to advise on close air supprt. Under the VNAF the TACS became more decentralized, each military region headquarters controlling its aircraft through its own air division. Trade-offs of air power between regions took place only when the TACS requested them.[28]

---

* This lesson had been vividly pointed out in January 1965 at the battle of Binh Gia. (See Chapter III.)

During March the enemy stirrings over the border in Cambodia, Laos, and North Vietnam signaled another imminent invasion. It came on the 30th when North Vietnamese Army forces launched a 3-pronged offensive spearheaded by heavy tanks and mobile armor units.* One force struck south across the demilitarized zone (DMZ), bent on conquering the northern provinces and seizing the ancient citadel of Hue. The second attack knifed from the Tri Border Area into the Central Highlands, seeking to capture population centers in the interior and cut South Vietnam in two. The third prong stabbed from Cambodia toward An Loc and Saigon. Vicious fighting enveloped on all three fronts.[29]

The Communists scored their greatest success in the northern provinces. In quick order they captured the province and city of Quang Tri and pushed on to Hue. Meanwhile the Air Force had recalled tactical fighter and B-52 units from the United States, and support operations were in full swing. To bolster the VNAF at Hue, Navy, Marine, and Air Force fighter-bombers joined B-52's in massive assaults on enemy positions. At night USAF gunships constantly harassed the attackers. This effort saved Hue and the foe was gradually shoved back to Quang Tri. South Vietnamese troops retook Quang Tri City only after the full force of tac air had dug the Communists out of their shelters.[30]

The battle for the Central Highlands also began well for the Communists but turned sour. Their Russian-built T-54 tanks and heavy armor rumbled across the highlands, winning control of huge chunks of Kontum province. The offensive bogged down close to the capital, Kontum City, as USAF fighters and gunships aided the beleaguered ARVN troops. In the open countryside the enemy soldiers fell easy prey to the airstrikes, the fire from the AC-119's and AC-130's being especially deadly. Two successive attacks on the capital were beaten off and by 1 June the worst was over. The attackers slowly retreated from their captured positions.[31]

---

* The invasion was supposedly under the leadership of Gen. Vo Nguyen Giap, North Vietnam's Defense Minister.

The most crucial engagement of the 3-pronged offensive erupted at An Loc, during the enemy's thrust toward Saigon. Firepower, position, and sheer numbers were all on the side of the Communists. On the first day the ARVN troops were driven into a small area in the southern part of the city, leaving most of their artillery pieces behind during the hasty retreat. Surrounded and cut off save by air, their resupply became extremely difficult because of the tiny parachute drop zones. To make matters worse, the North Vietnamese brought in many sophisticated AA weapons, including multiple-barrel 37-mm and twin-barrel 57-mm guns, plus SA-7 Strella surface-to-air missiles. This array of firepower compelled the low-flying AC-119K's and Army Cobra helicopter gunships to move out. Forward air controllers in the slow-moving OV-10's and 0-2A's likewise found low-altitude work too risky. They went to above 10,000 feet AGL where the Strellas and AA fire lost their punch.[32]

Jet strike pilots found the shoulder-fired Strellas less of a problem than the heavy concentrations of AA fire around An Loc. To evade the SA-7, the pilot kept airspeed beyond 450 knots and pulled 4 G's in a tight climbing turn to above 10,000 feet AGL. On the other hand, the mass fire from 37-, 57-, and 85-mm guns often required him to release his bombs from 6,500-7,000 feet. This somewhat diminished accuracy.[33]

AC-130 Spectres, newly armed with Pave Aegis 105-mm howitzers, plugged the gap left by the AC-119K's and Army Cobras. Less vulnerable to the ground fire, the Spectre could strike enemy positions from 6,500-12,000 feet AGL with scant loss in precision. Time after time the AC-130's wracked the Communist troops with the lethal "105's"--often only 10-15 yards from the friendlies. Soon ground commanders swore by Pave Aegis's ability to hurt the enemy. A Spectre pilot reported that one ARVN commander told him to "go north along the main street for three blocks, turn east there, and hit the second house from the corner."[34]

At the peak of the struggle for An Loc, it kept five forward air controllers busy handling the airstrikes. Even then, fighters at times were stacked up 10 deep, waiting their turn to come in. To help sort things out, the TACC designated one controller as the senior, or King, FAC. The King maintained contact with the ground commanders and the ABCCC. He assigned controllers to specific zones of responsibility, shunting aircraft between them as the ground situation altered.[35]

B-52 operations at An Loc tilted the scales to victory. The big bombers flew numerous close air support missions, hitting enemy positions nearly next door to the friendlies and wiping out many mortar and AA artillery sites. Their phychological impact was enormous. For example, when Communist forces spilled into nearby villages to rouse local support, the villagers frequently fled. They feared the B-52's might bomb them to get at the enemy.[36]

By August the battle for An Loc had all but ended, and it was clear the North Vietnamese offensive had failed. The country-wide effort cost the enemy an estimated 120,000 casualties and the best part of his heavy armor. The VNAF and ARVN generally fought well--better than the Communists thought they would. Vietnamese pilots (many with more than 4,000 combat hours under their belts) showed great skill in striking the enemy. During all of 1972 they flew more in-country sorties than USAF pilots.[37]

(U) In the spring of 1972, President Nixon had enlarged American efforts to halt the Communist offensive in South Vietnam. He ordered the renewed bombing of North Vietnam by strike aircraft and B-52's. On 8 May he approved the mining of North Vietnam's harbors and river inlets, to further impede the flow of war supplies south. These interdiction actions continued through the summer and early fall.

The A-7D Makes Its Bow

On 10 October 1972 a squadron of the Air Force's newest aircraft, the A-7D Sluf, joined the 354th Tactical Fighter Wing at Korat Royal Thai AFB. Built by Ling Temco Vought, the A-7D was a modified version of the Navy's A-7A. The Sluf flew its first combat mission on the 16th with promising results.[39]

Conceived as a general purpose light attack aircraft, the A-7D carried up to 16,000 pounds of ordnance on eight external stations. Its internally mounted M-61 Gatling gun and two Sidewinder missiles allowed some air-to-air and ground strafing. The 14,500-pound thrust of the self-starting Rolls Royce T-41A jet engine gave the Sluf a top true airspeed of 575 knots.* Foam filled fuel tanks, armorplating, and an intermeshed triple hydraulic system helped protect the plane from ground fire.[40]

A remarkable integrated and computerized navigation/ weapon delivery system let the A-7D pinpoint bombs better than any other jet fighter-bomber in SEA. The system included a digital computer, forward-looking radar (FLR), doppler radar, air data computer, armament station control unit, and heads-up display (HUD). On a windscreen in front of the pilot, the HUD flashed all information needed to control the Sluf and deliver bombs or 20-mm shells on the target--altitude, climb or descent rate, airspeed, and attitude. With his head out of the cockpit, the pilot could devote his attention to the target and the threat. The system worked well for straight-and-level bombing, radar offset bombing, dive-bombing, and computed gunfire.[41]

During strike missions the A-7D crews adopted the tactics of the other jet fighters. Following takeoff they formed up in 2-ship flights and climbed to a cruise altitude of 24,000 feet AGL. The lead pilot contacted the DASC for target information, the FAC's call sign, and the rendezvous point. After join-up with the controller, the crews reviewed target requirements and the sequence of weapon drops. Flying into the target area, the fighters descended to orbit altitude (8,000-12,000 feet) and swung into a floating wheel pattern. To bomb, the Sluf pilots dove steeply ($30°$ - $60°$) and gunned to 450-500 KIAS. They shallowed their dive to under $30°$ and cut airspeed to 250-300 knots for rocket and napalm attacks. The accuracy of the integrated bombing system permitted the pilots to release their weapons at 3,000-4,000 feet, well beyond the range of small-arms fire. They went lower only when cloud ceilings dictated.[42]

A few drawbacks detracted from the A-7D's close air support performance. A long takeoff roll (over 8,000 feet on hot days with a full load) kept the Sluf from using a number of smaller airfields in the combat zone. Thus it took longer in responding to immediate air requests. In flight the aircraft maneuvered sluggishly

---

* The A-7D commonly cruised at 280 KIAS (430-440 knots TAS). Its best combat radius was 400 nautical miles, plus 30 minutes of loiter time.

when fully loaded, requiring a larger than normal turn radius. Moreover, slow acceleration rendered the plane more vulnerable in medium to high-threat areas. The A-7D nevertheless proved to be the Air Force's best close air support aircraft, and plans called for using it in that role after the war.[43]

The End of American Combat

(U) The A-7D had scarcely flown its first combat missions in October 1972 when Henry Kissinger, Special Assistant for National Security Affairs, returned from Paris to inform the nation that "peace is at hand." The negotiations dragged on for 2 more months, however, with North Vietnam unwilling to agree upon a timetable for withdrawing forces and repatriating prisoners of war. On 18 December President Nixon therefore ordered B-52 raids against Hanoi and the Haiphong seaport area. For 11 days the giant bombers pummeled railroad yards, power plants, munition depots, and military bases. Finally on the 29th, North Vietnam's negotiators came back to the conference table. A 9-point cease-fire agreement was hammered out and agreed to on 23 January 1973. It became effective on the 27th and American prisoners of war began returning home. The last American combat soldier left South Vietnam on 28 March. All USAF tactical aircraft were out by 31 May. Except for airlift support in Cambodia, U.S. combat operations in Southeast Asia ended on 15 August. For the Americans, the longest war in their history was over.[44]

EPILOGUE

(U) Testifying on 17 April 1973 at hearings of the House Armed Services Committee, Gen. Creighton W. Abrams, Jr., MACV Commander (1968-1972) lauded Air Force close air support. He stressed that two or three squadrons of USAF jet fighters packed far more hitting power than any combination of helicopters--in terms of payload and bombs and rockets on the target. General Abrams pointed out there was "nothing in the Army" like the Air Force's command and control system--in fact, "nothing anywhere in the world like it." He concluded that close air support was

> one of the reasons why you don't have to hold a division in reserve. The only thing that is in reserve is what isn't in contact with the enemy. . . it is not only the airplane, it is that whole system . . . the Air Force has.[1]

(U) Such praise was not easily earned. When the Air Force entered the Vietnam War in 1961, it was ill-prepared to give the close air support needed. Since World War II, nuclear deterrence had been the centerpiece of U.S. military policy. Both the air fleet and tactical doctrine were built around a fast, hard-hitting conflict that would be decided chiefly in the air. Consequently, swift tactical fighters and high-flying jet bombers stood by, set for quick strikes on the enemy's lines and deep within his heartland. Limited, prolonged ground operations seemed out of place in this scheme. Hence air-ground coordination and planning withered. The Tactical Air Control System fell into neglect and near disuse. World War II close air support aircraft aged and slipped into the mothball fleet in the Arizona desert, with no replacements on the drawing boards. Stockpiles of conventional weapons dwindled, siphoned into the hands of friendly nations. Moreover, many seasoned aircrewmen left the Air Force, taking along a wealth of knowledge and experience gleaned from two wars.

(U) The expanding conflict in South Vietnam during the early 1960's spurred the Air Force to action. Aging aircraft, hastily jerked out of mothballs or borrowed from the Army and Navy, were modified for combat. Old bombs, bought back from other nations and drawn from shrunken stockpiles, were shipped to SEA. The TACS was revamped and introduced into South Vietnam. Forward air controllers forsook the ground for the air and found directing airstrikes easier. Jet fighter pilots retrained in propellor-driven aircraft, relearning close air support tactics almost forgotten. Finally, ground commanders had to be convinced that tactical air power surpassed their often inadequate organic firepower in destroying enemy targets.

(U) In 1965 newer weapon systems began appearing in South Vietnam. Jet fighters flew close air support missions, cutting response time. Fixed-wing gunships hammered and at times decimated enemy units. High-flying B-52's dropped massive bombloads on Communist soldiers without warning. The starlight scope, infrared detectors, and side-looking airborne radar made the enemy's life miserable at night, and saved many friendly troops from ambush and disaster. The OV-10 FAC aircraft rendered close air support more flexible.

Even so, a striking feature of the early war years was the extent that the Air Force modified old aircraft and equipment to meet close air support needs. Attrition took its toll of these aged planes, the Communists countering their tactics and shooting quite a few down. The answer seemed to lie in the development of an aircraft expressly for close air support. Thus the Chief of Staff, Gen. John P. McConnell, directed on 8 September 1966 that planning for the new plane (the A-X) begin.[2]

By March 1968 the Air Force had already issued the A-X concept formulation package. It envisioned a twin-engine jet aircraft, hauling 16,000 pounds of bombs and rockets on 10 external stations, plus an internal 30-mm cannon capable of killing tanks. To take off with a 6,500-pound bombload from 1,000-foot runways, a high-lift wing was specified. The combat radius conceived was 250 NM with 2 hours of loiter time. For improved response to immediate air requests, the required cruise speed was 300-400 knots. Armorplating, redundant flight controls,* and a fully foamed fuel system were to shield against heavy ground fire. A simply designed navigation system would permit all-weather flight. A simple heads-up display was to yield a bombing accuracy of less than 100 from the

---

* Fluctuations or loss of hydraulic pressure would not affect the flight controls.

center of a target.* Lastly, the A-X would be designed to later accept a laser spot-seeker for dropping laser-guided bombs.[3]

When in May 1970 the Air Force sought design proposals, Boeing, Cessna, Convair, Lockheed, Northrop, and Fairchild Industries complied. The designs of Northrop and Fairchild were selected, and in December they received the go-ahead for building prototypes. In October 1972 the Air Force started flight-testing the Northrup A-9A and Fairchild A-10A, opting for the latter on 28 February 1973. A single-seater, the A-10A featured a low wing, twin tails, and engines mounted on each side of the fuselage, just behind and above the wing.ǂ [4]

(U) Meanwhile, the Air Force began tailoring the Tactical Air Control System to the evolving demands of modern war. Plans called for the continued use of forward air controllers, both in the air and on the ground. Close air support tactics would be regularly reviewed and updated to meet current and anticipated threats. These actions and the development of the A-10A underlined USAF intent to maintain and refine close air support. Unlike the Vietnam War, a future conflict would brook no delay in applying such support--most likely amid enemy air attacks as well as ground fire. The Air Force well knew the extent of the challenge and stood ready to meet it.[5]

---

* The planned strafing accuracy of the A-X was 15 feet or less. Its best altitude for dive-bombing and strafe would be 1,500-3,000 feet AGL, but it could attack on the deck if need be.

ǂ In 1974 the Air Force firmed up plans for a flyoff between the A-10A and the A-7D Sluf, to find out if the A-10A was really needed for close air support. The answer proved to be yes, and the Air Force accepted the A-10A in 1975.

SOURCES AND NOTES

Material for this study came from four general sources: official records (chiefly Air Force); manuscript histories; interviews; and certain published works.

Official Records

The author used applicable information from the files of the Secretary of the Air Force, available as retired materials at the National Federal Records Center, Suitland, Maryland.

Records of the Tactical Control Branch of the Tactical Control Division, Director of Operations, at Headquarters Air Force provided numerous messages, letters, and studies not found elsewhere. Letters, messages, and other miscellaneous correspondence (involving major commands and other organizations below Air Force level) were acquired from the Albert F. Simpson Historical Research Center, Maxwell AFB, Alabama. The Tactical Air Warfare Center at Eglin Air Force Base, Florida, and the Historical Research Center furnished other valuable information. The Tactical Air Warfare Center was most helpful in revealing information on early Air Force involvement in South Vietnam and the development of initial close air support tactics. The Historical Research Center made available all unit histories and other reports concerning Southeast Asia. The Air University Library, Air War College, and Air Force Command and Staff College also supplied useful information. The author is also appreciative of the help given by the Army's Office of Military History in the form of reports and studies.

Manuscript Histories

Project CHECO (Contemporary Historical Examination of Current Operations) reports, first narratives written by Air Force historians in the field during the war, were an excellent source and often pointed the way to additional valuable sources. Those touching upon close air support proved especially helpful. Also of considerable worth were Project Corona Harvest reports, studies and evaluations relating to Southeast Asia. These sources were available in the Office of Air Force History. The Corona Harvest collection at the Air Force Archives afforded many documents for further research.

Semiannual histories of Headquarters USAF directorates, major commands (chiefly Pacific Air Forces and Tactical Air Command), and lower units (air force, division, and wing) were helpful. The histories of Military Assistance Command, Vietnam, gave the author an understanding of the wider aspects of the SEA war and the infantryman's point of view concerning close air support.

Other history manuscripts consulted were a number of monographs (commonly called "bluebooks" or "blue covers"), published by the Office of Air Force History.

Interviews

The author relied heavily on interviews to fill gaps in other sources. During his research, he interviewed several dozen Air Force pilots, particularly those serving early in the war. They furnished rich details that could have been acquired in no other way. The Special Acquisitions Branch of the Historical Research Center has been another fertile source, having a reservoir of more than 600 typed interviews.

Published Works

Published works used were for the most part general in nature. They included various military magazines as well as articles from publications of the Air Force Office of Information. Their principal value lay in adding insight to topics already researched. Congressional publications, specifically those by the House Armed Services Committee, were useful in documenting information contained herein. RAND studies supplied a non-military perspective on the war.

Most of the above published material may be found in the Air Force Studies and Analysis Library and the Pentagon's Army Library.

ABSTRACT

This study traces the development of close air support tactics and operations in South Vietnam from 1961 through 1973.

The early years (1961-64) witnessed the buildup of Farm Gate operations and introduction of the Tactical Air Control System (Barn Door). Tactics evolved for the O-1 Bird Dog FAC and for such strike aircraft as the T-28 Trojan, B-26 Invader, and A-1E Skyraider. Ordnance problems were tackled and headway made.

During the buildup (1965-68) the O-2A Skymaster and OV-10 Bronco bolstered forward air control. Strike operations were strengthened by the F-100 Super Sabre, B-57 Canberra, F-4 Phantom, F-5 Freedom Fighter, and A-37 Dragonfly. Gunships (the AC-47 Spooky, AC-130 Spectre, AC-119G Shadow, and AC-119K Stinger) also gave excellent assistance to group troops. Support of Special Forces commenced. Inroads were made on problems of coordination, command, and control of tactical air power. Tactics were further refined to meet the changing needs of close air support.

In the final period (1969-73) the OV-10 acted as an armed FAC. The A-7 Corsair II entered the war. In 1973 the pullout of American troops began.

Lastly, the study discusses the A-10, a new close air support aircraft.

NOTES

Chapter I

1. John L. Frisbee and Edgar Ulsamer, "The Air War in Vietnam," Air Force Magazine, 55 (Sep 1972), 48-72; Maj Paul T. Ringenbach and Capt Peter J. Melly, The Battle for An Loc, 5 April-26 June 1972 (S) HQ PACAF, Project CHECO, 31 Mar 73).

2. TAC Rprt 73-13 (S), History of United States Air Force Close Air Support Command Control (Dir/Studies and Analys, DCS/Plans, TAC, 1 Mar 73), pp 1-2; JCS Study, Joint Staff Task Force Phase II Close Air Study, Vol III, Pt 1, History of Close Air Support Command and Control (S) (JCS, 1972), AF-1 to AF-3, A-1, A-2 [hereinafter cited as JCS Study].

3. See note above; Alfred Goldberg and Lt Col Donald Smith, Army-Air Force Relations: The Close Air Support Issue (C) (R-906-PR, The RAND Corp, Oct 1971), pp 1-3; Alfred Goldberg, A History of the United States Air Force, 1907-1957 (Princeton, N.J., 1957), p 21 [hereinafter cited as Goldberg, USAF History]; Robert F. Futrell, Ideas, Concepts, Doctrine: A History of Basic Thinking in the United States Air Force, 1907-1964 (ASI, AU, Jun 1971), I, 20-21.

4. JCS Study, A-1 to A-2; TAC Rprt 73-13 (S), 1 Mar 73, pp 3-4; Goldberg and Smith, Army-Air Force Relations: The Close Air Support Issue, pp 1-3; U.S. Army in the World War, 1917-1919, Vol IX: Meuse-Argonne Operations of American Expeditionary Forces (Hist Div, DA, 1948), 48.

5. See note above.
6. William D. Parker, A Concise History of the U.S. Marine Corps, 1775-1969 (HQ USMC, 1970), p 56; Lt Col James E. Daniel, Jr., Will the Attack Fighter Fulfill the Army's Close Air Support Requirements (U)(Army War College Carlisle Barracks, Pa., 23 Feb 72), pp 4-5; Robert Sherrod, History of Marine Corps Aviation in World War II (Washington, 1952), p 26.

7. The Rise and Fall of the German Air Force (1933-1945) (Asst Ch of Air Staff (Intel), British Air Ministry, 1948), pp 14-18; Gen der Flieger a. D. Paul Deichman, German Air Force Operations in Support of the Army (USAF Hist Study 163, New York, 1969), pp 131-34; Daniel, Will the Attack

Notes to pages 3-5

Fighter Fulfill the Army's Close Air Support Requirements, pp-4-5; TAC Rprt 73-13 (S), 1 Mar 73, p 5; A. Goutard, The Battle of France, 1940 (New York, 1959), pp 144-45; Alistair Horne, To Lose a Battle, France 1940 (Boston, 1969), pp 288-307, 332-35, 437.

8. Maj Ralph A. Rowley, USAF FAC Operations in Southeast Asia, 1961-1965 (S) (Ofc/AF Hist, Jan 1972), pp 2-3 [hereinafter cited as FAC Ops in SEA, 1961-1965]; Charles W. Dickens, A Survey of Air-Ground Doctrine (S) (Hist Study 34, TAC, Apr 1958), p 4.

9. War Department Basic Field Manual 31-35 (U), Aviation in Support of Ground Forces, 9 Apr 42, pp 1, 3; Dickens, A Survey of Air-Ground Doctrine, pp 5-6; Goldberg, USAF History, p 59; Goldberg and Smith, Army-Air Force Relations: The Close Air Support Issue, pp 1-3; Daniel, Will the Attack Fighter Fulfill the Army's Close Air Support Requirements, pp 4-5; JCS Study, A-12; TAC Rprt 73-13 (S), 1 Mar 73, pp 7-11.

10. See note above.

11. See note 9; FAC Ops in SEA, 1961-1965, p 3.

12. Goldberg and Smith, Army-Air Force Relations: The Close Air Support Issue, p 3.

13. Denis Richards and Hilary St. George Saunders, Royal Air Force 1939-1945, Vol II: The Fight Avails (London, 1954), 265-266; Working Paper (S), TAC, The Forward Air Controller (FAC), May 1958, p 3; Close Support of the Fifth Army (U) HQ MAAF, 1964-1965, Tab D; J. Farmer and M. J. Strumwasser, The Evolution of the Airborne Forward Air Controller: An Analysis of Mosquito Operations in Korea (The RAND Corp, Oct 1957), p 3 [hereinafter cited as Mosquito Ops in Korea].

14. The Employment of Air Power in the North African Campaign (U) (AF Hist Div, 9 Oct 51), p 44; Dwight D. Eisenhower, Crusade in Europe (New York, 1948), pp 261, 323.

15. JCS Study, A-20; FAC Ops in SEA, 1961-1965, pp 4-5; Mosquito Ops in Korea, pp 3-4; Memoirs by Harry S. Truman, Vol II: Years of Trial and Hope (Garden City, N.Y., 1956) p 337; Goldberg and Smith, Army-Air Force

Relations: The Close Air Support Issue, pp 4-5.

16. See note above.

17. JCS Study, A-23 to A-26; Truman, Years of Trial and Hope, p 337; Goldberg and Smith, Army-Air Force Relations: The Close Air Support Issue, pp 6-9.

18. JCS Study, A-23 to A-26; Brooke Nihart, "Sixty Years of Unresolved Problems," Armed Forces Journal, 107 (25 Apr 70), pp 19-26; Robert E. Futrell, The United States Air Force in Korea, 1950-1953 (New York, 1961), pp 12-13, 76-77; TAC Rprt 73-13 (S), 1 Mar 73, pp 32-35; FAC Ops in SEA, 1961-1965, pp 5-7; Mosquito Ops in Korea, pp 19-21; Truman, Years of Trial and Hope, p 337.

19. JCS Study, A-25 to A-30; TAC Rprt 73-13 (S), 1 Mar 73, pp 34-35; Nihart, "Unresolved Problems," pp 19-26; FAC Ops in SEA, 1961-1965, p 7; Futrell, Air Force in Korea, pp 73-80.

20. Goldberg and Smith, Army-Air Force Relations: The Close Air Support Issue, pp 10-13.

21. Ibid., pp 12-13; FAC Ops in SEA, 1961-1965, pp 7-8, 41; Mosquito Ops in Korea, pp 19-21; Dwight D. Eisenhower, The White House Years, Vol I: Mandate for Change (Garden City N.Y., 1963), p 454.

22. See note above; rprt, Close Air Support, Special House Subcommittee on Tactical Air Support, 89th Cong, 2d sess 44 (1966), pp 4862-63 [hereinafter cited as Pike Cmte Rprt]; Daniel, Will the Attack Fighter Fulfill the Army's Close Air Support Requirements, p 5.

23. Goldberg and Smith, Army-Air Force Relations: The Close Air Support Issue, pp 16-17.

24. Ibid.; JCS Study, A-33 to A-35; ACDC Study (U), A Short History of Close Air Support Issues (Institute of Special Studies, Ft Belvoir, Va., Jul 1968), pp 53-54 [hereinafter cited as ACDC Study].

25. Goldberg and Smith, Army-Air Force Relations: The Close Air Support Issue, p 17.

26. ACDC Study, pp 53-54.

Chapter II

1. ASI rprt (S), *Evaluation of Airpower in Southeast Asia, 1954-1964,* Vol II, Bk 1, 1961-1964, Aug 1970, pp 2-17 to 2-20 [hereinafter cited as *Airpower Evaluation*]; *A Report on the United States Air Force Tactical Air Support Requirements* (S), (USAF TAS Eval Bd, 1 Aug 62), Atch 2, pp 3-4 [hereinafter cited as *TAS Requirements*]; intvw (C), author with Col Ira L. Kimes, Dir/Ops, 26 Nov 73 [Kimes was a Farm Gate T-28 pilot and armament officer (Oct 1961-Feb 1962)]; Charles H. Hildreth, *USAF Counterinsurgency Doctrines and Capabilities, 1961-1962* (S) (AF Hist Div Ln Ofc, Feb 1964), p 6.

2. Intvw (S), Lt Col Valentino Castellina and Maj Samuel J. Riddlebarger, with Brig Gen Benjamin H. King, 4 Sep 69 [King was 4400th CCT Sq Comdr (1961-1962)]; *TAS Requirements,* pp 3-4.

3. See note above.

4. King intvw (S), 4 Sep 69; *FAC Ops in SEA, 1961-1965,* p 10; "A Program of Action for South Vietnam," 8 May 61 and National Security Action Memorandum 62, 11 May 1961, in *The Pentagon Papers as Published by the New York Times* (New York, 1971), pp 119-127.

5. Hist (S), 2d ADVON, Nov 1961-Oct 1962, pp xvii-xx, 10-13; *Airpower Evaluation,* pp 2-17 to 2-20; Hildreth, *USAF Counterinsurgency Doctrines and Capabilities, 1961-1962,* pp 12-13; Maj Terrence G. Wheeler, *Special Air Warfare Concept and Doctrine* (S) (ACSC, AU, 1969), p 10; memo (TS), SECDEF to CJCS, subj: 4400th CCTS, 3 Oct 61; King intvw (S), 4 Sep 69; Maj Victor B. Anthony, *Tactics and Techniques of Night Operations, 1961-1970* (S) (Ofc/AF Hist, Mar 1973), p 1 [hereinafter cited as *Night Ops in SEA*]; intvw (C), author with Col Jackson L. Thomason, Dir/Doctrine, Concepts, and Objectives, 11 Dec 73 [Thomason was an AGOS instr (1960-1962) and coauthored 13th AF OPlan 226-61 (Barn Door I)].

6. See note above; hist (S), 13th AF, Jul-Dec 1961, pp 75-76.

7. *Night Ops in SEA,* p 1; hist (S), 2d ADVON, Nov 1961-Oct 1962, pp xvii-xx, 7-9; hist (S), USAFSAWC, 27 Apr-31 Dec 62, pp 11-12; hist (TS), *Rules of Engagement in Southeast Asia, 1957-1965* (PACAF, Oct 1968); King intvw (S), 4 Sep 69; Kimes intvw (C), 26 Nov 73; hist (S), 13th AF, Jul-Dec 1961, pp 75-76.

8. Night Ops in SEA, p 1; hist (S), 2d ADVON, Nov 1961-Oct 1962, pp 7-9

9. Night Ops in SEA, pp 1-2; PACAF rprt (S), In-Country and Out-Country Strike Operations in Southeast Asia, 1 Jan 65-31 Dec 69, Vol II, Hardware: Strike Aircraft, 1 Dec 1970, pp 6-51 to 6-54 [hereinafter cited as Strike Aircraft].

10. Airpower Evaluation, pp 6-54 to 6-56; Strike Aircraft, pp 170-173; Night Ops in SEA, pp 2-3; rprt (U), TAC Spt Eval Bd, Characteristics of Aircraft Currently Employed in COIN Operations, 1 Aug 62, pp 15-17; intvw (S), Maj Victor B. Anthony, Ofc/AF Hist, with Maj Charles W. Brown, Dir/Plans, 14 Sep 70 [Brown was a Farm Gate T-28/B-26 pilot (May-Nov 1962)].

11. Night Ops in SEA, pp 1-2; hist (S), 2d ADVON, Nov 1961-Oct 1962, pp 8-9.

12. Night Ops in SEA, p 3; study (U), History of Night/All-Weather-Tactical Air Operations in World War II and Korea (AF Hist Ln Ofc, 1963); Futrell, Air Force in Korea, pp 258-260.

13. Night Ops in SEA, p 11; intvw (S), Maj Victor B. Anthony, Ofc/AF Hist, with Lt Col John R. Pattee, JCS, 18 Sep 70 [Pattee was a Farm Gate pilot (1961-1962)].

14. Presentation (S), Brig Gen Rollen H. Anthis, 2d ADVON Comdr, to SECDEF McNamara at Mar 62 SECDEF conf, subj: Air Operations, in hist (S), 2d ADVON 15 Nov 61-8 Oct 62, Doc 203; msg (TS), PACAF to CINCPAC, 062125Z Dec 61, subj: Concept of Employment of Farm Gate; Robert F. Futrell, Chronology of Significant Airpower Events in Southeast Asia, 1954-1967 (S) (AF Hist Div, Dec 1967), p 16 [hereinafter cited as Chronology].

15. Airpower Evaluation, pp 4-7, 4-8; TAC/TAWC rprt (TS), Tactical Air Control Systems in SEA, Vol I, Jan 1965-Mar 1968, 19 Nov 69, pp 5, 13-17 [hereinafter cited as TACS, Jan 1965 - Mar 1968]; hist (S), 13th AF, Jul-Dec 1961, I, pp 73-74; Thomason intvw (C), 11 Dec 73.

Notes to pages 11-14

16. Hists (S), 13th AF, Jul-Dec 1961, I, 73-74; Jan-Dec 1963, pp 72-73; 2d ADVON, Nov 1961-Oct 1962, p 90; 2d Air Div, Jan-Jun 1965, I, 64; Airpower Evaluation, pp 4-7, 4-8; Thomason intvw (C), 11 Dec 73.

17. Hists (S), 2d ADVON, Nov 1961-Oct 1962, pp 91-94; 13th AF, Jul-Dec 1961, I, 73-74; Airpower Evaluation, pp 4-7, 4-8; TACS, Jan 1965-Mar 1968, 11-17; Thomason intvw (C), 11 Dec 73.

18. Hist (S), 2d ADVON, Nov 1961-Oct 1962, pp 93-94.

19. Ibid., pp 95-96; Thomason intvw (C), 11 Dec 73.

20. Hist (S), 2d ADVON, Nov 1961-Oct 1962, pp 92-96; Maj Richard F. Kott, SEAsia Glossary, 1961-1970 (S) (HQ PACAF, Project CHECO, 1 Feb 70), pp 36-37.

21. Hist (S), 2d ADVON, Nov 1961-Oct 1962, pp 97-98; intvw (S), J. W. Grainger, 2d ADVON Historian, with Capt Donald V. MacKellar, ALO/FAC Sec, AOC, 29 Aug 62.

22. Hist (S), 2d ADVON, Nov 1961-Oct 1962, p 97; FAC Ops in SEA, 1961-1965, p 11; III Corps ALO rprt for Mar 1964 (C), Lt Col David S. Mellish, 15 Apr 64, p 4; EOT Rprt (S), Lt Col Robert L. Gleason, Comdr Det 2A, 4400th CCT Sq (17 Nov 61-2 Mar 62), 20 Mar 62.

23. Memo (S), Capts Thomas N. Cairney and Donald K. Evans, 2d ADVON FAC's, to 2d ADVON Comdr, subj: Summary of 2nd ADVON FAC Activities in SVN, 17 May 62, pp 1-8, p 1 of atch 3, atch 10; msg (S), JOC to 2d ADVON/13th AF, subj: Forward Air Controllers, 10 Mar 62; FAC Ops in SEA, 1961-1965, pp 15-16.

24. See note above; ltr (S), 2d ADVON FAC's to Dep Dir/JOC, subj: Utilization of T-28 for Airborne FAC's, 12 Apr 62; hist (S), 2d Air Div, Jan-Jun 1964, I, 63, II, 46; rpt (S), Capts Thomas N. Cairney and Donald K. Evans, 2d ADVON FAC's, to Dep Dir/JOC, 14 Feb 62, pp 3-4; Warren A. Trest, Control of Air Strikes in SEA, 1961-1966 (TS) (HQ PACAF, Project CHECO, 1 Mar 67),

pp 5-6; memo (S), Cairney and Evans, to 2d ADVON Comdr, 17 May 62, pp 3-4 of atch 3; intvw (S), J. W. Grainger, 2d ADVON Historian, with Maj Carl G. Schneider, Chief ALO/FAC Sec, AOC, 2 Jun 63; hist (S), TAC, Jul-Dec 1962, I, 99-100.

25. Airpower Evaluation, pp 4-7, 4-8; TACS, Jan 1965-Mar 1968, 5; intvw (S), author with Col David M. Murane, Dir/Doctrine, Concepts, and Objectives, 26 Nov 73 [Murane was CAS Duty Off, II ASOC, SVN (26 Feb 62-19 Feb 63].

26. Lt Col Donald F. Martin and Carl O. Clever, Contemporary Historical Evaluation of Counterinsurgency Operations, October 1961-December 1963 (TS) (HQ PACAF, Project CHECO, May 1964), Pt II, The Threat, pp 1-3; PACOM Weekly Intelligence Digest (S), Vols 19-62, 39-62.

27. Schneider intvw (S), 2 Jun 63; hists (S), TAC, Jul-Dec 1962, pp 528-532, Jan-Jun 1963, p 42; Chronology, p 16.

28. FAC Ops in SEA, 1961-1965, pp 26, 30; intvw (S), Kenneth Sams, 2d ADVON Historian, with Maj Julius R. Conti, Ch ALO/FAC Sec, AOC, 6 Aug 62; hists (S), TAC, Jan-Jun 1963, pp 587-88, 2d Air Div, Jan-Jun 1964, I, 76.

29. FAC Ops in SEA, 1961-1965, pp 25-27; msg 2CCR-62-162E (S), 2d ADVON to ASOC's I and II, May 1962; III Corps ALO rprt for Mar 1964 (C), Lt Col David S. Mellish, 15 Apr 64, p 5.

30. Capt Edward Vallentiny, VNAF FAC Operations in SVN (S) (HQ PACAF, Project CHECO, 28 Jan 69), pp 8-9, 19; Martin and Clever, Contemporary Historical Evaluation of Counterinsurgency Operations, October 1961-December 1963, Pt VI, Support Activities, p 28; EOT Rprt (S), Lt Col Bill A. Montgomery, I ASOC ALO, 27 Jun 65; hist (S), 2d Air Div, Jan-Jun 1964, IV, 22; FAC Ops in SEA, 1961-1965, pp 31-33.

31. SECDEF Confs (TS), 6 May 1963, p 3-k, 20 Nov 63, p A-1-4; Martin and Clever, Support Activities, pp 19-20; FAC Ops in SEA, 1961-1965, pp 31-32.

Notes to pages 15-17

32. Maj Louis Seig, Impact of Geography on Air Operations in SEA (S) (HQ PACAF, Project CHECO, 11 Jun 70), pp xi, 1, 11-15, 25-28.

33. Ibid.

34. Draft rprt (S), 2d Air Div, Farm Gate Tactics and Techniques, Jun-Dec 62 [ca Jan 1963, hereinafter cited as Farm Gate Tactics]; Night Ops in SEA, pp 16-18; Brown intvw (S), 14 Sep 70; intvw (S), Lt Col Vaughn Gallacher and Maj Lyn Officer, AU, with Maj Frank J. Gorski, Jr., Maxwell AFB, 5 Feb 73 [Gorski served as a Farm Gate T-28 pilot (1962-1963) in SVN, and flew A-26's out-country in 1964].

35. See note above; Airpower Evaluation, Bk 2, 6-58 to 6-58C; Capt Owen L. Dawson, Jr., and Lawrence G. Starkey, Air Ordnance for Counterinsurgency Operations in South Vietnam (U) (2d ADVON Ops Analys Paper 2A, 16 Jun 62); Kimes intvw (C), 26 Nov 73.

36. See note above.

37. See note 35; hist (S), 2d Air Div, Jan-Jun 1964, IV, 29-31; Dawson and Starkey, Air Ordnance for Counterinsurgency Operations In South Vietnam: Airpower Evaluation, Bk 2, 6-58C to 6-60.

38. See note above; Farm Gate Tactics; Capt Owen L. Dawson, Jr., and Bernard Kornhauser, Weapons Selection in the 2nd ADVON Theater of Operations (S) (2d ADVON Ops Analys Paper 1, 16 Mar 62); PACAF rprt (S), In-Country and Out-Country Strike Operations in Southeast Asia, Vol II, Hardware, Munitions, 1 January 1965-31 December 1969, 1 Dec 1971 [hereinafter cited as Hardware, Munitions].

39. See note above; Gorski intvw (S), 5 Feb 73.

40. Airpower Evaluation, Bk 2, p 6-62; Dawson and Starkey, Air Ordnance for Counterinsurgency Operations in South Vietnam; Farm Gate Tactics; Gorski intvw (S), 5 Feb 73; hist (S), 2d Air Div, Jul-Dec 1964, I, 42-43; L. E. Paterson, Evolution of the Rules of Engagement for Southeast Asia, 1960-1965 (TS) (HQ PACAF, Project CHECO,

20 Sep 69), p 16; hist (S), 2d ADVON, Nov 1961-Oct 1962, pp 138-146.

41. See note above.

42. See note 40.

43. Hardware, Munitions, 19-20, 22-23; Airpower Evaluation, Bk 2, 6-64; Farm Gate Tactics.

44. Airpower Evaluation, Bk 2, 6-64 to 6-68.

45. Ibid.

46. Night Ops in SEA, p 12; Brown intvw (S), 14 Sep 70; intvw (S), author with Maj Charles W. Brown, Dir/Plans, 28 Apr 71 [Brown served as Air Ops Off, CSD, SVN (Aug-Nov 1962].

47. Hist (S), 2d ADVON, Nov 1961-Oct 1962, pp 99, 127-133; FAC Ops in SEA, 1961-1965, p 25; Schneider intvw (S), 2 Jun 63.

48. See note as above.

49. FAC Ops in SEA, 1961-1965, p 15 (footnote), chap III; memo (S), Cairney and Evans, to 2d ADVON Comdr, 17 May 62, atch 10; Farm Gate Tactics, p 11; intvw (S), Maj Thomas J. Hickman, 2d Air Div Historian, with Capt Jerry Rhein, FAC pilot, 3 Jan 63; hist (S), 2d Air Div, Jan-Jun 1964, I, 68-69.

50. Hists (S), 2d ADVON, Nov 1961-Oct 1962, pp 111-14; 2d Air Div, Jan-Jun 1964, I, 74; MacKellar intvw (S), 29 Aug 62; intvw (S), J. W. Grainger, 2d Air Div Historian, with Capt John C. Artley, USAF FAC, 23 Feb 63; FAC Ops in SEA, 1961-1965, pp 59-61; Murane intvw (S), 26 Nov 73.

51. Night Ops in SEA, 1961-1965, p 61; hist (S), 2d Air Div, Jan-Jun 1964, I, 74; JCS Study, AF-115, AF-116; Murane intvw (S), 26 Nov 73; MacKellar intvw (S), 29 Aug 62; Airpower Evaluation, Bk 2, 6-35 to 6-37.

52. Capt Robert L. Vining, Air Operations in the Delta (S) (HQ PACAF, Project CHECO, 8 Dec 67), p 6; hist (S), 2d ADVON, Nov 1961-Oct 1962, p 100; intvw (S), Maj Dean S. Gausche and J. W. Grainger, 2d Air Div historians, with Maj Gen Rollen H. Anthis, 2d Air Div Comdr, 20 Aug 63; intvw (S), J. W. Grainger, 2d Air Div historian, with Capt Bryant L. Ruhman, ALO/FAC Sec, AOC, 3 Jul 63.

53. FAC Ops in SEA, 1961-1965, pp 65-67; Brown intvws (S), 14 Sep 70, 28 Apr 71.

54. FAC Ops in SEA, 1961-1965, pp 67-71; hists (S), 2d ADVON, Nov 1961-Oct 1962, pp 100-115, 2d Air Div, Jan-Jun 1964, IV, 25-27; Brown intvw (S), 28 Apr 71; MacKellar intvw (S), 29 Aug 62.

55. See note above.

56. See note 54; Chronology, p 47; Fact Sheet 47 (U), VNAF Air Request Net, 18 Jun 64; hist (S), 2d Air Div, Jan-Jun 1964, I, 66, 77-80, and II, p 46; EOT Rprt (S), Lt Col Milton R. Pierce, IV Corps ALO, 24 Jul 64; Kimes intvw (C), 26 Nov 73.

57. Hist (S), 2d ADVON, Nov 1961-Oct 1962, pp 103-5; FAC Ops in SEA, 1961-1965, p 95.

58. See note above; MacKellar intvw (S), 29 Aug 62; Rhein intvw (S), 3 Jan 63.

59. Hist (S), 2d ADVON, Nov 1961-Oct 1962, pp 103-5; FAC Ops in SEA, 1961-1965, pp 94-96; Kimes intvw (C), 26 Nov 73; intvw (S), author, et al, Ofc/AF Hist, with Lt Col Roy C. Dalton, JCS, 8 Feb 73 [Dalton was a Farm Gate B-26 pilot in SVN (Jul-Dec 1962) and a Water Pump FAC out-country (Nov 1965-May 1966)]; Gorski intvw (S), 5 Feb 73; Brown intvw (S), 14 Sep 70.

60. See note above.

61. Kimes intvw (C), 26 Nov 73; Gorski intvw (S), 5 Feb 73; Dalton intvw (S), 8 Feb 73; Airpower Evaluation, Bk 2, 6-70 to 6-73.

62. Hist (S), 2d ADVON, Nov 1961-Oct 1962, p 103; MacKellar intvw (S), 29 Aug 62; Gleason EOT Rprt (S), 20 Mar 62; Rhein intvw (S), 3 Jan 63.

63. See note above; memo (S), Cairney and Evans, to 2d ADVON Comdr, 17 May 62, pp 2-4 of atch 10; intvw (S), J. W. Grainger, 2d Air Div historian, with Capt Harwood D. Towner, TDY FAC, 3 Jun 63; hist (S), 2d Air Div, Jan-Jun 1964, IV, 18; EOT Rprt (U), Lt Col John J. Wilfong, 19th TASq Comdr (Jul 1963-Mar 1964), 30 Jun 64; final rprt (S), AF Test Unit--Vietnam, Operational Test and Evaluation, TACS in Republic of Vietnam, 25 Feb 64, p 12.

64. Rhein intvw (S), 3 Jan 63; Towner intvw (S), 3 Jun 63; Gorski intvw (S), 5 Feb 73.

65. See note above; hist (S), 13th AF, Jul-Dec 1963, I, 71; Farm Gate Tactics.

66. See note above.

67. Kimes intvw (C), 26 Nov 73; Gorski intvw (S), 5 Feb 73; Dalton intvw (S), 8 Feb 73; Airpower Evaluation, Bk 2, 6-70 to 6-73.

68. See note above; SAWC Working Paper (U), Special Air Warfare Strike-Recce Forces in Counterinsurgency (USAFSAWC, Oct 1964), pp 51-53 [hereinafter cited as SAW Strike-Recce Forces].

69. Gorski intvw (S), 5 Feb 73; Kimes intvw (C), 26 Nov 73; SAW Strike-Recce Forces, pp 50-51.

70. See note above.

71. Dalton intvw (S), 8 Feb 73.

72. Ibid.; Kimes intvw (C), 26 Nov 73; Brown intvw (S), 14 Sep 70.

73. Dalton intvw (S), 8 Feb 73; final rprt (C), Tactical Analysis of B-26 Aircraft in the Republic of Vietnam (Proj 63-2, 13th AF, 30 Apr 63), pp 19-21 [hereinafter cited as B-26 Analysis]; Airpower Evaluation, Bk 2, 6-75.

74. Dalton intvw (S), 8 Feb 73; B-26 Analysis, pp 19-21; SAW Strike-Recce Forces, p 52.

75. See note above.

76. Rhein intvw (S), 3 Jan 63; Kimes intvw (C), 26 Nov 73; msg (S), CINCPAC to JCS, 282020Z Aug 62; msg (S), COMUSMACV to CINCPAC, 290720Z Aug 62; FAC Ops in SEA, 1961-1965, p 95.

Notes to pages 33-35

77. See note above.

78. Airpower Evaluation, Bk 2, 6-70 to 6-73; hist (S), USAFSAWC, 27 Apr-31 Dec 62, pp 199-200; ltr (C), Det 2 Alpha to 2d ADVON Comdr, 4 Aug 62.

79. See note above.

80. See note 78.

81. Hildreth, USAF Counterinsurgency Doctrines and Capabilities, 1961-1962, p 25.

82. King intvw (S), 4 Sep 69.

83. Night Ops in SEA, pp 6-7, 15-16; Dalton intvw (S), 8 Feb 73; Gorski intvw (S), 5 Feb 73; hist (S), 2d Air Div, Jan-Jun 1964, IV, 43-44; Farm Gate Tactics; intvw (S), Maj Victor B. Anthony, Ofc/AF Hist, with Maj Roy H. Lynn, Jr., Dir/Ops Rqmts and Dev Plans, 9 Sep 70 [Lynn was a Farm Gate pilot in SVN during 1963].

84. See note above.

85. Night Ops in SEA, p 8; Lynn intvw (S), 9 Sep 70; Airpower Evaluation, Bk 2, 6-70 to 6-73.

86. Gorski intvw (S), 5 Feb 73; Kimes intvw (C), 26 Nov 73; Brown intvws (S), 14 Sep 70, 28 Apr 71; Lynn intvw (S), 9 Sep 70; Night Ops in SEA, pp 7-14; 2d Air Div Reg 55-18 (S), Procedures for Night Close Air Support, 2 Aug 63; SECDEF Conf (TS), 6 May 63, p 3-3, L. E. Paterson, Evolution of the Rules of Engagement for Southeast Asia, 1960-1965 (TS) (HQ PACAF, Project CHECO, 30 Sep 66), p 12; hist (S), 2d Air Div, Jan-Jun 1964, IV, 14; Trest, Control of Air Strikes in SEA, 1961-1966, pp 21-22.

87. See note above.

88. Lynn intvw (S), 9 Sep 70; hist (S), 24th TGp, Jan-Jun 1964, atch, C-47 Tactics [ca 1963-1964]; 2d Air Div Reg 55-18 (S), 2 Aug 63; hist (S), 2d ADVON, Nov 1961-Oct 1962, p 128; B-26 Analysis, p 37; Night Ops in SEA, pp 9-10, 11-14.

89. See note above; Kimes intvw (C), 26 Nov 73; Brown intvw (S), 14 Sep 70; intvw (S), Maj Victor B. Anthony, Ofc/AF Hist, with Lt Col John L. Piotrowski, Dir/Plans, 21 Sep 70 [Piotrowski was a Farm Gate pilot in SVN].

90. Brown intvw (S), 14 Sep 70; Piotrowski intvw (S), 21 Sep 70; Night Ops in SEA, pp 13-14.

91. Brown intvw (S), 14 Sep 70.

92. Ibid.; Piotrowski intvw (S), 21 Sep 70; Dalton intvw (S), 8 Feb 73; B-26 Analysis, pp 3-5, 37.

93. Dalton intvw (S), 8 Feb 73; B-26 Analysis, pp 3-5, 37; Night Ops in SEA, p 14.

94. Col Ray L. Bowers, The Air Force in Southeast Asia, Tactical Airlift (TS), comment ed (Ofc/AF Hist, 1971, 1973, 1975), Vol I, 1971, 125-26, Vol II, 1973, 399-400; Book of Actions in Southeast Asia, 1961-1964 (S), pp 24-25, in USAF Archives 6-4995-52; Lawrence J. Hickey, Night Close Air Support in RVN, 1961-1966 (S) (HQ PACAF, Project CHECO, 15 Mar 67), p 32; Night Ops in SEA, p 24.

95. EOT Rprt (S), Lt Col Harry G. Howton, 311th ACSq Comdr, 6 Sep 65; hist (S), 2d Air Div, Jan-Jun 1964, IV, 43-44.

96. Intvw (S), Maj Dean Gausche, Proj CHECO historian, with Lt Col Thomas E. Kennedy, 315th TAGp Comdr, 4 Feb 64; Night Ops in SEA, pp 24-25; Trest, Control of Air Strikes in SEA, 1961-1966, pp 21-22.

97. Night Ops in SEA, pp 24-26; PACAF Tactics and Techniques Bul 7 (U), Troop Carrier/Transport Tactics, 25 May 65; ltr (C), 6002d Stan/Eval Gp, subj: PACAF Tactics/Techniques (Bulletin #12), 17 Jun 65.

98. See note above.

99. Hist (S), 2d Air Div, Jan-Jun 1964, II, 16-17; Gleason EOT Rprt (S), 20 Mar 62; Night Ops in SEA, pp 8-11.

100. See note above.

Notes to pages 40-45

101. Hist (S), 2d Air Div, Jan-Jun 1964, IV, 44; Bowers, Tactical Airlift, II, 399-400; Night Ops in SEA, pp 15-16.

102. See note above.

103. Hist (S), 2d Air Div, Jan-Jun 1964, I, 11-16, IV, 13-14; hist (TS), Rules of Engagement in Southeast Asia, 1957-1965 (PACAF, Oct 1968), p vii.

104. Hist (S), 2d Air Div, II, 12-15.

105. Hist (C), 34th TGp, Jul-Dec 1964, pp 6-7; Airpower Evaluation, Bk 2, 6-75.

106. See note above; SAW Strike-Recce Forces, pp 47-48.

107. Airpower Evaluation, Bk 2, 6-75; SAW Strike-Recce Forces, pp 49-50.

108. Night Ops in SEA, p 13; Airpower Evaluation, Bk 2, 6-51 to 6-54.

109. Night Ops in SEA, p 16.

110. B-26 Analysis, pp 3-5; EOT Rprt (S), Maj William D. Palank, in Tab. I, hist (S), USAFSAWC, 27 Apr-31 Dec 62.

111. Hist (S), 2d Air Div, Jan-Jun 1964, I, 45-55; Airpower Evaluation, Bk 2, 6-51 to 6-56.

112. Hist (S), 2d Air Div, Jan-Jun 1964, I, 45-57.

113. Ibid., pp 45-55; Airpower Evaluation, Bk 2, 6-51 to 6-56.

114. See note above.

115. See note 113; Strike Aircraft, 171-77.

116. Hist (S), 2d Air Div, Jan-Jun 1964, I, 21-22, 40-55, 62.

117. Strike Aircraft, 109-115.

118. Ibid., 117-125; hists (S), TAC, Jan-Jun 1963, I, 63; 56th SOWg, Jul-Dec 1968, I, 23; 2d Air Div, Jan-Jun 1964, I, 40-47; Jul-Dec 1965, I, 89-90; hist (C), 34th TGp, Jul-Dec 1964, pp 8-10; Night Ops in SEA, pp 110-11; Airpower Evaluation, Bk 2, 6-56, 6-57.

119. Hist (S), 2d Air Div, Jul-Dec 1964, II, 39-41; hist (C), 34th TGp, Jul-Dec 1964, pp 7-10.

120. See note above.

121. See note 119.

122. Hist (S), 2d Air Div, Jul-Dec 1964, I, 44-45; hist (C), 34th TGP, Jul-Dec 1964, pp 7-10.

123. Hist (S), 2d Air Div, Jan-Jun 1964, II, 16-17; PACAF Tactics and Techniques Bul 15 (C), Daisy Cutter, FC-47, 22 Jul 65; hist (C), 34th TGp, Jan-Jul 1965, p 4; Night Ops in SEA, p 18.

124. Hist (C), 34th TGp, 1 Jan-8 Jul 64, pp 4-5; hist (S), 2d Air Div, Jul-Dec 1964, I, 47-48; Kenneth Sams, Escalation of the the War in Southeast Asia, July-December 1964 (TS) (HQ PACAF, Project CHECO, 1965), pp 49-52; hist (S), 2d Air Div, Jan-Jun 1964, IV, 31-34.

125. Sams, Escalation of the War in Southeast Asia, July-December 1964, pp 49-52; hist (S), 2d Air Div, Jul-Dec 1964, I, 49-50.

126. Hists (S), 2d Air Div, Jan-Jun 1964, IV, 31-34, Jul-Dec 1964, I, 42-43; hist (C), 34th TGp, 1 Jan-8 Jul 64, pp 4-5; Airpower Evaluation, Bk 2, 6-62; Hardware, Munitions, 19-24.

127. Kenneth Sams, First Test and Combat Use of the AC-47 (S) (HQ PACAF, Project CHECO, 8 Dec 65), pp 1-2; Lt Col Jack S. Ballard, Development and Employment of Fixed-Wing Gunships 1962-1971 (S) (Ofc/AF Hist, Jan 1974), p 18 [hereinafter cited as Gunships]; hist (S), 2d Air Div, Jul-Dec 1964, I, 45-47; Sams, Escalation of the War in Southeast Asia, July-December 1964, pp 52-55.

128. Hist (S), 2d Air Div, Jul-Dec 1964, I, 45-47; Gunships, p 21; Sams, Escalation of the War in Southeast Asia, July-December 1964, pp 52-55.

Notes to pages 50-54

129. Gunships, p 24.

130. Ibid., pp 25-27; Sams, Escalation of the War in Southeast Asia, July-December 1964, pp 52-55.

131. See note above.

132. Sams, First Test and Combat Use of the AC-47, pp 3-4; Gunships, pp 27-28.

133. Hist (S), 2d Air Div, Jul-Dec 1964, I, 62-63; Trest, Control of Air Strikes in SEA, 1961-1966, p 25; Sams, Escalation of the War in Southeast Asia, July-December 1964, pp 117-18.

134. FAC Ops in SEA, 1961-1965, pp 48-49.

135. See note above.

Chapter III

1. Chronology of Events Pertaining to US Involvement in the War in Vietnam and Southeast Asia (U) (MACV, 29 Sep 72) [hereinafter cited as MACV Chronology]; Adm U. S. G. Sharp and Gen William C. Westmoreland, Report on the War in Vietnam (As of 30 June 1968), Sec II, Report on Operations in South Vietnam, January 1964-June 1968 (Washington, 1968), pp 97-104 [hereinafter cited as Sharp and Westmoreland Report]; Charles B. MacDonald and Charles V. P. von Luttichau, American Military History, chap 29 (revised), The U. S. Army in Vietnam (DAMH), U. S. Army, 1969), pp 622-24.

2. See note above.

3. See note 1; Wesley R. C. Melyan, The War in Vietnam, 1965 (TS) (HQ PACAF, Project CHECO, 25 Jan 67), pp 14-16, 23-26; rprt (U), MACV, Lessons in Strategy, 25 May 68; MacDonald and Luttichau, American Military History, pp 623-27.

4. See note above; Sharp and Westmoreland Report, pp 97-104.

5. Illustrated History of the United States Air Force in Southeast Asia (U), comment ed (Ofc/AF Hist, Jul 1974), chap III [hereinafter cited as Illustrated History].

6. MacDonald and Luttichau, *American Military History*, pp 626-29; rprt (U), MACV, 25 May 68.

7. See note above; *Sharp and Westmoreland Report*, pp 113-136; *Illustrated History*, chap III; *MACV Chronology*.

8. See note above; rprt (U), MACV, 25 May 68; MacDonald and Luttichau, *American Military History*, pp 632-36.

9. See note above.

10. See note 8.

11. *MACV Chronology*; rprt (U), MACV, 25 May 68; *Sharp and Westmoreland Report*, pp 157-170.

12. See note above; *Illustrated History*, chap III.

13. See note above; Bernard C. Nalty, *Air Power and the Fight for Khe Sanh* (Ofc/AF Hist, 1973).

14. See note above.

15. Hist (TS), *Rules of Engagement in Southeast Asia, 1957-1965* (PACAF, Oct 1968), pp xxi, 106-7; hist (C), 34th TGp, 1 Jan-8 Jul 65, pp 1-3.

16. Team Report on Requirements for ALO/FAC/SCAR/Navigators and Aircraft in SEA (S), PACAF, 22 Nov 68, pp 2-3 [hereinafter cited as SEA FAC Requirements].

17. Rprt (S), *Analysis of Close Air Support Operations* (Dir/Doctrine, Concepts, and Objectives, 14 Aug 66), pp I-2, I-3; Goldberg and Smith, *Army-Air Force Relations: The Close Air Support Issue*, pp 24-27.

18. Rprt (C), Maj William E. Powers [unit unk], Airmobile Operations in 21st ARVN Division, 2 Aug 65.

19. Goldberg and Smith, *Army-Air Force Relations: The Close Air Support Issue*, pp 32-33.

20. Maj James B. Overton, FAC Operations in Close Air Support Role in SVN (S) (HQ PACAF, Project CHECO, 31 Jan 69), p 4.

21. Ernie S. Montagliani and Capt John R. Wohnsigl, The DASC's in II Corps Tactical Zone, July 1965-June 1969 (S) (HQ PACAF, Project CHECO, 31 Aug 69), p 3; Overton, FAC Operations in Close Air Support Role in SVN, pp 9-10.

22. Lt Col Thomas D. Wade, Seventh Air Force Tactical Air Control Center Operations (S) (HQ PACAF, Project CHECO, 15 Oct 68), pp 19-24; Capt Russell W. Mank, TACC Fragging Procedures (S) (HQ PACAF, Project CHECO, 15 Aug 69), p 2; MACV Dir 95-11 (C), Aviation, Joint Air-Ground Operations System (JAGOS), 21 Jun 66; hist data record (S), 7th AF TACC, Jan-Jun 1966; MACV Lessons Learned 77 (C), Fire Support Coordination in the Republic of Vietnam, 20 May 70, p C-3; TAC Rprt 73-13, (S), 1 Mar 73, p 64.

23. See note above.

24. USMACV Tactical Air Firepower Board Report (C) (MACV, 20 Oct 65), App 1, p 3 [hereinafter cited as Air Firepower Report]; ltr (U), CSAF to CSA, subj: Concept of Improved Joint Air-Ground Coordination, 19 Mar 65, atch 1, pp 1-5; Wade, Seventh Air Force Tactical Air Control Center Operations, pp 20-22; intvw (U), Lt Col Vaughan Gallacher, Sp Acq Br, AU, with Lt Col Joe Madden, HQ AU, 7 Feb 73 [Madden served in SEA as ALO, 1st Bde, 4th Inf Div (Apr 1967-Mar 1968)].

25. Ltr (U), CSAF to CSA, 19 Mar 65, atch 1, pp 4-5; Lessons Learned 77 (C), 20 May 70, pp C-1 to C-5, C-7 to C-9; Wade, Seventh Air Force Tactical Air Control Center Operations, pp 20-22; MACV Dir 95-11 (C), 21 Jun 66; Melvin F. Porter, Air Response to Immediate Air Requests in SVN (S) (HQ PACAF, Project CHECO, 15 Jul 69), pp 5-11; Air Firepower Report, App 1, pp 3-4; rprt (C), A Comparative Analysis of Air Force and Marine Corps Close Air Support Performance in South Vietnam (JCS CAS Study Gp, 19 Feb 66), pp 8-10 [hereinafter cited as Close Air Support Performance]; EOT Rprt (C), Brig Gen George W. McLaughlin, Dir/7th AF TACC (May 1968-May 1969), 25 Jul 69.

26. Capt Louis M. McDermott, III DASC Operations (S) (HQ PACAF, Project CHECO, 1 Aug 69), pp 6-8; Air Firepower Report, App 1, pp 1-35; Wade, Seventh Air Force Tactical Air Control Center Operations, pp 32-34.

27. See note above.

28. Close Air Support Performance, pp 8-10; Porter, Air Response to Immediate Air Requests in SVN, pp 5-8, 11; McLaughlin EOT Rprt (C), 25 Jul 69; MACV Lessons Learned 77 (C), 20 May 70, pp C-1 to C-5; EOT Rprt (C), Lt Col Donald G. Page, ALO 4th ARVN Corps (Mar-May 1965), Chief, Sp Proj Br, 7th AF TACC (May 1965-Jan 1966) [ca Feb 1966].

29. Lt Col Ralph A. Rowley, FAC Operations, 1965-1970 (Ofc/AF Hist, May 1975), chap III; Overton, FAC Operations in Close Air Support Role in SVN, pp 32-36; PACAF rprt (S), Task: Intelligence Collection, Subtask: Visual Reconnaissance in SEA, 1 January 1962-31 March 1968, 30 Sep 70, pp 49-52 [hereinafter cited as VR in SEA, 1 Jan 62-31 Mar 68]; draft rprt (S), Establishment of an Effective SEAsia Tactical Air Control System, 1 Jan 65-31 Mar 68 (Dir/Ops, undated), pp 2-22 to 2-24, 2-36.

30. Rowley, FAC Operations, 1965-1970, pp 51-54; Capt Joseph V. Potter, OV-10 Operations in SEAsia (S) (HQ PACAF, Project CHECO, 15 Sep 69), p 16.

31. Strike Aircraft, 111-13, 117-125.

32. Strike Aircraft, 1-13, 17-26; intvw (U), author with Col Donald H. Hooten, Dir/Ops, 4 Jun 73 [Hooten was 9th TFSq Comdr at Bien Hoa AB, SVN (Aug 1966-Aug 1967)].

33. Strike Aircraft, 21-30.

34. Strike Aircraft, 126-138; hist (TS), PACAF, Jan-Dec 1966, I, pt 1, 59-61, 318-325; Standard Aircraft Characteristics, B-57, AFG-2 (U), Vol I, Addn 39 (AFSC, Feb 1965), 1; PACAF Tactics and Techniques Bul 19 (C), 3 Sep 65, p 1; Night Ops in SEA, pp 123-25.

35. See note above.

Notes to pages 67-71

36. Hist (TS), PACAF, Jan-Dec 1966, I, 323-25; intvw (S), Maj Victor B. Anthony, Ofc/AF Hist, with Col James J. Gearhart, Dir/Ops, 18 May 71 [Gearhart served in SEA as Asst Ops Off and Flt Ldr, 13th and 8th Tac Bomb Sqs (1967-1969)]; EOT Rprt (S), Lt Col Kenneth S. Smith, 8th Tac Bomb Sq Comdr (Nov 1968-May 1969) [ca Jun 1969]; Night Ops in SEA, pp 124-25.

37. See note above.

38. See note 36.

39. USAF Management Summary Southeast Asia Review (S), 24 Jul 70, p 7; Strike Aircraft, 62-63; Night Ops in SEA, pp 132-34.

40. Strike Aircraft, 63-67, 95-106; Night Ops in SEA, pp 132-34.

41. See note above.

42. Strike Aircraft, 100-04; rprt (S), USAF 1970 Tactical Fighter Symposium (USAFTAWC, 4-8 May 70), pp 33-34

43. Strike Aircraft, 183-85, 188-197; Final Report (S), Combat Evaluation of the F-5 Aircraft "Skoshi Tiger" (TAC, Apr 1966), p i [hereinafter cited as Skoshi Tiger Evaluation]; hist (C), 35th TFWg, Jan-Jun 1966.

44. Strike Aircraft, 183-85, 188-197; Skoshi Tiger Evaluation, pp 1-8, 61, 67; hist (C), 35th TFWg, Jan-Jun 1966.

45. See note above.

46. Strike Aircraft, 142-150; AF Info Sheet (U), A-37, Jul 1967.

47. See note above; Final Report (S), Combat Evaluation of the A-37A Aircraft Combat Dragon (TAC, 1 Apr 68), pp 1-3, 12, 27.

48. See note above.

49. Intvw (U), author with Col Scott G. Smith, Dir/Ops, 10 Oct 73 [Smith was Dep Dir/7th AF TACC (Jul 1969-Jul 1970) and 432 TFWg Comdr (Apr 1972-Apr 1973)]; Strike Aircraft, pp 21-22; hist (S), 37th TFWg, Oct-Dec 1968, I, 23.

50. Maj A. W. Thompson, Strike Control and Reconnaissance (SCAR) in SEA (S) (HQ PACAF, Project CHECO, 22 Jan 69), pp 52-65; TAC/TAWC rprt (TS), Forward Air Control Operations in Southeast Asia, Vol II, 1 January 1965-31 March 1968, 10 Nov 69, 5c-5e; Working Paper 66/11 (C), 7th AF, An Evaluation of the Visual Reconnaissance Program in South Vietnam, 20 Sep 66, pp 5-12.

51. Intvw (C), author with Maj Richard L. W. Henry, Dir/Ops, 4-5 Jan 72 [Henry, 21st TASSq, was an ALO in Darloc and Binh Thuan Provinces, II Corps, SVN (16 Jan 68-12 Jan 69)]; intvw (U), author with Maj John F. Campbell, Dir/Ops, 4 Jan 72 [Campbell was a 22d TASSq ALO/FAC with ARVN in Kien Phong Province, IV Corps, SVN (31 Dec 68-19 Dec 69)]; Maj John R. Bode, Command and Control of Air-Delivered Fire Support in Vietnam (C) (ACS/Studies and Analysis, Sep 1970), pp 28-29; 504th TASGp Manual 55-3 (U), Forward Air Control Tactics Manual, 1 Mar 70, p 2-2.

52. See note above; MACV Lessons Learned 77 (C), 20 May 70, pp C-17 to C-20; Henry intvw (C), 4-5 Jan 72; intvw (C), author with Lt Col John R. Bode, ACS/Studies and Analysis, 4, 19 Jan 72 [Bode was a 19th TASSq ALO/FAC with 1st Bde, 25th Inf Div, Tay Ninh, III Corps, SVN (Oct 1968-Oct 1969)].

53. McDermott, III DASC Operations, pp 8-10; MACV Lessons Learned 77 (C), 20 May 70, pp C-17 to C-20; Bode, Command and Control of Air-Delivered Fire Support in Vietnam, pp 28-33; intvw (S), author with Lt Col Stuart E. Kane and Capt Gary Sheets, HQ TAC, 17 May 70 [Kane was ALO, 1st Cav Div (Jul 1965-Mar 1966), Sheets a FAC, 20th TASSq (Jul-Oct 1966) and TIS (Dec 1966-Feb 1967)]; Henry intvw (C), 4-5 Jan 72; Bode intvw (C), 4, 19 Jan 72; TACM/PACAFM/USAFEM 3-1 (S), CAS Strike Tactics, 30 Sep 71, pt II.

54. See note above; ltr (U), III Corps ALO to III Corps Army Staff, subj: Close Air Support in III CTZ, 10 Aug 67; intvw (U), author with Col John R. Stoner, HQ TAC, 18 May 70 [Stoner was ALO, 1st Cav Div, An Khe, SVN (Jul 1965-Feb 1966)]; PACAF Tactics and Techniques Bul 59 (U), FAC Procedures, Target Marking, 24 Mar 67; 504th TASGp Manual 55-3 (U), 1 Mar 70, pp 5-8 to 5-10.

55. Ltr (U), III Corps ALO to III Corps Army Staff, 10 Aug 67; Stoner intvw (U), 18 May 70; PACAF Tactics and Techniques Bul 59 (U), 24 Mar 67; 504th TASGp Manual 55-3 (U), 1 Mar 70, pp 5-8 to 5-10.

56. See note above; Overton, FAC Operations in Close Air Support Role in SVN, pp 19-20; PACAF Tactics and Techniques Bul 47 (U), Forward Air Controlling, 29 Aug 66; intvw (U), author with Maj Donald M. Nagel, Dir/Studies and Analysis, 22 Jul 70 [Nagel was a Sector FAC in Binh Thuan Province, II Corps, SVN (Sep 1965-Aug 1966)].

57. 504th TASGp Manual 55-3 (U), 1 Mar 70, pp 5-10, 5-11; tng manual (U), 4410th CCT Sq, The Airborne Forward Air Controller, 8 Feb 67, pp 8-10; tng manual (U), 4410th CCT Wg, 0-2A Phase Training Manual, Mar 1968, pp 21-23.

58. See note above.

59. See note 57.

60. See note 57; 504th TASGp Manual 55-3 (U), 1 Mar 70, pp 5-12 to 5-17; Bode intvw (C), 4, 19 Jan 72; intvw (U), author with Capt Walter L. Johnson, HQ AFSC, 14 Dec 71 [Johnson was a FAC with 2d ARVN Div, Quang Ngai, SVN (1 Jan 69-15 Dec 69)].

61. See note above.

62. See note 60.

63. See note 60.

64. See note 60; Rowley, FAC Operations, 1965-1970, chap IV.

65. 504th TASGp Manual 55-3 (U), 1 Mar 70, pp 5-17 to 5-21.

66. Ibid.; tng manual (U), 4410th CCT Sq, 8 Feb 67, pp 10-15

67. See note above; Overton, FAC Operations in Close Air Support Role in SVN, pp 19-20; Campbell intvw (U), 4 Jan 72; PACAF Tactics and Techniques Bul 47 (U), 29 Aug 66.

68. See note above.

69. Tng Manual (U), 4410th CCT Sq, 8 Feb 67, pp 14-15.

70. Intvw (S), Lt Col Barry L. Bonwit, Sp Acq Br, AU, with Lt Col William Gutches, HQ AU, 15 Jul 68 (Gutches served as Ops Off, 1st ACSq, at Bien Hoa and Pleiku, SVN (1965-1966)].

71. PACAF Tactics and Techniques Bul 33 (S), A-1 Tactical Employment in SEA, 10 Jan 66; AFM 3-5 (U), Special Air Warfare Tactics, 18 Mar 66, pp 65-68; intvw (U), author with Lt Col Gordon C. Bruner, Dir/Ops, and Maj Brooks G. Bays, Dir/Ops, 4 Jun 73 [Bruner commanded the 23d TASSq (Jul 1970-Jul 1971) and Bays served with 602d TFWg and 19th and 23d TASSqs (Feb 1966-Jan 1967)]; SAW Strike-Recce Forces, pp 65-68.

72. See note above; ltr (U), 3d TFWg to 510th TFWg, subj: Delivery Techniques, 23 Mar 68.

73. Lee Bonetti, et al, The War in Vietnam, July-December 1967 (S) (HQ PACAF, Project CHECO, 29 Nov 68), pp 28-29; Henry's Handy Hints (U), 3d TFWg [ca June 1968]; EOT Rprt (S), Capt Frank N. Assaf, 602d FSq (Commando) (19 May 65-19 May 66) [ca Jun 1966]; EOT Rprt (C) Col Abner M. Aust, 31st TFWg Comdr (2 May 68-8 Feb 69) [ca Mar 1969].

74. C. William Thorndale, VC Offensive in III Corps, October-December 1967 (C) (HQ PACAF, Project CHECO, 15 May 68), pp 14-16.

75. Assaf EOT Rprt (S) [ca Jun 1966].

76. Ibid.

77. Ibid.; PACAF Tactics and Techniques Bul 47 (C), Napalm Delivery Variations, 4 Mar 66.

78. See note above.

79. See note 77.

80. Hooten intvw (U), 4 Jun 73.

Notes to pages 84-88

81. Ibid.; EOT Rprt (U), Maj Leslie R. Leavoy, 416th TFWg Comdr (Nov 1965-Mar 1966) and 90th TFWg Comdr (Mar-Oct 1966) at Bien Hoa, SVN, 10 Sep 66.

82. Henry's Handy Hints (U), 3d TFWg, 3 Jun 68; 12th TFWg Manual 3-1 (S), Cobra Tactics Manual, 30 Apr 71.

83. Hooten intvw (U), 4 Jun 73; EOT Rprt (C), Capt Gary W. Fredericks, F-100 pilot, 3d TFWg (10 Nov 65-6 Nov 66) [ca Dec 1966]; EOT Rprt (C), Col Robert A. Ackerly, 3d TFWg Comdr (10 Nov 65-2 Nov 66 [ca Dec 1966]; hist (S), 3d TFWg, Apr-Jun 1968, p 30; hist (C), 35th TFWg, Jul-Sep 1969, pp 23-32; EOT Rprt (S), Col Leroy J. Manor, Comdr, and Col Benjamin H. Clayton, Vice Comdr, 37th TFWg (1 May 68-1 Apr 69) [ca May 1969]; ltr (U), Maj Lyn R. Officer, to Maj Ralph A. Rowley, Ofc/AF Hist, 15 Jun 73 [Officer flew F-100's with the 37th TFWg (Apr 1967- Apr 1968)]; PACAF Tactics and Techniques Bul 36 (C), F-100 Air-to-Ground Tactics, 17 Feb 66.

84. PACAF Tactics and Techniques Bul 36 (C), 17 Feb 66; TACM/PACAFM/USAFEM 3-1 (S), 30 Sep 71, pt II, pp 8-31, 8-35.

85. See note above; Fredericks EOT Rprt (C) [ca Dec 1966]; ltr (U), Maj Lyn R. Officer, to Maj Ralph A. Rowley, Ofc/AF Hist, 15 Jun 73.

86. TACM/PACAFM/USAFEM 3-1 (S), 30 Sep 71, pt II, p 8-35; PACAF Tactics and Techniques Bul 36 (C), 17 Feb 66; ltr (U), Maj Lyn R. Officer, to Maj Ralph A. Rowley, Ofc/AF Hist, 15 Jun 73; Hooten intvw (U), 4 Jun 73.

87. TACM/PACAFM/USAFEM 3-1 (S), 30 Sep 71, pt II, pp 8-28 to 8-31; Fredericks EOT Rprt (C) [ca Dec 1966]; PACAF Tactics and Techniques Bul 63 (C), F-100 Combat Tactics, 22 May 67; ltr (U), Maj Lyn R. Officer, to Maj Ralph A. Rowley, Ofc/AF Hist, 15 Jun 73; Hooten intvw (U), 4 Jun 73.

88. See note above.

89. See note 87.

90. Hist (C), 35th TFWg, Jul-Sep 1969, pp 23-32.

91. Strike Aircraft, pp 63-67, 95-106; intvw (U), author with Lt Col Samuel E. Fields, Dir/Ops, 3 Oct 73 [Fields was an O-2A FAC (2 mos) then F-4 pilot at Cam Ranh Bay, SVN (Mar-Oct 1968)]; intvw (U), author with Lt Col Clifford D. Peterson, Dir/Ops, 3 Oct 73 [Peterson served as an F-4 pilot and flight commander, 421st TFSq, Da Nang, SVN (Feb 1970-Feb 1971)].

92. See note above.

93. Hist Data Record(S), 416th TFSq, Jan-Jun 1966; PACAF Tactics and Techniques Bul 57 (S), MSQ-77 in SEA, 27 Feb 67; Kenneth Sams, The Fall of A Shau (S) (HQ PACAF, Project CHECO, 18 Apr 66).

94. Herman S. Wolk, USAF Plans and Policies, R&D for Southeast Asia, 1965-1967 (TS) (Ofc/AF Hist, Jun 1969), pp 57-58; Night Ops in SEA, pp 203-04.

95. Futrell, Air Force in Korea, p 329.

96. Wolk, USAF Plans and Policies, R&D for Southeast Asia, 1965-1967, pp 57-58; PACAF Tactics and Techniques Bul 57 (S), 27 Feb 67.

97. See note above.

98. See note 96; Night Ops in SEA, pp 204-05; Hist Data Record (S), 416th TFSq, Jan-Jun 1966.

99. See note above.

100. See note 98; PACAF Tactics and Techniques Bul 57 (S), 27 Feb 67.

101. SAW Strike-Recce Forces, pp 76-81; AFM 3-5 (U), 18 Mar 66, pp 87-95.

102. See note above.

103. Gutches intvw (S), 15 Jul 68; SAW Strike-Recce Forces, pp 88-90; AFM 3-5 (U), 18 Mar 66, pp 97-98.

104. SAW Strike-Recce Forces, pp 91-93; AFM 3-5 (U), 18 Mar 66, pp 97-98.

105. See note above.

106. 12th TFWg Manual 3-1 (S), 30 Apr 71.

107. Ibid.

108. Kenneth Sams and Lt Col Bert B. Aton, USAF Support of Special Forces in SEA (S) (HQ PACAF, Project CHECO, 10 Mar 69), pp 1-4, 11-16; Paul S. Ello, et al, US Army Special Forces and Similar Internal Defense Advisory Operations in Mainland Southeast Asia, 1962-1967 (S) (Tech Paper RAC-TP-354, Rsch Analys Corp, McLean, Va., Jun 1969), p 1-2; Rowley, FAC Operations, 1965-1970, chap VII.

109. See note above.

110. Intvw (S), author with Col Marvin C. Patton, Dir/Budget, 4, 15 Feb 72 [Patton was ALO, 5th SF Gp (May 1967-May 1968)]; intvw (U), author with Lt Col Kenneth L. Kerr, HQ USAF, 31 Mar 72 [Kerr was a Proj Delta FAC during 1966]; intvw (U), Lt Col Vaughn Gallacher and Mr. Hugh N. Ahmann, Albert F. Simpson Hist Rsch Cen, with Maj Richard L. Griffin, HQ AU, 24 Mar 72 [Griffin was a Sector FAC, ARVN 24th Sp Zone, Pleiku and Kontum, SVN (Sep 1966-Sep 1967)]; Sams and Aton, USAF Support of Special Forces in SEA, pp 13-16; Col Robert M. Lowry, Study of ALO/FAC Support of Special Forces (S) (HQ DASC Alpha, Aug 1968).

111. Intvw (S), author and Col Ray L. Bowers, Ofc/AF Hist, with Col Eugene P. Deatrick, JCS, and Col Eleazer Parmly, USA Hopkins University, 9 May 72 [Deatrick was 1st Ac q Comdr, Pleiku, SVN (Feb 1966-Feb 1967), Parmly was SF Advisor to Laos (May 1960-May 1961) USSF Det Comdr, I and III Corps (Aug 1966-Jul 1967)]; Lowry, Study of ALO/FAC Support of Special Forces; Sams and Aton, USAF Support of Special Forces in SEA, pp 66-69; Rowley, FAC Operations, 1965-1970, chap VII.

112. Rowley, FAC Operations, 1965-1970, chap VII; Smith intvw (U), 10 Oct 73; intvw (S), author with Col Eugene P. Deatrick, JCS, 3 Feb 72; Sams and Aton, USAF Support of Special Forces in SEA, pp 13-16; Porter, Air Response to Immediate Air Requests in SVN, pp 19-25; McLaughlin EOT Rprt (C), 25 Jul 69.

113. Rowley, *FAC* *Operations,* *1965-1970,* chap VII; Sams and Aton, *USAF* *Support* *of* *Special* *Forces* *in* *SEA,* pp 45-46, 52.

114. Patton intvw (S), 4, 15 Feb 72; intvw (U), author with Capt David L. Shields, F-100 pilot, Cannon AFB, N. Mex., 10 Jan 72 [Shields was a FAC, 5th SF Gp, Proj Delta (Sep 1967-May 1968)]; intvw (S), author with Maj Allen R. Groth, F-100 pilot, Cannon AFB, N. Mex., 10 Jan 72 [Groth was a 5th AF Gp FAC, Proj Delta (Dec 1966-Oct 1967)]; Griffin intvw (U), 24 Mar 72.

115. See note above.

116. Patton intvw (S), 4, 15 Feb 72; Shields intvw (U), 10 Jan 72.

117. See note above.

118. See note 116; Groth intvw (S), 10 Jan 72.

119. See note above; Porter, *Air* *Response* *to* *Immediate* *Air* *Requests* *in* *SVN,* pp 19-25.

120. See note above; Griffin intvw (U), 24 Mar 72; intvw (U), Maj Richard B. Clement and Dr. James C. Hasdorff, Sp Acq Br, AU, with Maj Thomas W. Scott, HQ AU, 7 Apr 72 [Scott was ALO/FAC, 3d Mobile Strike Force, 5th SF Gp (Feb-Jul 1969)]; intvw (U), author with Col James R. Lindsay, HQ WPAFB, 10 Apr 72 [Lindsay became the first ALO, 5th SF Gp (Abn) (Oct 1966-1967)].

121. See note 118.

122. Deatrick intvw (S), 3 Feb 72; Deatrick and Parmly intvw (S), 9 May 72; intvw (U), author with Col Monroe E. Blaylock, Dir/Ops, 14 Apr 72 [Blaylock served as an A-1E pilot, 1st ACSq (1965-1966)]; intvw (C), author with Maj James R. Thyng, Dir/Studies and Analys, 8 Feb 72 [Thyng flew A-1E's with 1st ACSq (Sep 1966-Aug 1967)].

123. See note above.

124. See note 122.

Notes to pages 102-105

125. Hists (TS), Dir/Plans, Jan-Jun 1967, pp 383-85, Jan-Dec 1966, pp 170-76, Jan-Jun 1968, pp 163-65; PACAF rprt (TS), Out-Country Strike Operations in Southeast Asia, 1 January 1965-31 March 1968, I, Sub Task IIc, Strike Operations in Laos, 5 December 1965-21 October 1967, pp 45-48; Praire Fire Training and Tactics Manual (S), 19 Jul 70; MR (TS), CINCPAC, subj: Prairie Fire, Jul 1967; Trest, Control of Air Strikes in SEA, 1961-1966, pp 66-68.

126. See note above.

127. See note 125.

128. See note 125.

129. Ltr (S), Maj Robert W. Moore, Dir/Plans, to Lt Col Ralph A. Rowley, Ofc/AF Hist, subj: The Air Force in SEA: Tactics and Techniques of Close Air Support Operations, 10 May 75 [Moore participated in Project Daniel Boone (1969-1970)].

Chapter IV

1. Lt Col Philip R. Harrison, Impact of Darkness and Weather on Air Operations in SEA (S) (HQ PACAF, Project CHECO, 10 Mar 69), pp 13-26, 37; Kenneth Sams, et al, The Air War in Vietnam, 1968-1969 (HQ PACAF, Project CHECO, 1 Apr 70), p 58.

2. Stoner intvw (U), 18 May 70.

3. Kane and Sheets intvw (S), 17 May 70; Harrison, Impact of Darkness and Weather on Air Operations in SEA, p 42.

4. Harrison, Impact of Darkness and Weather on Air Operations in SEA, pp 39-41, 62.

5. SEAOR 136, 7th AF, subj: Forward Firing Target Marking Device [undated, covering FY 1968 requirements]; Harrison, Impact of Darkness and Weather on Air Operations in SEA, p 40.

6. Harrison, Impact of Darkness and Weather on Air Operations in SEA, pp 41-42, 45, 47; hist (S), 7th AF, Jan-Jun 1968, I, pt 2, 339.

7. See note above.

8. 504th TASGp Manual 55-3 (U), 1 Mar 70, pp 14-2, 14-3; 23d TASSq Tng Manual 1 (U), FAC Night Operations, 1 Sep 68, p 34-36; hist (S), TAC, Jan-Jun 1966, I, 276.

9. Hist (S), 504th TASGp, Jul-Sep 1970, I, 29; 504th TASGp Manual 55-3 (U), 1 Mar 70, p 14-4; Capt Melvin F. Porter, The Defense of Attopeu (S) (HQ PACAF, Project CHECO, 16 May 66), p 4; intvw (U), author with Lt Col Frank M. Eichler, Dir/Studies and Analysis, 22 Jul 71 [Eichler was ALO, 3d Bde, 1st Inf Div, Lai Khe, II Corps, SVN (Feb 1966-Feb 1967)].

10. See note above.

11. Eichler intvw (U), 22 Jul 71; Capt Dorrell T. Hanks, Jr., Riverine Operations in the Delta, May 1968-June 1969 (S) (HQ PACAF, Project CHECO, 31 Aug 69), p 38; MACV Counterinsurgency Lessons Learned 59 (C), Image Intensification Devices, 13 Jul 66, p 9.

12. Porter, The Defense of Attopeu, pp 1-7, 12; Melvin F. Porter, Control of Airstrikes, January 1967-December 1968 (S) (HQ PACAF, Project CHECO, 30 Jun 69), pp 32-33.

13. Porter, Control of Airstrikes, January 1967-December 1968, pp 33-34; Capt Buddy L. Bowman, Night Avionics for 0-2A Aircraft (C) (APGC-TR-68-85, APGC, Eglin AFB, Fla., Jul 1968); hist (S), TAC, Jul-Dec 1967, pp 285-86; MACV Counterinsurgency Lessons Learned 59 (C), 13 Jul 66, p 9.

14. PACAF Tactics and Techniques Bul 65 (S), 0-1 Night Operations, 30 Jun 67; 23d TASSq Tng Manual 1 (U), 1 Sep 68, p 18.

15. TACM/PACAFM/USAFEM 3-1 (S), 30 Sep 71, pt II, p 8-46; 12th TFWg Manual 3-1 (S), 30 Apr 71; Harrison, Impact of Darkness and Weather on Air Operations in SEA, pp 17-26; Patton intvw (S), 4, 15 Feb 72; PACAF Tactics and Techniques Bul 65 (S), 30 Jun 67; 23d TASSq Tng Manual 1 (U), 1 Sep 68, P 21; tng manual (U), 4410th CCT Sq, 8 Feb 67, pp 6-7.

16. See note above; Porter, Control of Airstrikes, January 1967-December 1968, p 35; intvw (S), Maj Victor B. Anthony, Ofc/AF Hist, with Capt David L. Shields, F-100 pilot, Cannon AFB, N. Mex., 10 Jan 72; Rowley, FAC Operations, 1965-1970, chap VI.

17. 23d TASSq Tng Manual 1 (U), 1 Sep 68, pp 24-27; PACAF Tactics and Techniques Bul 65 (S), 30 Jun 67; 504th TASGp Manual 55-3 (U), 1 Mar 70, p 14-9; 12th TFWg Manual 3-1 (S), 30 Apr 71; Rowley, FAC Operations, 1965-1970, chap VI.

18. Tng manual (U), 4410th CCT Sq, 8 Feb 67, pp 9-13; Rowley, FAC Operations, 1965-1970, chap VI.

19. 504th TASGp Manual 55-3 (U), 1 Mar 70, pp 14-9, 14-10; 23d TASSq Tng Manual 1 (U), 1 Sep 68, pp 30-32; Harrison, Impact of Darkness and Weather on Air Operations in SEA, pp 37-51.

20. 23d TASSq Tng Manual 1 (U), 1 Sep 68, pp 29-33; 504th TASGp Manual 55-3 (U), 1 Mar 70, pp 14-9 to 14-11.

21. 12th TFWg Manual 3-1 (S), 30 Apr 71; TACM/PACAFM/USAFEM 3-1 (S), 30 Sep 71, pt II, pp 8-46, 8-47.

22. Final Report (C), OV-10 Aircraft Introduction, Evaluation, and Assistance Program in Southeast Asia (TAC, Nov 1968), p 64, figs A-23, A-24; TACM/PACAFM/USAFEM 3-1 (S), 30 Sep 71, pt II, pp 8-50, 8-51.

23. Ltr (U), Maj Lyn R. Officer, to Maj Ralph A. Rowley, Ofc/AF Hist, 15 Jun 73; Fredericks EOT Rprt (C) [ca Dec 1966]; Fields intvw (U), 3 Oct 73; 12th TFWg Manual 3-1 (S), 30 Apr 71; TACM/PACAFM/USAFEM 3-1 (S), 30 Sep 71, pt II, pp 8-46 to 8-51.

24. Gunships, pp 32-33, 45, 73-80; Sams, First Test and Combat Use of the AC-47, pp 6-8; hist (C), 34th TGp, 1 Jan-8 Jul 65, pp 3-4; hist (S), 6250th CSGp, 1 Jul-31 Dec 65, pp 16-17; Hickey, Night Close Air Support in RVN, 1961-1966, p 25; Night Ops in SEA, pp 27-29.

25. Quoted in Gunships, p 46.

26. Hist (S), 14th ACWg, Jan-Jun 1966; Night Interdiction (S) (HQ PACAF, Project CHECO, Rprt 20-9, Dec 1966).

27. Gunships, p 30; hist (S), 14th ACWg, Jan-Jun 1966, p 53; Hickey, Night Close Air Support in RVN, 1961-1966, p 25.

28. PACAF Tactics and Techniques Bul 15 (C), 22 Jul 65; Harrison, Impact of Darkness and Weather on Air Operations in SEA, p 92; Night Ops in SEA, pp 29-30; hist (S), 14th ACWg, Jan-Jun 1966, p 53.

29. PACAF Tactics and Techniques Bul 56 (U), C/AC-47 SEA Operations, 13 Feb 67, hist (S), 4th ACSq, Jan-Jun 1966, chap II.

30. Maj Richard F. Kott, The Role of USAF Gunships in SEAsia (S) (HQ PACAF, Project CHECO, 30 Aug 69), p 92; 504th TASGp Manual 55-3 (U), 1 Mar 70, pp 14-13, 14-14; Night Ops in SEA, pp 30-31.

31. See note above; Gunships, p 29; hist (S), 4th ACSq, Jan-Jun 1966, II, 1; PACAF Tactics and Techniques Bul 56 (U), 13 Feb 67; PACAF Tactics and Techniques Bul 15, 22 Jul 65.

32. PACAF Tactics and Techniques Bul 56 (U), 13 Feb 67; hist (S), 14th ACWg, Jan-Jun 1966; Sams, First Test and Combat Use of the AC-47, p 5.

33. Hist (S), 14th ACWg, Jan-Jun 1966.

34. Gunships, pp 51-54; hist (S), 14th ACWg, Jul-Sep 1966, pp 54-57.

35. See note above.

36. See note 34.

37. Gunships, pp 51-52, 57, 69-70; hists (S), 14th ACWg, Jul-Sep 1966, pp 54-7; Nov-Dec 1966, I, 25.

38. Night Ops in SEA, pp 35-36; Gunships, pp 33, 97-99; Kott, The Role of USAF Gunships in SEAsia, p 15; hist (S), 14th ACWg, Nov-Dec 1966, I, 21, 32-35.

39. Gunships, pp 88-98.

40. Ibid., pp 103-05.

Notes to pages 119-125

41. Ibid., pp 106-113; Night Ops in SEA, pp 149-153; Sams, et al, The Air War in Vietnam, 1968-1969, pp 49-53; Rprt 69-3 (S), Air Operations in Southeast Asia, Aug 1967-Jan 1969 (ASI, Jul 1969), p 28; hist (S), 8th TFWg, Jan-Mar 1969, pp 37-39; 7th AF OpOrd 543-69 (S), Aug 1968, p B-1; Kott, The Role of USAF Gunships in SEAsia, pp 25-34; Trends, Indicators, and Analyses (S), Dir/Ops, Apr 1968, pp 2-1 to 2-4 [hereinafter cited as TIA with appropriate date and page].

42. See note above.

43. See note 41.

44. TIA, Apr 1968, pp 2-1 to 2-4; Kott, The Role of USAF Gunships in SEAsia, pp 11-12, 36-40.

45. See note above.

46. See note 44.

47. Gunships, pp 110-131.

48. Ibid., pp 119-121.

49. Ibid., pp 238, 259, 270-273; Kott, The Role of USAF Gunships in SEAsia, pp 20-21.

50. Kott, The Role of USAF Gunships in SEAsia, pp 6-8.

51. Ibid.; pp 20-21, App I; hist (S), 14th SOWg, Oct-Dec 1968; Professional Approach (U), 14th SOWg, Nov 1969.

52. Professional Approach (U), 14th SOWg, Nov 1969.

53. Kott, The Role of USAF Gunships in SEAsia, App I.

54. Ibid., pp 36-40; see note 52; Sams, et al, The Air War in Vietnam, 1968-1969, pp 49-53.

55. Kott, The role of USAF Gunships in SEAsia, pp 36-40.

56. Ibid., pp 292-96.

57. John F. Kennedy Center for Special Warfare, The Viet Cong (S) (Ofc of ACS/G-2, USA, 2d revision, Nov 1965), chap IV; PACOM Weekly Intelligence Digest 25-67 (S), A Typical Viet Cong Pre-Attack Evaluation, 23 Jul 67; hist (S), 504th TASGp, Jul-Sep 1968, I, Doc 6; C. William Thorndale, Defense of Da Nang (S) (HQ PACAF, Project CHECO, 31 Aug 69), pp 13-14; Rowley, FAC Operations, 1965-1970, chap VI.

58. See note above.

59. Thorndale, Defense of Da Nang, p 14; EOT Rprt (S), Col Paul C. Watson, 366th TFWg Comdr (Jan 1968-Jan 1969) [ca Feb 1969], pp 41-42.

60. Maj A. W. Thompson and C. William Thorndale, Air Response to the Tet Offensive, 30 Jan-29 Feb 68 (S) (HQ PACAF, Project CHECO, 12 Aug 68), p 6; hist (S), 504th TASGp, Jul-Sep 1968, I, Doc 6; Maj A. W. Thompson, The Defense of Saigon (S) (HQ PACAF, Project CHECO, 14 Dec 68), pp 45-48; Thompson, Strike Control and Reconnaissance (SCAR) in SEA, p 56.

61. Thompson, The Defense of Saigon, pp 47-49.

62. Ibid., pp 45-49; Thompson and Thorndale, Air Response to the Tet Offensive, 30 Jan-29 Feb 68, p 6; Thompson, Strike Control and Reconnaissance (SCAR) in SEA, p 56; hist (S), 504th TASGp, Jul-Sep 1968, I, Doc 6.

63. Thompson, The Defense of Saigon, pp 49, 52-53, Strike Control and Reconnaissance (SCAR) in SEA, p 56.

64. Intvws (C), C. William Thorndale, Proj CHECO historian, with Maj Slayton L. Johns, Asst ALO, CMD, SVN, 18 Jul 68, Lt Col Donald J. Clemons, ALO, CMAC, SVN, 9 Aug 68, in Docs 8 and 11, Thompson The Defense of Saigon; pp 52-53.

65. Thorndale, Defense of Da Nang, p 20; Thompson and Thorndale, Air Response to the Tet Offensive, 30 Jun-29 Feb 68, pp 23-25.

66. Thompson, The Defense of Saigon, pp 50-53.

67. Ibid.

Notes to pages 128-130

Chapter V

1. Hist (TS), MACV, 1969, I, V-192, V-193; Illustrated History, chap III.

2. TAC/TAWC rprt (S), Tactical Air Control Systems in SEA, Vol II, April 1968-Dec 1969, 1 Sep 70, 431 [hereinafter cited as TACS, Apr 1968-Dec 1969]; VNAF TACS ALO/FAC Upgrading Plan (S), VNAF/7th AF, Mar 1969; James T. Bear, VNAF Improvement and Modernization Program (S) (HQ PACAF, Project CHECO, 5 Feb 70), pp 9-10; Illustrated History, chap III; USAF Management Summary Southeast Asia (S), 22 Mar 73, pp 37-38.

3. Capt Drue L. Deberry, Vietnamization of the Air War, 1970-1971 (S) (HQ PACAF, Project CHECO, 8 Oct 71), pp 4-5; Bear, VNAF Improvement and Modernization Program, pp 16-17.

4. TACS, Apr 1968-Dec 1969, 431; VNAF TACS ALO/FAC Upgrading Plan (S), VNAF/7th AF, Mar 1969; Bear, VNAF Improvement and Modernization Program, p 38; Capt Joseph G. Meeko, IV, Vietnamization of the Tactical Air Control System (S) (HQ PACAF, Project CHECO, 23 Sep 74), chaps II, III.

5. Study (C), Evaluation of the Adequacy and Timeliness of Immediate Close Air Support (7th AF, Jun 1969), pp 5-9.

6. Ibid.

7. Ibid.

8. Thompson, Strike Control and Reconnaissance (SCAR) in SEA, p 63; Lt Col Stuart E. Kane, Jr., The Armed FAC Controversy (U) (AWC, Maxwell AFB, Ala., Apr 1971), pp 4-5.

9. Shields intvw (U), 10 Jan 72; Kane, The Armed FAC Controversy, pp 5-9; Thompson, Strike Control and Reconnaissance (SCAR) in SEA, p 63; Groth intvw (S), 10 Jan 72; PACAF rprt (TS), In-Country Strike Operations in Southeast Asia, 1 April 1968-31 December 1969, 23 Oct 70, Vol I, Sub-Task 1e, 41-42 [hereinafter cited as In-Country Strike Ops,

1 Apr 68-31 Dec 69]; hist (S), TAC, Jul 1968-Jun 1969, I, 186 (footnote); TAC/TAWC rprt (TS), Forward Air Control Operations in Southeast Asia, 1 January 1968 - 31 March 1968, Vol II, pp 12-13; EOT Rprt (U), Lt Col Thomas P. Garvin, ALO 25th Inf Div (23 Dec 67-14 Dec 68), 14 Dec 68.

10. Kane, The Armed FAC Controversy, pp 5-6; George L. Weiss, "The Fabulous FAC's of Vietnam," Air Trails--Military Aircraft, 1970, pp 35-36.

11. Ed Blair, "Saga of a Fighting FAC," Airman, XIII (May 1969), 60-64; Medal of Honor Citation (U), Capt Hilliard A. Wilbanks, 24 Jan 68.

12. See note above.

13. Kane, The Armed FAC Controversy, pp 9-10; msg (S), 7th AF to CINCPACAF, subj: Armed FAC Aircraft, 20 Jan 67.

14. Kane, The Armed FAC Controversy, pp 10-12; Potter, OV-10 Operations in SEAsia, p 12.

15. Kane, The Armed FAC Controversy, pp 10-12, 14; Rowley, FAC Operations, 1965-1970, chap VI; Michael H. Jones, Survey of Air Force Responsiveness to Immediate ASAP Requests for Air Support (C) (7th AF, Dec 1969), p 3; Potter, OV-10 Operations in SEAsia, pp 12-14; hist (S), TAC, Jan-Jun 1969, I, pt 2, 335; Richard T. Sandborn, Lee E. Dolan, Jr., and Michael H. Jones, Armed FAC (OV-10A) Evaluation, RVN, Jun-Sep 1969 (C) (ACS/Studies and Analysis, Jul 1970), p 5; In-Country Strike Ops, 1 Apr 68-31 Dec 69, 4; Maj Maxwell R. Sidner, Misty Bronco, Final Report (C) (Exercise Dir 1, 7th AF, Jul 1969), pp ii, 1; hist (TS), MACV, 1969, I, V-199, V-200; TIA, Aug 1969, pp 1-16 to 1-18.

16. Sidner, Misty Bronco, Final Report, pp 3-5, 7-9; Potter, OV-10 Operations in SEAsia, pp 12-14; TIA, Aug 1969, pp 1-13, 1-16, 1-17; hist (TS), MACV, 1969, I, V-199, V-200; McDermott, III DASC Operations, pp 30-31; Evaluation of the Adequacy and Timeliness of Immediate Close Air Support, pp 3-4; Bode intvw (C), 4, 19 Jan 72; Jones, Survey of Air Force Responsiveness to Immediate ASAP Requests for Air Support, pp 1-2, 5-7.

17. *Evaluation of the Adequacy and Timeliness of Immediate Close Air Support*, pp 3-4; McDermott, *III DASC Operations*, pp 30-31; hist (TS), MACV, 1969, I, V-199,V-200; TIA, Aug 1969, pp 1-17, 1-19; Potter, *OV-10 Operations in SEAsia*, pp 13-15; hist (S), 7th AF, Jan-Jun 1969, I, pt 2, 356.

18. John H. Scrivner, ed, *A Quarter Century of Air Power, Studies in the Employment of Air Power, 1947-1972* (AU, Jun 1973), pp 185-86; *Time*, 1 Mar 71, pp 19-20; *Illustrated History*, chaps III, V.

19. See note above; Col J. F. Loye, Jr., Maj L. J. Johnson, and J. W. Dennison, *Lam Son 719, 30 January-24 March 1971: The South Vietnamese Incursion into Laos* (S) (HQ PACAF, Project CHECO, 24 Mar 71), pp xii, xv, 82-85; After Action Report (S), XXIV Corps, Operation Lam Son 719, 30 January - 16 April 1971 (MCJ 3-32), 14 May 1971, pp 2-8 [hereinafter cited as After Action Report, Lam Son 719]; hist (S), MACV, 1971, II, E-17; Working Paper (S), 7th AF, in rprt (S), PACAF, Commando Hunt I, May 1971, pp 117-19.

20. See note above.

21. See note 19; After Action Report, Lam Son 719, pp 7-12, 82-89, 94-95, 106, App G-9; Loye, Johnson, and Dennison, *Lam Son 719, 30 January - 24 March 1971*, pg 11.

22. See note above.

23. Loye, Johnson, and Dennison, *Lam Son 719, 30 January - 24 March 1971*, pp 3-4, 11-15, 28-34, 80-82, 103-09; *Illustrated History*, chaps III, V.

24. Loye, Johnson, and Dennison, *Lam Son 719, 30 January-24 March 1971*, pp xvi, 103-09; *Illustrated History*, chaps III, V.

25. See note above.

26. See note 24; hist (S), MACV, 1971, II, E-32 to E-34; After Action Report, Lam Son 719, App 1-F-6.

27. See note above; hist (TS), PACAF, Jul 1969-Jun 1970, pp 154o, 154p; Deberry, *Vietnamization of the Air War, 1970-1971*, pp 29-33; Rowley, *FAC Operations, 1965-1970*, chap X; Bear, *VNAF Improvement and Modernization Program*, pp 33, 35, 38.

28. MR (U), Maj Gary L. Boyer, Dir/Ops, subj: Tactical Air Operations in RVN, 7 Jun 72; background paper (S), Lt Col Jack C. Strasser, Dir/Ops, subj: Tactical Air Control System in RVN, 20 Jul 72; msg (C), CSAF to CINCPACAF, TAC, and AFGP 311144Z May 72, subj: SEAsia Air-Ground Operations; Rowley, FAC Operations, 1965-1970, chap X.

29. Capt David K. Mann, The 1972 Invasion of Military Region I: Fall of Quang Tri and Defense of Hue (S) (HQ PACAF, Project CHECO, 15 Mar 73), pp 1-3, 69-71; hist (S), MACV, 1971, II, secs J, K, L.

30. See note above.

31. Capt Peter A. W. Liebchen, Kontum: Battle for the Central Highlands, 30 March-10 June 1972 (S) (HQ PACAF, Project CHECO, 27 Oct 72), pp 33-39, 42-49, 57-62, 84-87; Illustrated History, chap III, hist (S), MACV, 1971, II, sec K.

32. Ringenbach and Melly, The Battle for An Loc, 5 April-26 June 1972, pp 55-56; intvw (C), author with Lt Col Barrett V. Johnson, Dir/Ops, 4 Oct 74 [Johnson flew F-4's with 497th TFSq, Ubon, Thailand (12 Jan 72 - 12 Jan 73)].

33. See note above.

34. Ringenbach and Melly, The Battle for An Loc, 5 April-26 June 1972, pp 55-66.

35. Ibid.

36. See note 34; Illustrated History, chap III.

37. Illustrated History, chap III.

38. Hist (S), 354th TFWg, Oct-Dec 1972, chronology.

39. Rprt (S), F-X Effort, Analysis, and Conclusions (OSD/HQ USAF, 1 Dec 67), III, 47; Goldberg and Smith, Army-Air Force Relations: The Close Air Support Issue, pp 30-31; TIA, Mar 1970, III, 1-3 to 1-6; intvw (S), Maj Lyn R. Officer and Hugh N. Ahmann, Sp Acq Br, AU, with Capt Jerry Fleming, HQ AU, 21 Feb 73 [Fleming was an A-7D pilot, 354th TFWg, Korat AB, Thailand(1972)]; John L. Frisbee, "How the

A-7D Rewrote the Book in SEA," Air Force Magazine 56 (Aug 1973), 30-36; Capt Thomas G. Ryan, "That Super-Accurate Sluf, the A-7D Corsair II, "Air Force Magazine 55 (Mar 1972), 27-32.

40. See note above.

41. Fleming intvw (S), 21 Feb 73; Frisbee, "How the A-7D Rewrote the Book in SEA."

42. See note above.

43. Fleming intvw (S), 21 Feb 73; Government Provided Information for Design Studies (S), Close Air Support Activity Aircraft (A-X) (HQ USAF, 10 Apr 67), pp 1-1 to 1-4; background paper (S), ACS/Studies and Analys, subj: The Air Force A-X Close Air Support Aircraft, 4 May 71; TIA, Oct 1971, X, 1-2 to 1-6.

44. Illustrated History, chap III.

EPILOGUE

1. "Chief of Army Praises Air Force Close Air Support Systems," The Air Reservist, Feb 1974, p 3; AF Policy Letter for Commanders (U), 1 Jan 74, pp 1-2.

2. Hist (S), AFSC, Jul 1970-Jun 1972, pp 190-195; TIA, Oct 1971, X, 1-2 to 1-6; Air Force A-X Concept Formulation Package (S), 1 Mar 68 (revised 1 May 68), I; background paper (S), ACS/Studies and Analysis, 4 May 71; Edgar E. Ulsamer, "A-X Lethal, Accurate, Agile, and Cheap," Air Force and Space Digest 53 (Jan 1970), 33-39.

3. See note above.

4. TIA, Oct 1971, X, 1-2 to 1-6; hist (S), AFSC, Jul 1970-Jun 1972, pp 200-06; hist (S), AFSC, Jul 1972-Jun 1973, pp 201-04.

5. Ltr (S), Dep/Dir Ops Forces, Dir/Ops, to Ofc/AF Hist, subj: Historical Study, "The Air Force in Southeast Asia: FAC Operations 1965-1970," 9 Apr 75.

GLOSSARY OF TERMS AND ABBREVIATIONS

A-1	Single-engine (reciprocating) strike aircraft developed by Douglas Aircraft at the close of World War II; categorized as a slow mover, the aircraft had several missions in SEA with both the USAF and VNAF.
A-26	Strike aircraft of the 56th Special Operations Wing, Nakhon Phanom RTAFB, Thailand, operating in Laos; call sign Nimrod
A-37	A modified version of Cessna's twin-engine T-37 pilot trainer
AC-47	The C-47 transport converted into a gunship by adding the General Electric SUU-11A minigun; the AC-47 had several nicknames: Puff the Magic Dragon, Dragon Ship and Spooky
AC-119G	Gunship with call sign Shadow
AC-119K	Gunship with call sign Stinger
AC-130	Gunship with call sign Spectre
AA	antiaircraft
AAF	Army Air Forces
AAGS	Army Air-Ground System (for close air and reconnaissance support)
AARN	Army Air Request Net
AB	airbase
ABCC	Airborne battlefield command and control center; usually a C-130 deployed in support of out-country air operations, it was an extension of Seventh Air Force Command Center.
abn	airborne
ACDC	Air Combat Developments Command
acft	aircraft
ACGp	Air Commando Group
acq	acquisition

ACS	Assistant Chief of Staff
ACSC	Air Command and Staff College
ACSq	Air Commando Squadron
actg	acting
acty	activity
ACW	aircraft control and warning
ACWg	Air Commando Wing
ADF	Automatic direction finder; it automatically and continuously measures the direction of arrival of the received signal; data are usually displayed visually
Adm	Admiral
adv	advance, advanced, advancement
adverse weather	Weather in which military operations are generally restricted or impeded
ADVON	advanced echelon
advsy	advisory
AEF	American Expeditionary Forces
aerosp	aerospace
AF	Air Force
AFAG	Air Force Advisory Group
AFAT	Air Force Advisory Team
AFB	Air Force Base
AFGP	Air Force Advisory Group, MACV
AFLC	Air Force Logistics Command
AFR	Air Force Regulation
AFSC	Air Force System Command; Air Force Specialty Code
AGCP	air-ground cooperating party
AGL	above ground level
AGOS	Air-Ground Operations School
AIRA	air attache
Air America	A contract airline that flew for the Central Intelligence Agency in SEA
air commando	Air Air Force member engaged in counterinsurgency operations

(This page Unclassified)

Barn Door	Code name for first element of the Tactical Air Control System, introduced into South Vietnam in January 1962 to establish an effective network
Barrel Roll	(S) Interdiction and close air support operations in eastern Laos (beginning 14 Dec 64), later reduced to the area of northern Laos (3 Apr 65); the operations were under 2d Air Division and later, Seventh Air Force control; most recently, Barrel Roll refers to strikes against personnel and equipment from North Vietnam
BDA	Bomb damage assessment; the term encompasses the determination of the effect of all air attacks on targets (e.g., bombs, rockets, or strafe); also referred to as "battle damage assessment"
bde	brigade
beddown	A unit's deployment
Bird Dog	The O-1 FAC aircraft
bk	book
Black Crow	(S) An ignition system detection sensor used on AC-130 and AC-123 Black Spot aircraft
Blindbat	Nickname of C-130 FAC/flareship aircraft operating in southern Laos; eventually Blindbat became the nickname for all C-130 flare missions [see Lamplighter]
BLU	Bomb Live Unit; applies to various ordnance, e.g., the bomblets dropped from dispensers and special purpose bombs
bn	battalion
boresight line	An optical reference line used in harmonizing guns, rockets, or other weapon launchers
bomb	bombardment
br	branch
Brig Gen	Brigadier General
bul	bulletin

alft	airlift
Alleycat	The EC-130 ABCCC at night in Barrel Roll, northern Steel Tiger, and the panhandle of North Vietnam
ALO	air liaison officer
AM	Amplitude modulator; modulation in which the amplitude of a carrier is varied
AmEmb	American Embassy
ammo	ammunition
amph	amphibious
AMTI	airborne moving target indicator
analys	analysis
AOC	air operations center
AOCC	air operations coordination center
APGC	Air Proving Ground Center
app	apppendix
Arc Light	(S) B-52 operations in SEA, initially missions were flown from Andersen AFB, Guam; Kadena AB, Okinawa; and U-Tapao RTAFB, Thailand; later, all Arc Light missions were flown from U-Tapao
armt	armament
arty	artillery
ARVN	Army of Republic of Vietnam
ASD	Aeronautical Systems Division
ASGp	Air Support Group
ASI	Aerospace Studies Institute
ASOC	air support operations center
asst	assistant
ATC	Air Training Command
atch	attachment
AU	Air University
AWC	Air War College
B-57	Strike aircraft developed by the Martin Company for night intruder missions; nicknamed Canberra
Barky	Call sign for forward air controllers of the 20th Tactical Air Support Squadron, operating in Military Region I, Republic of Vietnam, during Lam Son 719

C-123	Fairchild Provider transport used in airlift and as a FAC/flareship; call sign Candlestick used in latter mission
C-130	Multi-engine transport developed for the Air Force by Lockheed; nicknamed Hercules
ca(circa)	about
Canberra	The B-57 strike aircraft
Candlestick	(S) Call sign for the C-123 FAC/flare aircraft in Laos
CAP	combat air patrol
Capt	Captain
cardinal points	north, south, east, and west
CAS	Controller American Source, close air support
cav	cavalry
CBU	cluster bomb unit
CCT	combat crew training
CEA	Circular error average; the bombing error in a given bombing attack, expressed as the average radial distance of the bomb impacts (or mean points of impact) from the center of the target
CEG	Combat Evaluation Group
cen	center
centerline	A line running along the longitudinal center of any given object, as along a runway, an airplane fuselage, or a rocket
CG	Commanding General
ch	chief
CHAAG	Chief, Army Advisory Group
chaff	Radar confusion reflectors consisting of thin, narrow, metallic strips of various lengths and frequency responses, used to reflect echoes for confusion purposes
chap	chapter
Charlie	Nickname for the Viet Cong, commonly used by military personnel

CHJUSMAGTHAI	Chief, Joint United States Military Advisory Group, Thailand
Christmas Tree	A SEA Operational term referring to normal (noncombat) lighting of an aircraft
CIA	Central Intelligence Agency
CIDG	Civilian Irregular Defense Group
CINCPAC	Commander in Chief, Pacific Command
CINCPACAF	Commander in Chief, Pacific Air Forces
CINCPACFLT	Commander in Chief, Pacific Fleet
CINCSTRIKE	Commander in Chief, United States Strike Command
CJCS	The Chairman, Joint Chiefs of Staff
CMAC	Capital Military Advisory (Assistance) Command
cmbt	combat
CMD	Capital Military District
cmte	committee
COC	combat operations center
COIN	counterinsurgency
Col	Colonel
Combat Bronco	SEA evaluation of the OV-10 in a FAC role (1968)
Combat Cover	A proposed SEA evaluation of the OV-10/AC-119 armed FAC/gunship missions
comd	command
comdr	commander
Commando Sabre	(S) Operations begun in June 1967 to test jet aircraft in the FAC role; the F-100 was used instead of slower FAC aircraft in higher threat areas
COMSEVENTHFLT	Commander, Seventh Fleet
COMUSMACV	Commander, United States Military Assistance Command, Vietnam
CONARC	Continental Army Command
conf	conference
concept formulation phase	The period extending from determination of a broad objective until the system program is established in the program element structure of the Five Year Defense Program

CONUS	Continental United States
Corona Harvest	United States Air Force project to collect documents on the SEA conflict for historical purposes
counterinsurgency	Those military, paramilitary, political, economic psychological, and civic actions taken by a government to defeat subversive insurgency
Covey	(S) Call sign of O-2 and OV-10 FAC's of the 20th Tactical Air Support Squadron, operating in North and South Vietnam and Laos
CP	command post
CRC	control and reporting center
Cricket	(S) Operations in Laos of O-1E and AC-47 FAC aircraft and the C-130 ABCCC
Cricket West	(S) Missions flown in northern Steel Tiger West by O-2 Nail FAC's from the 23d Tactical Air Support Squadron at Nakhon Phanom, Thailand, with Laotian Army observers (X-rays) aboard to supplement Raven FAC's
CRP	control and reporting post
C/S	Chief of Staff
CSA	Chief of Staff, United States Army
CSAF	Chief of Staff, United States Air Force
CSD	Combined Studies Division; operated by the U.S. State Department, it included U.S. Army Special Forces and Farm Gate personnel
CSF	Composite Strike Force (Special Forces)
CSGp	Combat Support Group
CTOC	corps tactical operations center
CTZ	Corps Tactical Zone; usually abbreviated "Corps," e.g., III Corps
CW	continuous wave

DA	Department of the Army
DAF	Department of the Air Force
Daisy Cutter	(S) MK-82 (500-pound HE) or MK-84 (2,000-pound HE) bombs with fuze extenders; designed to explode at the surface to kill personnel, damage materiel, and to defoliate
Daniel Boone	MACV support reconnaissance commando (RECONDO) teams
DARN	direct air request net (radio)
DASC	direct air support center
DCS	Deputy Chief of Staff
dead reckoning	Finding one's position by means of a compass and calculations based on speed, time elapsed, effect of wind, and direction from a known position
def	defense
dep	deputy
dept	department
det	detachment
dev	development
DF	direction finder
dir	director, directorate, directive
direction finding	Procedure for obtaining bearings of radio frequency emitters with the use of a highly directional antenna and a display unit on an intercept receiver of ancillary equipment
div	division
DME	distance measuring equipment
DMZ	demilitarized zone
doc	document
DOD	Department of Defense
doppler radar	A radar system that differentiates between fixed and moving targets by detecting the apparent change in frequency of the reflected wave due to motion of the target or observer

DR	dead reckoning
dry pass	An orientation pass with no ordnance drop
DTG	date-time group
DTOC	division tactical operations center
E&E	evasion and escape
ECM	electronic countermeasures
ed	edition, editor
Elephant FAC	Ground FAC team with English-speaking personnel; it could communicate both ground-to-air and ground-to-ground
EOT	End of Tour
ETA	estimated time of arrival
et al (et alii)	and others
eval	evaluation
EW	electronic warfare
EWO	electronic warfare officer
eyeball reconnaissance	Reconnaissance by sight rather than by radar and sensors
Eye Glass	(S) A night observation device (NOD)--also called starlight scope--that could compensate for motion of targets; used on Gunships II and III, this direct-viewing scope detected targets by intensifying images through use of ambient (surrounding) moonlight or starlight
F-4	Strike aircraft nicknamed Phantom
F-5	Strike aircraft nicknamed Freedom Fighter
F-100	Strike aircraft nicknamed Super Sabre
FAC	forward air control, forward air controller
FAG	forward air guide
fairing	An auxiliary member or structure on an aircraft that reduces drag
Farm Gate	Replaced Jungle Jim in December 1971 as covert USAF mission to train VNAF personnel

fast movers	high-performance aircraft
FC	fire control, force commander
FCC	fire control center
FDC	fire direction center
FDCC	fire direction control center
FFV	Field Forces Vietnam
FGp	Fighter Group
fig	figure
fire arrow	Could be made of many materials; metal gas cans filled with gasoline-soaked sand were often used; ignited, it was easy to see at night; hamlet defenders relayed to flare/strike aircraft the enemy's position with reference to the fire arrow
Fire Fly	A-1E strike aircraft in Barrel Roll, used for forward air control as well as strikes
1st Lt	First Lieutenant
Fishhook	The protrusion of Cambodia into Military Region III
flak	Bursting shells fired from AA guns
flak-suppression fire	Fire used to suppress AA fire immediately prior to and during an air attack on enemy positions
FLAR	folding fin aircraft rocket
flare	To drop flares
flechette	small steel dart
flight-following	The task of keeping in contact with specified aircraft to determine en route progress and/or flight termination
FLIR	forward-looking infrared
FLR	forward-looking radar
flt	flight
FM	frequency modulation, field manual
FO	forward observer
FOB	forward operating base
FOL	forward operating location
fr	from
frag	Fragmentation operations order; the daily supplement to standard operations order governing the conduct of the air war in Southeast Asia, it contained mission number and function, type of ordnance, time on target, and other instructions; "to frag" means to issue a fragmentation operations order covering the details of a single mission

FSCC	fire support coordination center
FSE	fire support element (division and higher)
FSO	fire support officer (United States Army)
FSq	Fighter Squadron
ft	foot, feet, fort
FTD	field training detachment
ftr	fighter
Funny Bomb	A 500- or 750-pound incendiary bomb cluster (M-31/32 and M-35/36 munitions)
FWF	free world forces
FWg	Fighter Wing
FY	fiscal year
G	The measure or value of the gravitational pull of the earth or of a force required to accelerate or decelerate any freely movable body at the rate of about 32.16 feet-per-second; to pull "3 G's" means to be subjected to a G-force of 3 G's
G-2/G-3 Air	Intelligence and Operations (corps and division level)
Gen	General
GLO	ground liaison officer
GP	general purpose
gp	group
GVN	Government of South Vietnam
Hammer	Call sign of FAC's from the 23d Tactical Air Support Squadron (augmented), operating over the Lam Son 719 operations area of Laos
hard ordnance	General purpose bombs to achieve blast or cratering effect
HE	high-explosive (iron bomb)
HF	high frequency
high-drag bomb	Weapon equipped with fins that increase its time of fall; for low-altitude delivery
Hillsboro	The EC-130 ABCCC in southern Steel Tiger during the day

hist	history, historical
Hobo	Call sign of 56th Special Operations Wing A-1 aircraft operating in Laos from Nakhom Phantom RTAFB, Thailand
HQ	headquarters
HUD	heads-up display
IAS	Indicated airspeed, i.e., airspeed read from the face of the indicator in the aircraft's cockpit
ibid.	in the same
IFF	Identification, friend or foe; a method for determining the friendly or unfriendly character of aircraft and ships by other aircraft or shps, and by ground forces using electronic detection equipment and associated IFF units
IFR	instrument flight rules
Igloo White	A surveillance system consisting of hand-implanted and air-delivered sensors, relay aircraft, and an infiltration surveillance center; Igloo White was formerly Muscle Shoels
incl	inclosure, include
in-country	That part of the Southeast Asia conflict within South Vietnam
inf	infantry
info	information
in-line engine	An internal-combustion, reciprocating engine in which the cylinders are arranged in one or more straight rows; distinguished especially from a radial engine
instr	instructor
intel	intelligence
in the clear	In plain text; said of a message not transmitted in cipher or code

in trail	Aircraft directly behind one another
intvw	interview
IP	Initial point--a well-defined point, easily distinguished visually and/or electronically, used as a starting point for the bomb run to the target
IR	infrared
iron bomb	A high-explosive bomb
ITACS	integrated tactical air control system
JAGOS	joint air-ground operations system
JAOC	joint air operations center
JATO	jet-assigned takeoff
JCS	Joint Chiefs of Staff
JGS	Joint General Staff (RVN)
jinking	An aircraft maneuver in which a series of rapid turn reversals and abrupt changes of roll and/or pitch attitude at random intervals prevent an enemy gunner from tracking the aircraft
JOC	joint operations center
Jungle Jim	Original covert training and reconnaissance program in RVN (code name later changed to Farm Gate)
JUSMAG	Joint United States Military Advisory Group
JUSMAGTHAI	Joint United States Military Advisory Group, Thailand
karst	A limestone region marked by sinks and interspersed with abrupt ridges, irregular protuberant rocks, caverns, and underground streams
KBA	killed by air
KIA	killed in action
KIAS	knots, indicated airspeed
kicker	A gunship/flareship crewmember charged with dropping the flares
kilometer	Equals 3,280.8 feet, above two-thirds (.62) of a mile
knot	A speed of 1 nautical mile of an hour (a nautical mile equals 6,076.115 feet or 1,852 meters)

LAU-59	A lightweight, clyindrical, 7-tube, expendable rocket launchers; tubes were reusable
Lamplighter	Nickname of C-130 aircraft operating in northern Laos; eventually Blindbat became the nickname for all C-130 flare missions
Lao	Laotian
LARA	light armed reconnaissance aircraft
laser	Light amplification by stimulated emission of radiation
LAU	launching mechanism
ldr	leader
lead	The head of an aircraft formation
Leaping Lena	U.S. Special Forces and indigenous forces who conducted long-range reconnaissance/interdiction missions; they acted as hunter-killer teams to conduct small search-and-destroy operations, initially in I and IV Corps; Leaping Lena became Delta in December 1964
LF	low frequency
Lima Site	Aircract landing sites (dirt strips) in Laos used as resupply points
link	A metal part that links one cartridge to another to form an ammunition belt
LLLTV	low-light level television
ln	liaision
LO	liaison office, liaison officer
LOC	line of communication
log	logistic; also a ground flare used by FAC aircraft to create a reference point during night strikes
loose trail	Aircraft directly behind one another and spaced fairly far apart
loran	Long-range electronic navigation system that uses the time divergence of pulse-type transmissions from two or more fixed stations; also called long-range navigation

LRP	long-range patrol
LRRP	long-range reconnaissance patrol
Lt Col	Lieutenant Colonel
LTD	laser target designator
Lt Gen	Lieutenant General
ltr	letter
LZ	landing zone
MAAF	Mediterranean Allied Air Forces
MAAG	Military Assistance Advisory Group
MAAGAF	Military Assistance Advisory Group, Air Force
MAC	Military Airlift Command
MACTHAI	Military Assistance Command, Thailand
MACV	Military Assistance Command, Vietnam
MAGAF	Military Assistance Group, Air Force
Maj	Major
Maj Gen	Major General
MAP	Military Assistance Program
marginal weather	Weather which is sufficiently adverse to military operations so as to require the imposition of procedural restrictions
meter	Equals 39.37 inches
MIA	missing in action
mil	military
Misty	Call sign for F-100F FAC's flying out of Phu Cat and Tuy Hoa Air Bases, RVN
mm	millimeter(s)
mph	miles-per-hour
MR	Military Region, memorandum for record, modification requirement
msg	message
MSQ	mobile search special
MTI	moving target indicator
Mule Team	Early logistical support in RVN
mush	To fly partly stalled with controls sluggish or ineffective
Nail	Call sign for FAC's of the 23d Tactical Air Support Squadron operating in Laos, out of Nakhon Phanom RTAFB, Thailand

napalm	A petroleum jelly fire bomb
nape	napalm
nav	navigation, navigational, navigator, navigate
NCO	noncommissioned officer
Night Owl	Night combat operations in SEA; the delivery of ordnance by F-4's under their own flare illumination; also call sign for 497th Tactical Fighter Squadron, Ubon RTAFB, Thailand
Nimrod	Call sign for A-26 aircraft of the 56th Special Operations Wing, Nakhon Phanom RTAFB, operating in Laos
NKP	Nakhon Phanom, a city and RTAFB in northeastern Thailand
NM	nautical mile
NOD	night observation device (e.g., starlight scope)
NVA	North Vietnamese Army
NVN	North Vietnam
NWC	National War College
O-1	FAC aircraft nicknamed Bird Dog
O-2A	FAC aircraft nicknamed Super Skymaster
OV-10	FAC aircraft nicknamed Bronco
OCMH	Office of the Chief of Military History
ofc	office
off	officer
OJT	on-the-job training
omnirange (omni)	A radio aid to air navigation that creates an endless number of paths in space through 360° of azimuth
on the deck	minimum altitude
opl	operational
OPlan	Operation Plan
OpOrd	Operation Order
ops	operations
ord	ordnance
orgn	organization
OSAF	Office of the Secretary of the Air Force
OSD	Office of the Secretary of Defense
OT&E	operational test and evaluation
OUSAIRA	Office of the United States Air Attache
out-country	That part of the Southeast Asia conflict outside South Vietnam, i.e., Laos and North Vietnam

(This page, Unclassified)

p	page
PACAF	Pacific Air Forces
panel code	A prearranged code for visual communications by use of marking panels (usually between friendly units)
para	paragraph
paradrop	Delivery by parachute of personnel or cargo from an aircraft in flight
Parrot's Beak	The tip of the Cambodian salient west of Saigon, South Vietnam
Pave Spot	A night observation device with boresighted laser target designator, used in the OV-10 aircraft
Pave Way	(S) The F-4 aircraft using various guidance devices: Pave Way I (laser); Pave Way II (electro-optical); Pave Way III (infrared)
PCS	permanent change of station
perch	An airborne position assumed by a fighter/bomber aircraft in preparation for or anticipation of an air-to-ground strike maneuver; the term was usually associated with fighter-escorted strike or FAC missions
pers	personnel
PI	photointelligence
pickle	To release a bomb or expend ordnance by depressing a button (pickle)
pilotage	Navigation by reference to checkpoints
pipper	The center or bead of a gunsight
POL	petroleum, oil, and lubricants
pp	pages
Prairie Fire	(S) MACV support reconnaissance commando (RECONDO) teams, normally organized to assess ground battle damage and locate lucrative targets for tactical airstrikes; they frequently worked behind enemy lines
prgm	program

proj	project
psychological operations (PSYOP)	Psychological warfare and those political, military economic, and ideological actions planned and conducted to create in neutral or friendly foreign groups the emotions, attitudes, or behavior to support the achievement of national objectives
pt	part
RAF	Royal Air Force (United Kingdom)
real time	The absence of delay, except for the time required for the transmission by electromagnetic energy, between the occurance of an event or reception of the data at some other location
recce	Reconnaissance, to reconnoiter
reciprocal	Opposite in direction; said of a bearing, course vector, or the like; e.g., a reciprocal bearing is the one taken plus or minus $180°$
recon	Reconnaissance, to reconnoiter
RECONDO	reconnaissance commando
ref	reference
reference altitude	The altitude assigned to a mission for control and separation of aircraft in the target area
reference point	A prominent, easily located point in the terrain
reg	regulation
regional forces (RF)	South Vietnamese local defense forces
regt	regiment
ret	retired
reticle	A system of lines, dots, crosshairs, or wires in the focus of an optical instrument
RFC	Royal Flying Corps
RHAW	radar homing and warning
RLAF	Royal Laotian Air Force
RLG	Royal Laotian Government
roadrunners	Indigenous personnel, dressed as enemy and working along infiltration routes in enemy-held territory (1966)

ROC	required operational capability
ROE	rules of engagement
ROK	Republic of Korea
RP	Route Package
rpm	revolutions per minute
rprt	report
rqmts	requirements
rsch	research
RTAFB	Royal Thai Air Force base
rules of enge engagement	Directives issued by competent military authority delineating the circumstances under which United States forces will begin and/or continue combat engagement with other forces met
RVN	Republic of Vietnam
RVNAF	Republic of Vietnam Armed Forces
2d ADVON	2d Advanced Echelon
SAC	Strategic Air Command
SAF	Secretary of the Air Force
safe	An ordnance term meaning "won't explode" or "will not fire"
salvo	The release of several bombs or rockets simultaneously (or in close train) from one or more aircraft at a single target
SAM	surface-to-air missile
SAR	search and rescue
SAWC	Special Air Warfare Center
SCAR	Strike control and reconnaissance; also applied to pilot FAC's without tactical fighter experience who were not authorized to conduct strikes with United States troops-in-contact; they were assigned out-country.
scramble	To take off as quickly as possible (usually followed by course and altitude instructions)
SEA	Southeast Asia
SEAITACS	Southeast Asia Integrated Tactical Air Control System
SEAOR	Southeast Asia Operational Requirement

sec	second
SECDEF	Secretary of Defense
2d Lt	Second Lieutenant
SECSTATE	Secretary of State
SF	Special Forces
SFGA	Special Forces Group, Airborne
shack	A direct or perfect hit
Shadow	Call sign of AC-119G gunship
shelf life	The period of time that an item can be stored and stay suitable for use
Shining Brass	Cross-border reconnaissance into Laos and the DMZ; called Prairie Fire after 1 March 1967
SIF/IFF	selective identification feature/identification, friend or foe
skin paint	A radar indication caused by the reflected radar signal from an object
Skyraider	A-1 strike aircraft
Skyspot	(S) MSQ-77 and TPQ-10 ground radars and control used to direct aircraft on bomb runs
slant range	The line-of-sight distance between two points not at the same elevation
SLAR	side-looking airborne radar
slick	Low-drag weapon; unarmed troop-carrying helicopter
slow movers	Relatively slow-moving aircraft
SLR	side-looking radar
small arms	All arms, including automatic weapons, up to and including .60-caliber and shotguns
Snort	Call sign for OV-10 FAC's
socked in	To be closed or unusable because of no visability; said of a place, an airbase, or the like
SOF	special operation force
soft ordnance	Ordnance suitable for use against soft or unprotected targets, e.g., napalm and cluster bomb units

SOG	Studies and Observation Group
SOGp	Special Operations Group
sortie	One aircraft making one takeoff and landing to conduct the mission for which it was scheduled
SOSq	Special Operations Squadron
SOWg	Special Operations Wing
sp	special
Special Forces	Military personnel with cross-training in basic and specialized military skills, organized into small multiple-purpose detachments with the mission to train, organize, supply, direct, and control indigenous forces in guerrilla warfare and counterinsurgency operations, and to conduct unconventional warfare operations
Spectre	Call sign of AC-130 gunship
sponson	A projection from the side of an aircraft to house guns or other items
Spooky	Call sign of AC-47 gunship
Spotlight	Report of a moving target derived from sensors and passed by a FAC or the ABCCC
spt	support
sq	squadron
SSB	single sideband
SSZ	specified strike zone
stan/eval	standardization and evaluation
starlight scope	An image intensifier using reflected light from the stars or moon to identify targets
Steel Tiger	(S) The geographic area in southern Laos designated by Seventh Air Force to facilitate planning and operations; the term also referred to strikes in southern Laos against personnel and equipment from North Vietnam
Steve Canyon	(S) Code word used in South Vietnam for covert FAC operations in Laos (volunteers were USAF FAC's)
stf	staff

stmt	statement
stn	station
strike lead	The pilot leading a fighter formation
strobe light	A light that produces short intense flashes
subj	subject
sup	supply, supplement
Super Sabre	F-100 strike aircraft
Super Skymaster	O-2A FAC aircraft
survivability	The probability the aircraft would not be lost if hit
svc	service
SVN	South Vietnam
sweep	To search out and clear the enemy from a specific area
sys	system
T-28	Strike aircraft nicknamed Zorro
III MAF	III Marine Amphibious Force
tac	tactical
TAC	Tactical Air Command
TAC Air	A term used in Southeast Asia to encompass all aircraft sorties other than B-52 and strategic airlift
TACAN	tactical air navigation (radio navigation system)
TACC	tactical air control center
TACLO	Tactical Air Command liaison officer
TACP	Tactical air control party; a subordinate operational component of a tactical air control system designed to provide air laison to land forces and for the control of aircraft
TACS	Tactical air control system; the organization and equipment necessary to plan, direct, and control tactical air operations and to coordinate air operations with other Services; it is composed of control agencies and communications-electronics facilities which provide the means of centralized control and decentralized execution of missions
TADC	tactical air direction center
TAGp	Tactical Airlift Group
Tally Ho	An intensified interdiction campaign in southern Route Package I, using O-2 FAC's in the western mountains and F-100F's in the eastern lowlands (1966)

(This page Unclassified)

TAOC	tactical air operations center
TAOR	tactical area of responsibility
TARN	tactical air request net (U.S. Marines)
TAS	true airspeed, tactical air support
TASE	tactical air support element (U.S. Army)
TASGp	Tactical Air Support Group
Task Force Alpha (TFA)	(S) A filter point for sensor information received under the Igloo White/Commando Hunt concept; it was organized in 1967 at Nakhon Phanom RTAFB, Thailand, under command of Seventh Air Force
TASSq	Tactical Air Support Squadron
TAWC	Tactical Air Warfare Center
TAWg	Tactical Airlift Wing
TCGp	Tactical Control Group
TCMSq	Tactical Control Maintenance Squadron
TCSq	Tactical Control Squadron
TDY	temporary duty
Tet	The Lunar New Year holiday observed in Vietnam and other Asian countries; it occurs early in the Julian year
TFSq	Tactical Fighter Squadron
TFWg	Tactical Fighter Wing
TGp	Tactical Group
TIA	Trends, Indicators, and Analyses
TIC	troops-in-contact (with the enemy)
Tiger/Tiger Hound	(S) Southern Steel Tiger south of 17° north latitude, for FAC employment (1965-1968); it was redesignated Steel Tiger South and its northern border moved southward
tight trail	Aircraft directly behind one another and spaced fairly close
TIS	Theater Indoctrination School
tng	training
TOC	tactical operations center
TOT	time-over-target
transceiver	A radio transmitter-receiver that uses many of the same components for both transmission and reception

transponder	Radio transmitter-receiver which transmits identifiable signals automatically when the proper interrogation is received
Tri-Border Area	The area west of Dak To, South Vietnam, at the convergence of the Cambodia, Laos, and South Vietnam borders
Tropic Moon III	Follow-on B-57 program for night attacks in high-threat areas, forerunner to the B-57G
Truscott White	(S) A United States Army operation in an area near the Laotian and Cambodian borders, West and southwest of Dak To, South Vietnam (1968); the operation's objective was to deny the enemy unrestricted use of the roadnets by destroying installations, personnel, and equipment; the Air Force added tremendous firepower to the operation
TRWg	Tactical Reconnaissance Wing
TSN	Tan Son Nhut Air Base, Republic of Vietnam
TUOC	tactical unit operations center
UHF	ultra high frequency
undercast	A layer of cloud beneath an aircraft
unk	unknown
US	United States (of America)
USA	United States Army
USAF	United States Air Force
USAFE	United States Air Forces in Europe
USAFSAWC	United States Air Force Special Air Warfare Center
USAFSOC	United States Air Force Special Operations Center
USAFSOF	United States Air Force Special Operations Force
USAFTAWC	United States Air Force Tactical Air Warfare Center
USAID	United States Agency for International Development
USASF	United States Army Special Forces
USMC	United States Marine Corps
USN	United States Navy
VC	Viet Cong; Vietnamese Communists

VFR	visual flight rules
VHF	very high frequency
VNAF	Vietnamese Air Force
VNSF	Vietnamese Special Forces
vol	volume
VOR	VHF omnirange (for navigation)
VR	visual reconnaissance
War Zone C	A Viet Cong stronghold northwest of Saigon, roughly encompassing northwestern Tay Ninh Province
War Zone D	A Viet Cong stronghold north-northwest of Saigon, embracing an area centered on the intersection of the borders of Binh Long, Phuoc Long, and Bin Duong Provinces
Water Pump	(S) Detachment 1, 56th Special Operations Wing, Udorn RTAFB, Thailand
wg	wing
wind sheer	A condition created by collision of winds from different directions
wing-loading	In stress analysis, the gross weight of an airplane divided by the wing area
wing root	The very base of an aircraft wing where it joins and blends into the fuselage
Wolf	Call sign of F-4 FAC's assigned to the 8th Tactical Fighter Wing, Ubon RTAFB, Thailand
WP	White phosphorous; plasticized white phosphorous munitions were used as marking rockets or bombs by FAC's who directed airstrikes
WPAFB	Wright-Patterson AFB

wpn	weapon
WRAMA	Warner Robins Air Materiel Area
WRCS	weapon release computer set
Z	Zulu Time (Greenwich Mean Time)
Zorro	Call sign of T-28 and A-1 aircraft assigned to the 56th Special Operations Wing, Nakhon Phanom RTAFB, Thailand

DISTRIBUTION

HQ USAF

1. SAFOS
2. SAFUS
3. SAFFM
4. SAFRD
5. SAFIL
6. SAFMR
7. SAFGC
8. SAFLL
9. SAFOI
10. SAFOII
11. SAFAAR
12. AFCC
13. AFCV
14. AFCVA
15. AFCCN
16. AFCVS
17. AFIGPP
18. AFJA
19. AFIN
20. AFPR
21. AFPRE
22. AFPRM
23. AFPRP
24. AFRD
25. AFRDG
26. AFRDM
27. AFSAG
28. AFSAMI
29. AFLG
30. AFLGF
31. AFLGP
32. AFLGX
33. AFLGY
34-35. AFXOD
36. AFXOOF
37. AFXOOSR
38. AFXOOSL
39. AFXOOSLA
40. AFXOOSLB
41. AFXOOSLC
42. AFXOOSLD
43. AFXOOSNB
44. AFXOXF
45. AFXOFT
46. AFXOFTF
47-48. AFXOXXP
49. NGB

MAJOR COMMANDS

50-51. AFLC
52-53. AFSC
54-55. ATC
56-57. MAC
58-60. PACAF
61-62. SAC
63-66. TAC
67-68. USAFE
69. USAFSS
70. AULD

OTHER

71-75. USAF Air Ground Operation School, Eglin AF Auxilary Field, FL 32544

76-78. USAFTFTAWC (TAC) Eglin AFB, FL 32542

79. USAF TFWC TAC Nellis AFB, NV 89191

80-81. AFSHRC

82. CHECO (DAD)

83-100. AF/CHO (Stock)

Printed in Great Britain
by Amazon